WANNABE

Reckonings with the
Pop Culture That Shapes Me

AISHA HARRIS

HarperOne

An Imprint of HarperCollins*Publishers*

HarperCollins books may be purchased for educational, business, or sales promotional use. For information, please email the Special Markets Department at SPsales@harpercollins.com.

FIRST EDITION

Designed by SBI Book Arts, LLC

Library of Congress Cataloging-in-Publication Data has been applied for.

ISBN 978-0-06-324994-3

23 24 25 26 27 LBC 5 4 3 2 1

WANNABE

For Ari

Contents

Introduction

THANK YOU, REBECCA BUNCH

There's a scene in the final season of the brilliant musical comedy series *Crazy Ex-Girlfriend* where Rebecca Bunch is lamenting her long list of well-documented destructive behaviors. Her friend and roommate, Heather, attempts to console her by saying that the worst thing about Rebecca is the fact that she flushes her tampons down the toilet.

"I'm sorry about the tampons," Rebecca reluctantly concedes. "Again, I didn't know you weren't supposed to flush them; I will wrap them in toilet paper and leave them in the trash to smell, like you want."

"Well, you could also just—take out the trash," Heather replies calmly but slightly irked.

I love this exchange, and think about it a lot for a few reasons. The

1

deliveries by Rachel Bloom as Rebecca and Vella Lovell as Heather are *chef's kiss*—the product of an established, familiar rapport, which feels utterly true to who these characters are and how their relationship has evolved over the course of several seasons.

And it encapsulates part of what made *Crazy Ex-Girlfriend* such a subversive delight—its weirdness and frankness in discussions of women's bodies and points of view. (This is a show, after all, in which a recurring gag involves characters singing bits of a song called "Period Sex.")

But the main reason I'm obsessed with this moment is because it concretely altered my life—my *womanhood*. In it, I stumbled upon a stunning revelation: that you are *not*, in fact, supposed to flush tampons down the toilet.

Yes, *I* was Rebecca Bunch. An early thirty-something with years of tampon-wearing experience, I had been painfully unaware that my bathroom trips while on my period rendered me a menace to society, if only for a few minutes every few months. Who knows how many plumbing systems I'd clogged or how many bodies of water I'd polluted with my ignorance? I shudder from a place of deep and immense shame at the thought of having left behind a never-ending trail of slowly degrading sanitary products in an untold number of sewage pipes. (Thank the medical gods for inventing the kind of birth control that can effectively eliminate periods! These days, I basically never have to worry about this anymore.)

I've learned a lot of lessons about myself and how the world works in this way—inadvertent self-formation by way of popular culture. I've devoured countless hours of movies, shows, books, music, and theater over the course of my life, first solely as a consumer and then later as

2

a professional critic and podcaster; I guess it was bound to work out that I'd fix my garbage disposal habits thanks to an encounter with a fictional TV character. Pop culture is also how I've worked through more existential issues, like a complicated relationship with my own name and my commitment to never having kids. When I'm searching for meaning, validation, or a challenge, I'll often find it through an exchange between fictional characters or in the lyric of a transformative album.

The truth is, most of our lives bear the imprints of the pop culture we consume, whether the consumption is casual or, as in my case, obsessive. (A song that lives rent-free in my head: "Muffin Top," from *30 Rock*.) The stuff that entertains us—or just merely distracts us—often finds a way of seeping into our "real" lives. It can be as frivolous and fleeting as "the Rachel" haircut from *Friends*, as enduring as doing the Cha-Cha Slide at weddings, or as singular and all-encompassing as Beatlemania. Sometimes it's inspiring, like seeing Sidney Poitier win the Oscar or reading books about a group of smart and enterprising tween and teen girl babysitters. In other cases, it's insidious, like the way decades' worth of baked-in copaganda on shows like *Cops* and *Law & Order* have primed Americans to feel overly sympathetic toward law enforcement.

It's nearly impossible to escape this world untouched by pop culture: moviegoing, TV watching, music listening. It doesn't all just happen to us—it helps *shape* us and informs how we move about the world, whether we're conscious of it or not. But *how* we interact with it has shifted in some significant ways, creating infinitely new possibilities for both connection and division. And of course, our social mores shift, too. I'm a middle millennial who was born at the end of the 1980s but came of age in the 1990s and early 2000s. My generation—the "killers" of cable TV, the auto industry, and casual dining, among other capitalistic entities of yore—often gets a bad rap for being overly concerned with relating to and seeing ourselves in pop culture. We're labeled vapid (the so-called selfie generation) and unhealthily obsessed with things like representation and cultural appropriation because we tend to be the loudest critics when, say, Tilda Swinton is cast in a role that was originally conceived as an Asian character (as in *Doctor Strange*) or J. K. Rowling spouts yet more trans-exclusionary rhetoric. Bill Maher can barely make it a week without sneering about "woke millennials" and our "cancel culture." (Naturally, this ire has begun to trickle down to Gen-Z, who have spent virtually all their sentient lives online and are rejecting labels and traditional identities at increasingly higher rates than millennials.)

But we're just embracing the reality of pop culture's indisputable impact on our society, only now with the added benefit of more diversity, more immediacy, and a bigger platform (social media) than generations prior. We're looking inward and looking back on many of the ideas and values we were taught by our parents, our teachers, our peers, and yes, our culture and recognizing that a lot of what we've been taught to accept or ignore was wrong.

"Movies do not change, but their viewers do," Roger Ebert wrote in 1997.[1] He was referring to Fellini's *La Dolce Vita* and how each time he experienced the film, he identified with the central character differently and in a way that was dependent upon whatever stage of life he was in at that moment. He's right, of course. We can all relate to the experience of a song or movie hitting you differently at different points in your life. Now that I'm around the same age as three of the *Sex and the City* women were during its original run, I watch the show very differently than I did when I was sixteen, and that's a *good* thing. (No more wildly unrealistic expectations of what dating and socializing is like as a young adult in a big city!)

As we individuals grow and change, so does the *collective* audience. And that collective audience always includes the next era of creators who might have the opportunities to do things differently, as we've seen lately with the likes of Issa Rae, Bo Burnham, Jerrod Carmichael, the Daniels, and Greta Gerwig, all of whom are pushing boundaries and breaking new ground. Pop culture shapes us, and we shape it right back in an invigorating feedback loop of creativity and interpretation.

It's worth embracing this.

Like most people, there are times when I just want to turn my brain off for a few hours, lose myself in entertainment, and never think about any of it again. But most often when I experience something, I want to dig into it. I want to understand how it all fits into the bigger picture, i.e., culture and history and life and all that. When I react a certain way to something I watch or listen to, I want to figure out why. When I sense a trend emerging, I want to put it in context. I love wrestling with and unpacking the irrepressible cultural forces that have moved me or made me cringe, made me proud or insecure, or just left me utterly confused. For me, there is a thrill in engaging on a deep level until I've made some sense of it all. The essays in this book are an invitation into that wonderful, maddening process and the tensions that come with it, all through the prism of one Black, suburban, 1990s-kid-turned-thirty-something, city-dwelling journalist who, on the very rare occasion when she does need a tampon these days, no longer flushes said tampon down the toilet.

1

ISN'T SHE LOVELY

Chance the Rapper paused on the other end of the phone line. It was merely a couple of seconds, but in the moment, it felt long enough to me to be a little awkward—especially because I couldn't read his facial expressions.

Had I unintentionally poked a beehive with my questions? I wondered in the space of that loaded pause.

It was summer 2019, and I'd successfully pitched my editor at the *New York Times* the idea of a lighthearted Q&A with the artist about his well-documented love of *The Lion King*—he's rapped about the movie on many different occasions—pegged to Disney's upcoming CGI remake. I figured it'd be fun to shoot the shit with the jovial rapper, who has frequently sprinkled *Lion King* shout-outs like "Call me Mr. Mufasa; I had to master stampedes" into his lyrics.

He was as chill and chatty in conversation as I'd expected him to be. He proclaimed *The Lion King*'s superiority over *Hercules* because the latter "just takes you to a bunch of different places until you just get to the end and it's like, 'Was it worth it?'" This is the correct take. But about ten minutes in, he let slip that he'd served as a consultant for the remake's director, Jon Favreau. This was news to me; at the time, there were only rumors he might have contributed to the movie's soundtrack—nothing beyond that.

When I asked him to elaborate on this "consultant" work, I could sense that *he* could sense that I'd unwittingly stumbled upon a news scoop. His guard went up a little, and he hesitated ever so slightly. "I don't know how much you know about my involvement with the movie, so could you just tell me that before I start talking?" he asked politely.

I mentioned the scuttlebutt regarding his possible musical input, and that I was aware of a previous interview he'd given a couple of years prior about auditioning for the voice role of Simba.

"When does this piece come out?" he followed up tentatively.

"Probably a day or two before the movie," I responded, trying to conceal my nervousness that he might immediately shut down the interview.

And then there was that pause.

Eek.

"Sorry, I never got . . ." he trailed off. "What's your name?"

I was confused. That was *not* where I thought this interaction was headed. "Oh—Aisha."

Another pause. Then: "Oh, Aisha?"

"Yes."

"Yeah . . . Can I ask you—are you Black?"

His tone was sheepish, echoing the deeply self-conscious mode we'd both apparently fallen into for the moment. I was slightly flustered, temporarily knocked off my guard.

"Yes, I'm Black," I responded, my face scrunched up in bewilderment. For a second, I was grateful he couldn't see me.

"Okay. I didn't know that . . . Earlier you were saying stuff about being Black, and I didn't know . . . and now I know."

Another pause.

"So can I just say that I fill a small role in the movie without that being a separate story that comes out ahead of this piece?"

This was not the first time someone had heard just my voice and didn't realize I was Black or was at least unsure about it; I've been told I "sound white" many times in my life. To be clear, I don't mean this in the "exceptional Negro" way—you know, how certain self-hating Black people try to signal how "different" they are from other Black people and complain about being teased for "acting white" because they "speak proper." Rather, my accent and the timbre of my voice—a product, I guess, of Midwestern roots by way of Mississippi on my dad's side and New England roots by way of Baltimore on my mother's—don't often automatically connote "Black American" for some people I encounter. Think more Kerry Washington than, say, Niecy Nash.

For instance, a couple of months after I joined NPR's *Pop Culture Happy Hour* as a host, a listener tweeted that they thought I sounded just like my cohost, Linda Holmes, who is lovely and someone I admire greatly but who is, unlike me, white. The observation stung a bit, because the last thing I wanted was to carbon copy her style. But I reassured myself, *Hey, I'm still trying to rediscover my podcast voice, its range, my cadences, my groove, and maybe I'm unintentionally mimicking her style as I do so. It's okay. I can work on that.*

But then, a week or two later while I was on the phone with my mom, she complimented me on my hosting duties while also noting that she'd started listening to a recent episode thinking I was the host, only to realize halfway through that it was actually Linda she was hearing. I hadn't even appeared in that episode at all. My own mother! (Love you anyway, Mom.)

Even in my writing, I've been mistaken for white by virtue of the publications featuring my work having predominantly white staff. Early into my first journalism job as a culture writer at *Slate*—back when I was still masochistic enough to read that cesspool under articles known as the comments section—I recall coming across a reader huffily dismissing a piece I wrote as the ignorant rantings of a white person. I can't for the life of me remember what I wrote, only how shocked I was at the time that someone would think I was white. Another reader chimed in to say, "Actually, I'm pretty sure the writer is Black."

I assume this person just didn't bother reading the byline, like a lot of readers. If my voice doesn't give it away first, my name is the first clue for strangers that I might be Black. In Chance's case, it seems to me he was trying to suss out whether or not he could trust me with this accidental revelation about his involvement with the new *Lion King*. If he confirmed that I'm Black, maybe he'd feel a little more at ease?

Depending upon the person, their assumptions, and the context, "Aisha" makes me Black. Or it makes me a Black Muslim. (I'm not Muslim, though I can't count how many chatty cabdrivers have tried to use my name as an entry point to a conversation by inquiring as much. I get that they are just trying to be friendly, but *Please, dude, it's five a.m., the sun isn't even up yet, and the last thing I want to do before boarding my flight today is have you mansplain to me that Aisha was one of the prophet Mohammad's favorite wives* is a thought I've had So. Many. Times.) Or it makes me a person with a "hard-to-pronounce" name. (It's pretty straightforward: eye-EE-shuh.) Or it's an excuse to sing a corny song by a one-hit-wonder boy group. (More on that later.)

But at my youngest, I understood only these things about my name: My parents picked it out because my dad especially wanted his children to have African names; it means "life" in Swahili; and the name "Aisha" is mentioned in Stevie Wonder's "Isn't She Lovely"—a tune that was often spun on vinyl or sung by my parents in our household.

I was born to Frank and Teresa in New Haven, Connecticut, at the end of the 1980s, smack-dab in the middle of what I've been told was a brutal winter, back when snow was still A Thing that happened with great frequency in the Northeast in January. I share a birthday with Mary J. Blige and Alexander Hamilton, whose name, like mine, has been the subject of a popular corny song. (*Hamilton* on the whole is dope and all, but the opening number is essentially tedious slam poetry filtered through show tune bravado. Fight me.)

My parents' names are pretty basic—"mainstream," as it were. "Frank and Teresa" could be an Italian-American couple from the Bronx. Theirs are the kind of "white-sounding" names that those infamous studies have found are more likely to get a callback from potential employers than "Black-sounding" names with the same résumés and qualifications.

A 2003 CBS News article stated that "Carries and Kristens had callback rates of more than 13 percent, but Aisha"—oh hey, it's me!—

"Keisha and Tamika got 2.2 percent, 3.8 percent and 5.4 percent, respectively."[1] (Although, I've talked to enough Black people with white-sounding names to know that whoever's hiring you is going to figure out you're Black eventually, so if they're prejudiced, a callback doesn't even really make that much of a difference.)

By the time my big head came along in 1988, the trend of Black American parents giving their children names that deliberately departed from white Anglo culture was in full swing. In one study published in 1995, data from the Illinois Department of Public Health for all in-state births between 1916 and 1989 was used to examine "unique" naming patterns among Black Americans. (A "unique" name is defined here as one given to "no other child born in that year who is of the same sex and race.")[2] The researchers concluded that a significant increase in unique names given to Black American girls—and a prominent but not as pronounced increase for Black boys—from the early 1960s into the 1980s could be explained in part by an increase in interest in African culture and heritage: Cassius Clay becoming Muhammad Ali, the publication of several popular books of African names targeted at parents beginning around the early 1970s, and of course, Alex Haley's groundbreaking historical novel about Kunta Kinte, a young eighteenth-century Gambian sold into slavery in *Roots: The Saga of an American Family*, and its record-breaking miniseries counterpart. Apparently "Kizzy," the name of Kunta Kinte's daughter, jumped into the top twenty for Black girl names in Illinois the year after the book came out.[3] (I kind of love this name, and knowing this little tidbit now, I feel cheated that I've yet to meet anyone named Kizzy despite the fact much of my dad's family is from Illinois.)

In another study published in 2004 by the Harvard University Society of Fellows and National Bureau of Economic Research, University of Chicago, researchers found that over the course of several years in the 1970s, Black girls born into segregated California neighborhoods "went from receiving a name that was twice as likely to be given to Blacks as whites to a name that was more than twenty times as likely to be given to Blacks." Black boy names also trended in this direction, though not as drastically, they added.[4]

I would come to understand that my name was "unique," at least within the predominantly white and suburban circles in which I frequently found myself—in a public elementary school in Hamden, Connecticut, where I was one of only a handful of Black kids in our entire grade, in my extracurricular activities, and in nearly every first-time interaction with a white stranger. Among my grade-school peers, I knew multiple Nicoles, Erins, Maggies, and Stef/Stephanies. There was always a healthy assortment of Alicia/Alesha/Alishas, white and Black, and perhaps their relative abundance is the reason why people's brains so frequently conjure up that letter L and plop it into my name as though it were the letter of the day on *Sesame Street*.

In the grand scheme of things that caused me anxiety as a child, this was pretty low on the list. Unlike the white girls who asked me if they could stick their grimy little kid fingers in my hair while simultaneously sticking their grimy little kid fingers in my hair, the mispronunciation of my name didn't feel like a deliberate attempt to "other" me. The contortion and fumbling and invention of syllables and sounds are just what happens when someone encounters the unfamiliar. It is what it is, and before I learned you should always just ask someone up front how they pronounce their name if you're unsure, I certainly stumbled over other people's names, too.

But when you're a kid, and the majority of your schoolmates are white, it still *feels* like you're being "othered." The nervous anticipation that would build up inside me whenever a new substitute teacher was doing roll call at the beginning of class—that was real. In such a situation, I knew just what was going to happen. When they approached my name on that sheet of paper, they would either (a) go full Lena Dunham and confidently screw it up royally, only to half-heartedly apologize later, or (b) pause and scrunch up their face while self-deprecatingly admitting they "have no idea" how to say my name, then ask me to pronounce it.

Of course, it's been just as mangled in written form. And I'm not only talking about the baffling misspellings I've discovered upon receiving my Starbucks drinks; those baristas will turn even the "simplest" of names like Amy into "Ay Mee," as if they were channeling the *Key & Peele* "Substitute Teacher" sketch, in which Keegan-Michael Key's character, accustomed to teaching at a predominantly Black high school, mispronounces his white students' names during roll call. (I can no longer see the name Aaron and not hear it as "Ay-ay-ron." Sorry to Ay-ay-rons everywhere.)

"Asia." "Aysha." "Eyesha." "Ayesha." "Iesha." These are the spellings I've been given on name tags at events, on to-go receipts for food back when it was still normal to call in orders and speak with a live human being over the phone rather than use an app. It's a pleasant surprise when someone actually spells or says it correctly without my input. Those people get bonus points from me. They could put mayo on my sandwich after I've specifically stated "no mayo"—thrice, because I've been burnt before—and they'd still get bonus points from me. It's a relief when my name feels "easy."

Which brings me to "Iesha"—the aforementioned corny song that has prompted a decent number of millennials and Gen-Xers with a good memory to start instantly singing upon our introduction.

For those who have mercifully forgotten or are blissfully unaware of "Iesha," it's a lightweight New Jack Swing–era ditty rap-sung by Another Bad Creation, a group composed of mostly prepubescent boys—they ranged in age from eight to thirteen years old at the time of their very brief peak—who were supposed to be hip-hop's answer to New Edition. In fact, ABC, as they were also known, had a direct New Edition connection: one of the six members was a nephew of Ralph Tresvant, and Michael Bivins helped produce their debut album.

Basically, ABC was the Muppet Babies' version of New Edition. The New Edition Babies, if you will.

The babies rap-sing (featuring ad-libs from Bivins) about the girl they "neva had" and "wanna get to know" better. It's inoffensive insomuch as a song in which preteen boys wailing about falling in love while on the monkey bars or playing Nintendo can be. But my god, I hate "Iesha." The production is a sparser, subpar rip-off of Bell Biv DeVoe's "Poison," released only months earlier; the music video cuts between the kids riding go-karts and furiously thrusting their pelvises as if they were baby Bobby Browns.

Maybe if I'd been just a bit older when the song came out in 1990 (I was two, just a few years younger than the youngest New Edition Babies member!), I might have swooned over this ragtag collection of boys and dreamed of being pushed by them in the tire swing on the playground and trading Juicy Juice boxes at lunch. But alas, I missed this train and only associate them with making the misspelling of my name much more likely thanks to the song's fleeting popularity. (It peaked at number nine on the Billboard Hot 100.)

I deserve better than this dumb song about puppy love, I often told myself.

In my disdain for that trite drivel, I clung to the need to distance myself from it in any way possible. I accomplished this by summoning the African ancestors and Stevie, who in stark contrast to the New Edition Babies, was a one-time musical boy genius who managed the nearly impossible feat of morphing into a musical man genius.

One of the books my parents used to help pick out names for me and my younger sister was *Golden Names for an African People,* by the Chicago-born writer and performer Nia Damali, published in 1986. I could flip through it and find our names there with little check marks penciled in next to them—markings that carried with them the rich prophecy of our existence preceding our entrances into the world. There were other check marks beside other names, like Layla, pronounced LAH-ee-lah, meaning "born at night" in Swahili, and Akilah, pronounced AH-kee-lah and meaning "intelligent one who reasons" in Arabic. But they weren't the names my parents ultimately chose.

Aisha. Life. That was it. It's beautiful.

The introduction for *Golden Names for an African People*—which, according to the copyright page in my parents' edition, had by then already sold over twenty-five thousand copies—borrows closely from the template of many of its counterparts within the genre of African baby name books. For one, there's an attempt to establish one's name as "godly," imbuing it with a spiritual connection to a higher power. This seems like a pleasant sentiment for some people to have, but to an agnostic such as myself, this means absolutely nothing. Ah, well.

Perhaps more crucial to the purpose of the book is framing these names as a spiritual tether to the African ancestors from whom Black Americans have been separated because of colonialism, slavery, and so on. "Through these names we choose we are reconnecting the umbilical cord between ourselves and our Motherland, Africa," writes Babatunde Khalid Shabazz Abdullah in the book's preface. "And our future generations will not only know their stolen past but will also be able to plan their future."

How . . . vivid! That's actually quite tame compared to the language of other books I've come across, where the flair for the dramatic gives way to an unintentional reinforcement of exoticizing the African continent and perpetuating stereotypes. The 1993 book *African Names: Names from the African Continent for Children and Adults* claims "the mere mention of an African name" might "conjure up images of vast savannas and endless deserts, dense forests and palm-fringed beaches, of golden ancient kingdoms and proud warriors . . ." (It keeps going, but I'll spare you. Yeesh.)

Anyway, *Golden Names* includes florid explanations of African naming rituals and considerations and the ways African names are inspired and influenced by newborns' perceived personalities.

Before I was even born, my dad knew he wanted to instill in me pride in being Black and feeling beautiful. "Aisha" was the first step.

The subsequent steps involved many other cultural influences: Black dolls only in our household; storybooks like *Tar Beach*, Faith Ringgold's lushly illustrated ode to Harlem's rooftops; and *The People Could Fly*, Virginia Hamilton's majestic collection of Black American folktales. Sunday mornings were spent listening to WBLS FM's oldies programming block, where they played everything from Billie Holiday to the Jackson Five to Luther Vandross, while one of my parents made pancakes or waffles from scratch. And there were home screenings of the PBS documentary *Eyes on the Prize* and all ninety million hours of *Roots*, taped on VHS from one of the cable rebroadcasts.

As I've already noted, *Roots*, Alex Haley's tome about Kunta Kinte, a young Gambian who's sold into American slavery in the eighteenth century, and his descendants was said to have been responsible for a number of Black parents naming their newborn daughters Kizzy. But anyone familiar with the 1977 TV adaptation surely remembers that one of its most iconic scenes involves LeVar Burton's Kunta being brutally whipped for refusing to accept the new name—Toby—bestowed upon him by his white master. (Toby! Just thinking of that name makes me angry because it feels like such an especially offensive, egregious act of humiliation and degradation, even for a white slave master. Sorry to Tobey Maguire—if it's any consolation, your Spider-Man's the best on-screen version besides Miles Morales, even if you were way too old to be playing a high-schooler at the time.)

That scene has been famously parodied to death by everyone from the Wayans family to Dave Chappelle, but when considered in its original context, it means far more than what has been mined for laughs. It's about how a name is the only thing left even in the darkest of moments, even when all else—your home, your family, your freedom—is lost. It's the belief that what you are called is tied to your lineage, to your ancestors, to your origins, and that bond is sacred.

As with the miniseries, Haley's book opens with the birth of Kunta in the village of Jufureh in The Gambia in 1750. Immediately, he weaves a mood of divinity, reverence, and tradition as he describes "ancient custom" and the painstaking task for Omoro, the father, in deciding upon the name of his firstborn son over the course of seven days. "It would have to be a name rich with history and with promise," Haley writes, "for the people of his tribe—the Mandinkas—believed that a child would develop seven of the characteristics of whomever or whatever he was named for."[5]

Omoro's choice of the name Kunta is in honor of the child's late grandfather Kairaba Kunta Kinte, described as the village's holy man and as having saved Jufureh from a famine. The naming ceremony includes the recitation of the names of Kairaba's forefathers.

In the miniseries, an enslaved Kunta is tied up, beaten into submission, and, battered and weakened, finally utters the name "Toby," a moment that feels powerful and singular. His persistent defiance in the face of violence is courageous and symbolic; Kunta is the stand-in for every Black person sold or born into slavery, the bridge between Black Africans and Black Americans, and a testament to how our culture persists and refuses to fold under the shameful tyranny of white supremacy but instead shifts and morphs as all customs do, sometimes out of necessity for survival or just because that's the way of the world. (Or both.) When Kunta says "Toby," it's so he can live another day. And even if he gives that satisfaction to his master, the resistance is the point, just as, to that master, the cruelty is the point.

The idea that a name isn't just a name, especially for Black people, is all over American pop culture. In one of *The Wire*'s best scenes, Marlo Stanfield, the slithering, ruthless drug kingpin who refuses to play by the rules of the streets and pisses off every other kingpin in town because of his recklessness, insists "My name is my name!" when he learns that, unbeknownst to him, his nemesis Omar Little called him out in the streets for not stepping to him directly. (*Breaking Bad*'s Walter White has a similar character-defining moment in season five, in which he pulls the ultimate badass power play and demands that an associate speak his nickname—Heisenberg, a nom de guerre in ode to the twentieth-century German physicist Werner Heisenberg. Fictional crime lords, it seems, are very precious about their names.)

Musicians love to ask, "What's my name?" in their songs, and the question is almost always rhetorical and an assertion of dominance. For the rapper DMX, it's meant to be menacing. (He definitely *is* terrifying on that track, but I chuckle every time I hear the line where he barks menacingly "I'M NOT! A NICE! PER-SON!" Okay then, DMX! RIP.) When Snoop Dogg or Rihanna poses the question, it's more playful and cocky. ("Hey boy, I really wanna see if you can go downtown with a girl like me!" sings the Bajan princess in her second-best Aubrey Graham collaboration. "Work" is number one, of course.) To speak someone's name as they want it to be spoken is the ultimate sign of respect and acknowledgment.

In the 1990s, Prince changed his name to a confusing and unpronounceable symbol, supposedly in protest of music executives at his then-label Warner Bros. and the industry's predatory contracts for artists—an attempt at a power play to get out of his contract and protect his moniker and his craft so they could no longer profit off it. (It didn't work.)[6] Beyoncé reasserted herself and marked a turning point in her career as a masterful marketer and visionary in 2013 with her self-titled album. That was her *fifth* solo studio album, and she was already one of the biggest pop stars in the world; choosing to name it simply *Beyoncé* was a statement of purpose and rebirth.

You may also recall that in *The Lion King*, just the mere mention of Mufasa's name sends shivers down the spine of Shenzi, one of the hyenas voiced by Whoopi Goldberg. ("Ooh, say it again!" she giddily implores

Banzai while simultaneously convulsing from the sound. I guess "Mufasa" is Shenzi's kink?)

Our culture loves names and loves to attach self-worth to them, which explains why it irked me to be linked to that New Edition Babies song. Iesha, my fictional namesake, was also my nemesis. "Yes, I've definitely heard this song before," I'd retort, attempting to hide my mild exasperation. "But Another Bad Creation spells it wrong, and actually, *my* name means 'life.'"

And then, I'd add, with a barely concealed smirk and a smug air of self-satisfaction, "Also, my parents named me after a *Stevie Wonder song.*"

Like most people who lived through the 1970s and had good musical taste, my parents owned many Stevie albums—vinyl, of course—including what is considered by many to be his crowning achievement among crowning achievements, *Songs in the Key of Life.* It's a sprawling sonic voyage across themes of love, world peace, and Black history, with nearly every facet of the artist's musical sensibilities and proclivities represented on this double LP: Socially Conscious Stevie ("Pastime Paradise," "Village Ghetto Land"), Lovey-Dovey Stevie ("Knocks Me Off My Feet"), Jammin' On the One Stevie ("I Wish," "Sir Duke").

Of course, there's also Schmaltzy Stevie, where he really lays on the fructose corn syrup, and earnestly so. On *Songs in the Key of Life,* "Isn't She Lovely" is that track, and while it doesn't belong near any respectable list of top twenty-five Stevie numbers, it's endearing enough to not skip over when listening to the album from beginning to end, as one must.

Plus my name gets a shout-out. And to be frank, that's all I really care(d) about.

Stevie wrote "Isn't She Lovely" in celebration of his firstborn child, Aisha, who arrived during the creative period that birthed *Songs in the Key of Life.* The track is joyous and cute, featuring cooing and crying ad-libs from baby Aisha herself and a pleasant harmonica solo as the bridge. There's no real chorus but, rather, three verses that find Stevie tossing about fawning adjective after fawning adjective—the epitome of the proud parent. You can just picture him in the delivery room, beaming broadly alongside an exhausted wife, who just spent hours in labor doing all the hard work, and exclaiming these lyrics at any nurse or doctor or human in the hospital within earshot that day: *"Isn't she lovely?!"* he asks. (Rhetorically, of course.) *"Isn't she precious?!" "Isn't she wonderful?!"*

The lyrics are so fawning and basic they could reasonably flow from the lips of any parent, ever—and have from many. I imagine that's a huge part of its appeal for listeners—how it captures an ostensibly universal feeling about what it's like to become a new parent.

You're proud! You're excited! You want the whole world to know that you had sex once and now there exists a human being who didn't exist before! (Yes, yes, nowadays there are several ways to make babies without having sex. But Stevie's lyrics specifically call out Aisha's mom to gush about how they "conceived" their daughter "from love.")

My dad is one such parent who sang this song to his own daughter, *moi*. Not unlike Stevie's Aisha, I was his firstborn, and he was incredibly enthusiastic about becoming a father. A few months after I was born, he wrote in a notebook about the wonder of experiencing fatherhood for the first time. I'm not entirely sure I know many people who have gotten as much pure joy out of parenting as my father has, and "Isn't She Lovely" maps perfectly onto my dad's personality.

But as widely appealing as this song is, there's one simple line that's deeply personal to me, and it's the kind of line that will probably skate right on past you if you're just casually listening to it. "Life is Aisha," Stevie sings in the final verse, "the meaning of her name."

That's *my* name. That's *my* way of spelling it. That's *my* way of pronouncing it.

And *that's* why my parents were inspired to call me Aisha, I wanted the world to know. Not because of a bunch of rug rats who were in possession of dubious musical talent, but an actual, true musical legend. A twenty-five-time Grammy winner. A creator who has provided the soundtrack to countless birthday parties (if you're Black and your friends and family don't break out into his version of the "Happy Birthday" song while blowing out the candles, are you really Black?), weddings, and weekend brunches. An artist whose influences and imitators stretch far and wide, from Michael Jackson to *American Idol* contestants who have wrongly assumed the only way to perform one of his songs is to murder it via a string of disastrous vocal runs. The man who's responsible for one of the greatest *Sesame Street* collaborations of all time. Go ahead and let the gloriousness of that "Superstition" performance and banter with Grover wash over you. I promise it will make you happy.

"Actually," I'd interject—anytime someone begins a sentence with "actually," the arrogance levels are high—"my name is spelled *A-i-s-h-a*, and my name means 'life.' And my parents named me after a *Stevie Wonder* song."

At some point during my adolescence, these words began casually dancing off my tongue with that barely concealed smirk, and the haughtiness was all right there in the text for anyone to see. By then I'd begun to latch on to an understanding of what most adults considered "great" based on my parents, teachers, and best-of lists assembled mostly by white-guy boomers and Gen-Xers in legacy publications like *Rolling Stone*, as young, impressionable people are wont to do. Stevie is undeniably and universally deemed great; white people, I noticed early on, were just as likely as Black people to extol his many virtues and jam out to his songs, in part because of his Motown origins (white boomers LOVE Motown; see *The Big Chill*) and because his talent for earworms is undeniable. Ditto young and old. To me, having such a specific personal connection to one of his songs was validating—a way to feel simultaneously unique and less "weird" among my peers.

I was a little Rob Gordon from *High Fidelity* in training, developing an unhealthy penchant for mocking what I perceived as others' plebeian tastes.

I was also a little Toni Childs in training—Toni being the bougie, stuck-up friend of the four besties on the TV show *Girlfriends*. The one who openly looked down on Maya for being more 'hood and less refined and was unabashed in her horrifying colorism. (In a season-one episode, she refuses to date a dude because he's as dark as she is, and she doesn't want to have dark-skinned babies. Yeah . . .) Shunning "Iesha" wasn't just about proving I had a mature cultural palate; it was also about distancing myself from the "ghetto," not unlike Toni.

Ah yes, the "ghetto"—that catchall word used to describe poverty, blackness, run-down infrastructure, a bad attitude, the 'hood, and anything not "good" or up to standards. By the time I'd reached the sixth grade, throwing around the word "ghetto" was just par for the course, kind of like how anything and everyone these days can be deemed "woke" or "canceled" or a Karen. I put a lot of the blame, perhaps unfairly, on Pras, Mya, and Ol' Dirty Bastard; in the summer of 1998, the song "Ghetto Supastar" was inescapable on pop radio. (It's catchy, though.)

Whatever the reason, it seemed every kid I knew back then said "ghetto," and white kids at my very white school especially loved to say it. I couldn't put my finger on it at the time, but something about hearing them use that word (and the word "wigger," which I eventually inferred correctly was a way to describe a white person who "acts Black") made me deeply uncomfortable. And I knew, within this very white school environment, I definitely didn't want to be viewed as ghetto.

A name is a quick way to signify status, and plenty of TV shows and movies taught me to draw a connection between negative depictions of blackness and their character names. On *Martin*, one of the show's most famous recurring characters was Sheneneh Jenkins, a teeth-sucking, neck-rolling stereotype of a ghetto Black woman—no manners, no sense of decorum, quick to violence. That Sheneneh is played by Lawrence in drag is part of a grand tradition of Black male comedians imagining a certain kind of Black woman who is inherently masculine and undesirable (to heterosexual men). This woman is rarely portrayed by a light-skinned comedian, and certain body parts are usually accentuated through padding and/or tacky, ill-fitting clothing. Truthfully, the likes of Sheneneh and Jamie Foxx's cross-eyed Wanda character on *In Living Color* don't feel too far off from the Welfare Queen or Mammy caricatures. Sheneneh is ridiculous and uncouth; her name only reinforces this and suggests this was predetermined by her origins. She in turn attracts the same kind of people in her life; her colleagues and friends' names include Bonquisha and Laquita.

The Steve Harvey Show—the 1990s sitcom, not the talk show of the same name—included Lovita the high school secretary, a less mean-spirited and more well-rounded ghetto girl stereotype than Sheneneh but a ghetto girl stereotype nonetheless. A running gag was the reveal of Lovita's relatives' names, which included Duracell, Bruschetta, and Clinique.

There's a mercifully long-forgotten 2001 song called "Shaniqua" by two white dudes from Jersey who looked like they could've been reject members of Limp Bizkit. In it, one of these dudes inherits the old phone number of someone named Shaniqua and fields calls from people trying to reach her. It's not explicitly clear whether or not Shaniqua is Black (the video features a parade of women across various races and ethnicities), but the wigger-like dialect ("Shaniqua don't live here no more!" goes the chorus) implies an attempt at gaining street cred off a name heavily associated with blackness. There was Bon Qui Qui, a sassy recurring character on *MADtv*, who was basically the Latina reincarnation of Sheneneh, except she "worked" at a fast food joint. (I put "work" in quotation marks because she's lazy and frequently talks back to her manager when asked to do simple tasks. That's it. That's the joke.)

As recently as 2017, *Saturday Night Live* made fun of Black names in a sketch featuring Leslie Jones, Sasheer Zamata, and guest host Octavia Spencer, who plays a woman suing her former employers for theft of intellectual property. She claims the company has named its products after her family members, like Seasonique (birth control) and Cymbalta (antidepressant). That's it. That's the joke.

Seeing that connection between unusual Black names and so-called ghetto attitudes over and over does something, or at least it did something to me. I unconsciously began to understand how certain names and superficial traits served as markers of class, and they became linked to my own internal anti-blackness. Is Aisha a name bound by the same level of stigma as Sheneneh or Bon Qui Qui or La-ah (pronounced lah-DASH-uh)? No, especially since it is incredibly popular among

Muslim women, and I can't tell you how many people have told me my name is "beautiful" or "lovely." (Isn't that lovely? Stevie, they agree with you!) And for whatever it's worth, the New Edition Babies' fictional "Iesha" is set up as a girl who's desired rather than a punch line.

But kids naturally want to fit in. They absorb, consciously and unconsciously, bullshit stereotypes and preconceived notions about race, gender, socioeconomics, and on and on. They internalize ideas about masculinity and femininity and learn to assume that things they see and hear from adults are true, because they are adults and supposedly know better than kids do. And thus my convoluted thinking went: *"Iesha" is lowbrow, "Isn't She Lovely" is highbrow, and I want to be seen as the latter.*

Iesha is a made-up Black name; Aisha has meaning and purpose.

I carried this dichotomy in the back of my mind for years.

At the end of 2016, while I was still a staff writer at *Slate*, our culture team put together an editorial package that was the brainchild of one of my colleagues: "Wonder Week," an homage to—you guessed it— the one and only Stevie Wonder. That year had been particularly brutal for pop music fans with the losses of formative artists like David Bowie and Prince, and so the point of Wonder Week was to honor one of our legends, while he was still alive and healthy, with a series of essays unpacking his wide-ranging influence.

I jumped at the chance to contribute and wound up writing three pieces: a song primer for beginners, if such people actually existed, an investigation into whether or not people who aren't Black sing his "Happy Birthday" song during celebrations (spoiler—in my informal polling, most white people had never even heard of it!), and an ode to his talents as a comedian in interviews and stints on shows like *Saturday Night Live*. But another essay I had in mind was intended to be kind of like this one you're reading now—about how I've grown to appreciate my name because of its connection to "Isn't She Lovely."

I hadn't even pitched the idea to the rest of the team yet when I decided to give my dad a call and have him recount the backstory of how he'd been inspired by *Songs in the Key of Life* to name me Aisha.

"Well, I was aware that his daughter's name was Aisha at the time, but I don't think that's where I got your name from," he said.

record scratch

"Wait—really?" I stammered, confused.

"As I recall, a friend of mine had a girlfriend whose daughter was named 'Aisha,' and I'd liked that name. It was also in one of those books of African names your mom and I bought."

"Oh."

Womp. Womp.

This . . . was *not* the story I remembered my dad telling me years ago; I could've sworn he'd heard the song and decided that one day if he were to ever have a daughter, he would name her Aisha. Or was it that while my mom was pregnant with me, he was listening to the album and thought, "Oh, this could be a great name for my daughter"? Or maybe I'm remembering it all wrong, and I only recall him playing the song a lot when I was a kid, and somehow I just *assumed* that's how I got my name. In reality, it wasn't so poetic as I'd thought.

I was flabbergasted. Had I . . . Haley'd myself?

Allow me to explain. Less than a year after *Roots* was published and the miniseries broke television history records, Alex Haley's research and reporting were called into question in Mark Ottaway's exposé in *The Sunday Times of London,* as noted in an article in the *New York Times.* The article claimed that Haley's assertions of ancestral ties to a man named Kunta Kinte, whose story was passed down in part by Haley's grandmother, were dubious at best and that the griot with whom the author consulted while visiting The Gambia to research his book had told Haley what he wanted to hear, not what could actually be proven. (According to the article, the griot's widow confirmed that he'd known in advance of Haley's plans to visit the village.)[7]

To add fuel to the criticism, multiple writers accused Haley of plagiarism. Margaret Walker Alexander, a college professor, filed an unsuccessful suit against Haley, alleging similarities to her 1966 novel *Jubilee,* which was based on the life of her great-grandmother. And in 1978, Haley settled a lawsuit with Harold Courlander, a white writer and anthropologist, over similarities to several passages in *The African,* a novel about an African boy who is kidnapped by French traders and sold into slavery.[8]

Recounting his research methods in the final pages of his tome, Haley wrote, ". . . by far most of the dialogue and most of the incidents are of necessity a novelized amalgam of what I *know* took place together with what my researching led me to plausibly *feel* took place."[9] Yet at the time of publication, *Roots* was classified as a work of nonfiction on the *New York Times* bestseller's list and elsewhere, which also helps explain why these doubts of its veracity have cast such a long shadow over the book, even as it continues to be celebrated. Over the years, Haley would both concede to some of his detractors' critiques and push back against them, referring to the book as a "faction"—a melding of fact and fiction. When he was interviewed by the *New York Times* about

Ottaway's article, he admitted to there being "dozens" of unintended errors in *Roots* but argued that the spirit of the book remained true and significant—his "carefully researched, laboriously developed" book would work to counter the pervasive narrative of a "Tarzan-and-Jane image of Africa."[10]

What I find so fascinating about the critical saga surrounding Haley's *Roots* are the ways in which it resists simple black-and-white conclusions. Was it a straight-up, intentional fabrication on Haley and his publisher's part, or was it a historical biography about a real family that took liberties with facts here and there? Does it matter either way if the results were mostly positive? In countless interviews, he evangelized the importance of Black Americans seeking their own roots and history just as he had. "An absence of pride changes to presence of pride, and the effect of pride can make every difference in the world," he told journalist John Callaway in a 1976 interview.[11]

He wasn't wrong: *Roots* inspired curiosity among countless Black people in part because it flew in the face of over a century's worth of incendiary, devastating images of blackness and grossly inaccurate portrayals of slavery, from minstrels to *Birth of a Nation* to antebellum-period Blaxploitation flicks like *Mandingo*. The act of excavating and recounting Black history through a lens like Haley's is a form of activism in its own right, standing in opposition to white supremacy. There's a reason Black Americans have been so obsessed with imagining ourselves as African royalty in pop culture, from *Coming to America* to Michael Jackson's "Remember the Time" video to *The Lion King* to Beyoncé's *Black Is King* to Wakanda. To render African culture a source of pride, however imperfect, is an act of resistance.

But Haley was also a writer in search of a narrative, and he found one in his grandmother's stories of Kunta Kinte. The need to accomplish something most Black descendants of enslaved people can only dream of doing—tracing one's lineage all the way back to the African continent—evidently led him to fudge ethical standards and overcorrect, both for The Culture™ and for the purposes of his own ego. The negative consequences of spinning this tall tale shouldn't be ignored either; it planted unrealistic expectations in Black people about their own prospects for success in finding their ancestors and certainly played an indirect part in generating the dubious multibillion-dollar industry of DNA ancestry testing. "I, we need a place called Eden," he reportedly told Ottaway, the author of that dissenting *Sunday Times* article. "My people need Pilgrim's Rock."

Indeed, I'd Haley'd my own origin story without even knowing it. Sure, there's not a one-to-one correlation between Haley's embellishment of Kunta's story and me imagining how I got my name; yet I believe the impulses are born from the same core place: a desire, a *need* to own our narrative. In my case, my memory was unconsciously influenced by the need to be palatable to others and feel empowered by my blackness. "Isn't She Lovely" was *my* Pilgrim's Rock, the antithesis of a corny New Jack Swing song by some kids from the 'hood. Before I was even aware of the concept of respectability politics (and spent many years learning to reject it), I'd already absorbed it as a mindset.

This is the power of anti-blackness. It can make us seek ways of coping and engendering pride that turn out to be at least partially damaging to our own psyche or, in Haley's case, the psyche of others. It may make us feel better in the moment, but in service of what? It elides the truth, and it's exhausting.

Yet it's also a thoroughly universal impulse. Just think of all the myths predominantly white Western culture has been primed to believe in: Christopher Columbus's "discovery" of the New World, the origins of Thanksgiving, the Lost Cause, the American Cowboy, the American Dream, capitalism, the War on Christmas. Years, sometimes centuries later, what were once facts have hardened in the cultural imagination into something other than what they originally were, having morphed and become about as reliable as a phrase passed along in the midst of a game of telephone. They've become convenient tales of bravado and pride, frequently in service of upholding white supremacy.

So, yeah. The revelation from my dad was kind of deflating! Like, I could feel air leaving my body and see myself melting into the shape of a flat, floppy pancake right there in my office chair. Who was I, even, if I wasn't the girl whose name was pulled directly from one of the greatest albums of all time? How was I going to respond now whenever some unoriginal stranger decided to start singing that goddamn "Iesha" song? Just grin and bear it, and let them think they're cool when they're not?

I'm being dramatic. I promise I have not spent sleepless nights contemplating my years-long self-deception, though perhaps I've spent quite a few waking moments shaking my head at myself for plucking this tale seemingly from out of nowhere. I'm sure I've sounded insufferable to those acquaintances who've had to hear this defensive retort from me about Stevie Wonder. Nobody wants to continue a conversation with the "Well, actually" person. That person is always annoying. Don't be that person.

By the time my dad and I had this conversation, I was pushing thirty and in a position to reflect on why I'd convinced myself of this fictional backstory all those years. I'd wrestled myself away from my Rob from *High Fidelity* phase (at least as best as I could—I do continue to struggle with this sometimes, especially when I meet anyone who still goes to Dave Matthews Band concerts) and had long since pried myself from the Toni Childs from *Girlfriends* state of mind. I'd gotten better at putting my pretentiousness and bougie inclinations in check. In college I'd immersed myself in environments with more—and more varied—Black and brown people, where my name didn't feel like a big deal and where there might even be other Aishas or someone who knew another Aisha. I'd encountered writers and scholars and professors and thinkers who were able to express pride without resorting to condescension toward other aspects of Black life—people like James Baldwin, Zora Neale Hurston, Toni Morrison, Charles Burnett, dream hampton, Spike Lee, and Kimberlé Crenshaw.

A couple of years after my personal myth was shattered, I saw the film *The Last Black Man in San Francisco*, a drama about a young Black San Francisco native named Jimmie Fails, who is frustrated and embittered by the rapid gentrification of the city. He's particularly fixated on the Victorian-style home he grew up in and which his grandfather built—a factoid Jimmie tells anyone and everyone who will listen (including, at one point, a group of passersby immersed in an architectural tour). As of late, however, it has been occupied by an older white couple, and Jimmie obsessively monitors their upkeep of the structure, frequently trespassing on the grounds to restore the details of its exterior design as he remembers them being when he lived there.

When the house suddenly becomes vacant—the children of the couple are fighting over its fate following the death of their mother—Jimmie becomes a squatter in his childhood residence, moving back in with his family's old furniture provided to him by his aunt. Here he can relive his memories and his family history and feel as though he's taken back ownership of what's rightfully his. It's a small comfort—a fantasy, but a comfort nonetheless. That's the function of a fantasy, anyhow.

But—spoiler . . . sorry if you haven't seen it yet; you've now been warned . . . 'k bye—during the performance of a one-man play put on by his best friend Monty inside the house's attic, Monty reveals to Jimmie and the rest of the audience that the house is not, in fact, the product of Jimmie's grandfather's blood, sweat, and tears. The house was actually built in the 1850s. It's "just" a home that was once owned by a Black family and no longer is.

It turns out Jimmie's always known the truth about the house. Over the years, he's held up this mythic ownership as a shield from the reality he doesn't want to face while clinging to the hope that one day he might be able to live in the home again. He's told himself and others this myth so much that he'd almost forgotten it wasn't true.

His mother understands what drove him to carry this on for so long and so deeply: "This was ours, and then it wasn't. So you just tell yourself what you need to make you feel like it still is. Shit, I did it, too. It makes you feel . . . special."

That's the motivation: the need to feel special. The need to combat seemingly labyrinthine and insurmountable forces of anti-blackness—disenfranchisement, redlining, the racial wealth gap. I'm not saying what Jimmie did is right or even healthy; obsessing over something you cannot change and lying to yourself about it is no way to live! It will fester and break you down and wreak havoc on your life! But . . . I get it. We all need something to believe in.

But then, you've eventually got to let it go. Or, bare minimum, channel that energy more productively. I may have uncovered the insidiousness of the stigma against Black-sounding names, but until that wake-up call about how I got my name, I was still living in a sort of denial. Monty's climactic reveal in *Last Black Man* sticks with me, both because of the performer Jonathan Majors's transfixing intensity and the conviction with which his character forces Jimmie to confront the truth:

> Let us give each other the courage to see beyond the stories we were born into. Let us all really look at Jimmie Fails, IV. Self-taught historian, carpenter, gentle, loving man, a true survivor. Jimmie, how many places have you lived? And if they kick you out tomorrow, you would still be all those things! You exist beyond these walls; you extend beyond your forefathers; you're not this house!

Monty's words come from a place of love and empathy for his friend. It's the wake-up call Jimmie needs to begin to heal, to not carry so much pain.

I, too, needed to realize that I'm much more than my origin, and that I can only appreciate it on my own terms, not concern myself about what it means to others. I'd Haley'd myself, but I didn't need to continue doing so.

On the other hand, I don't need to beat myself up about having done so, either. I think of the filmmaker Sarah Polley's fascinating *Stories We Tell*, a documentary uncovering long-held secrets and revelations about her family. Part of the brilliance of the film is how interviews with family members and friends reveal the various inconsistencies in the perspectives and retellings of events that took place long before Polley herself was even born.

At one point, Polley lays out her motivations for making the film, saying, "I'm interested in the way we tell stories about our lives, about the fact that the truth about the past is often ephemeral and difficult to pin down, and many of our stories, when we don't take proper time to do research about our pasts—which is almost always the case—end up with shifts and fictions in them, mostly unintended."

There's no malice or blame-casting to be found in Polley's thesis, only curiosity and, occasionally, bewilderment. She leaves room for each of these points of view to be a kind of truth, even if the facts aren't quite there. She leaves room for understanding and grace.

Which is why, after that conversation with Chance the Rapper where he asked me to tell him my name, then sheepishly asked if I was Black, I couldn't help but laugh to myself about how those two things seemed to be inextricably intertwined. At the end of the interview, I felt compelled to ask him if I'd sounded white to him; "I wasn't offended" by the earlier question about my race, I assured him. I was only curious.

"It wasn't at all that you sounded white," he said. "I don't know how to explain this . . . If you had never said the thing about Black characters in *The Lion King* and stuff, to be honest I probably never would have guessed that you were Black, but I think . . ." And then he switched gears, presumably a bit embarrassed about it all. "It really doesn't matter. I really appreciate your interview, getting on the call with you."

I mean, he was right. It really didn't matter. My name is my name, I'm Black, and I've long since become comfortable with both. I don't need any song, good or bad, to define my existence. I'm at peace and thankful for life.

Life is Aisha, the meaning of her name.

2

BLACKETY-BLACK

How to Be a Critic (of Black Art*)

*i.e., any work of art involving and/or about Black people

**Do** judge as to whether it's serving up positive or negative representation. If it's positive, that's good. If it's negative, that's bad.

More specifically, if the work involves drug dealers, gang members, Black-on-Black crime, promiscuity, deadbeat dads, baby mamas, poor people, high school dropouts, lower-middle-class people, blue-collar workers, homeless people, disabled people, abusive men, effeminate men, masculine women, sassy women, men in drag, the prolific usage of "nigga," slavery, rappers, the 'hood, domestic workers, hustlers, gamblers, drunks, strippers, and/or fried chicken—this is not an exhaustive list, by the way—then it is to be condemned and avoided at all costs. For decades upon decades, Black people have been plagued by these harmful stereotypes in media and culture, which have greatly contributed to our relative lack of progress in producing more upstanding entrepreneurs, doctors, lawyers, CEOs, scientists, coders, and classically trained musicians within our communities.

There's nothing to be gained by telling more stories about these kinds of characters, unless, of course, it's a story about pulling oneself up by one's bootstraps and overcoming adversity, aka The Struggle™, or if there's a redemption arc deliberately baked into the narrative where the negative stereotypical characters either see the error of their ways and fix themselves and/or are counterbalanced by a critical mass of upwardly mobile/bougie Black characters. (This is why Tyler Perry is acceptable, even if he's cross-dressing as a giant, gun-toting mammy. Also, just look at how many jobs he's given many of our best Black performers all these years—surely that's gotta count for something.)

Some examples of negative Black art, or NBA for short—not to be confused with the National Basketball Association—exemplifying these traits include: *Empire*, *The Boondocks*, *The Color Purple*, *Sweet Sweetback's Baadasssss Song*, *Porgy & Bess*, *Slave Play*, "WAP" by Cardi B and Megan Thee Stallion.

Conversely, any work about Black people that does not include the above-mentioned pestilences should be considered a win for the culture, no questions asked. Systemic racism is very real, yes, but there are plenty of us who are moving on up or have already moved on up—the third-generation Alphas and AKAs, the Ivy League grads, the ones who came from two-parent households, the single adults with no kids/no criminal record/excellent credit, the Black nerds, the judges, the good cops, the

Black lady therapists, the surgeons . . . where are all *those* stories? Why aren't *they* being told?

When encountering Black art out in the wild, be on the lookout for Black Girl Magic, Black Love, Black Excellence, and the direct involvement of Common and/or John Legend. These are signs of positive Black art (or PBA, though not to be confused with the Professional Bowlers Association)—the kind of art we should all get behind. That's what is needed to uplift the race and take our place as the kings and queens of the world that we were always destined to be.

Some examples of PBA include: *Black Panther*, Beyoncé's *Homecoming*, *The Cosby Show*, your local spoken word poet who addresses every Black person as "queen" or "king."

<u>Do</u> be wary if white people or the "wrong" kind of Black people are overly enthusiastic about it.

Here's how it goes: A Black person makes something. Maybe that thing is purported to be about capturing an essence of Black culture and existence—"authentically" and "unapologetically Black," if you will. Maybe it deals with super-serious issues like police brutality, microaggressions, or unwed mothers. Or maybe it doesn't come with all those bells and whistles and hype; it's simply something made by a Black person.

Either way, it's been made and reproduced for the general population, perhaps with the kind of heavy promotion and fanfare that once eluded the vast majority of Black creatives no matter their field. And suddenly, it's *really* popular with white people and many others across the racial/ethnic spectrum, not just Black people. In fact, the artist has "crossed over," as they say, beloved and praised by white critics staffed at fancy, elite institutions who put them on their year-end best-of lists, awarded top prizes by historically exclusive organizations, and feverishly and breathlessly discussed at progressives' dinner parties as a way to demonstrate cultural cachet. If this artist is a musician, their music gets the mostly white crowd to go apeshit at the frat party or in the club; if a comedian, their jokes—many of them about their blackness—leave white audience members howling a bit too much with laughter. Even white middle-age suburban moms love them, having seen them once on *The Ellen DeGeneres Show*.

If any of this is happening, be afraid. Be *very* afraid. Fear the sellout, the shuck-and-jiver, the coon who's more than eager to tap-dance for the white folks (and white-adjacent folks) so they can be the biggest stars in the world, because that's who these artists are. They're performing for white approval and being anointed as the Golden Black Child of the moment because of it. They aren't making art for Black people, even if they claim it to be, because what they're doing is corny, watered-down, exploitative, and *real* Black people know it. They absolve white people of all their injustices committed against Black people; they perpetuate anti-Black stereotypes, and for that, they deserve very pointed side-eyes. And the Black people who *do* love these works aren't to be trusted, either, because those are the "pick-me" Negroes who are always The One Black Friend in their social circle or the only Black person in The Room Where It Happens, and they're more than content with that state of things; in fact, they revel in it.

You don't want to keep company with the likes of Van Jones, do you? Then stop supporting Lizzo; she makes music for white ladies who SoulCycle and say *"Yassss qweeeeen"* after one-too-many White Claws.

Real blackness, that Donny-and-Roberta blackness, that *blackety-blackness*, is uncompromising and wholly exempt from dilution and exploitation by whiteness. It's difficult, actually, to exactly describe what authentic blackness is, but you know it when you see it. It's Solange singing "Don't Touch My Hair"; Doughboy lamenting to Tre how the media "don't know, don't show, or don't care about what's goin' on in the 'hood"; that classic photo of Maya Angelou and Amiri Baraka dancing; David Ruffin in *The Temptations* TV movie with the sick burn, "Ain't nobody comin' to see you, Otis!"; Soul Glo.

Even if white people can be entertained by some of those things, they can't *love* them like *real* Black people do and can't appreciate them in the same way. That's the only standard that matters, truthfully. (On a related note, if a white person is at the helm of this art, it's automatically got a strike against it. That's it. Those are the rules, sorry. For every *Jeffersons* or *Coming to America*, there's a million *Song[s] of the South*. White people can't be trusted to tell our stories . . . except on the rare occasions when they can.)

<u>Do</u> protect Black artists and their work at all costs, at all times. In mixed company, at least.

On the red carpet at an awards ceremony, Issa Rae once said, "I'm rooting for everybody Black."

It was the proclamation heard 'round the world, the modern-day equivalent of James Weldon Johnson's "Lift Every Voice and Sing," James Brown's "Say It Loud—I'm Black and I'm Proud," Nina Simone's "To Be Young, Gifted, and Black." It was the essence of twenty-first-century

Black pride and yet more confirmation that Rae, creator of one of the best shows of the last decade, is unabashedly down for the cause.

It's only right we take her at her literal word and support all Black artists and art, no matter how questionable, incompetent, or just plain offensive they might be. The script may be shoddy, a role or two may be woefully miscast, the jokes might not be hitting the way you know they're supposed to hit. But you shouldn't dare speak ill of them outside of close inner circles and definitely not on social media or in publications where art is reviewed.

Because that's absolutely what she meant by "rooting for everybody Black." We've gotta be ride-or-dies for each one of our skinfolk because a rising tide lifts all boats, and we're all in this together, and if one of us suffers bad criticism, then we all suffer because they'll just stop letting Black people make stuff. If we don't support us, who will? No one, that's who! Remember what Ice Cube said in *Boyz n the Hood*: "Either they don't know, don't show, or don't care about what's goin' on in the 'hood." "They" is the mainstream media, i.e., white people, i.e., those who want to keep us down.

And think about it: Issa made this statement at the 2017 Emmy Awards ceremony, an event where whiteness abounds. That year was notable, with an unusually high number of Black nominees and some historic wins, including Donald Glover as the first Black person to win for directing a comedy series and Lena Waithe becoming the first Black woman to win for writing a comedy series. That never would've happened if we gave negative or even mixed reviews to Black work. It's just basic math.

This edict might seem contradictory to the previously stated guidelines—after all, plenty of Black people have made anti-Black art, and plenty of Black people are into the kinds of Black artists who are immensely appealing to white people. But at the end of the day, we've still got to hold this art to a lower standard to make up for racism. There's that saying that goes something like, *I don't agree with what you said, but I'll defend to the death your right to say it.* It's totally the same thing: *I think your movie is crap, but I will shut down any hater who spews slander against your work online, because if I don't, we'll lose all the Black art, forever.*

Do assume this Black movie you loved has a low Rotten Tomatoes score because no Black critics have had a chance to weigh in. Alternatively, assume this thing you hated/find extremely problematic is not being critiqued harshly enough because no Black critics have had a chance to weigh in.

As a general rule of thumb, professional Black critics don't exist at major publications—at least not the kinds that like the same things you do; these are the ones who tend to have the "acceptable" points of view on race and everything else.

So after you've watched that god-awful Oscar-baity slavery movie that "everyone" seems to be raving about ad nauseum and does indeed get nominated for a bunch of Oscars, tweet about how Black voices are "SO NEEDED" to counter the overwhelming whiteness of criticism. (Do not Google to see whether any Black critics actually did cover the movie and perhaps even wrote glowingly of it because your point must stand. Black critics don't exist!)

If you do, however, happen to encounter a professional Black critic in the wild, and it turns out they criticized a heartwarming tale of Black uplift that you enjoyed and didn't think too deeply about, confront them in a tweet or slide into their DMs to question their blackness and wonder why they've gotta be such an FBI informant about their dislike of it. It's absolutely this person's fault that this movie with a predominantly Black cast and crew doesn't have an absolutely perfect score on Rotten Tomatoes and Metacritic—those two arbiters of taste and pillars of online criticism. And they don't get to ruin your good time by harping on the extensive plot holes or lazy dialogue or undercooked characterizations.

• • •

The year 2016 was a pretty crappy one, for obvious reasons. Trump, of course, but also that was the year Brexit was decided, several high-profile terrorist attacks occurred, and seemingly every significant cultural figure decided they were done with this thing called life (Prince, Bowie, Carrie Fisher, Debbie Reynolds, George Michael, Muhammad Ali, Leonard Cohen, and Harper Lee, just for starters).

But 2016 was also a great year for blackness, culturally speaking. It might have even been a peak year for blackness. These are just a few of the things that were released or made their debut in that dumpster fire of a 366-day period:

- Beyoncé's *Lemonade*
- Solange's *A Seat at the Table*
- *Queen Sugar*
- *Atlanta*

- *Insecure*
- *Moonlight*
- Rihanna's *Anti*
- *13th*

I'm not going to pretend as if there was any cosmic or coordinated force that led to such a murderers' row of artistry in such a short amount of time—production schedules, individual creative work-flows, and Jay-Z's infidelity happen on their own timelines with no regard for what everyone else is doing. But what a year for blackness! It's not that Black art had waned before then, because it never can; yet it does feel like a turning point when so many different expressions of blackness found popularity, critical acclaim, and, later, influence on a huge scale all at the same time. As the world was burning, some of the biggest works that would come to help define American culture in the twenty-first century thus far were emerging and thriving. If that isn't Black, I don't know what is.

Since then, a relative abundance of Black creativity has emerged, and it's been simultaneously invigorating and befuddling to exist in this current moment. Across all mediums, there's arguably a broader canvas upon which storytellers have been able to work and a wider variety of modes: Boots Riley and Terence Nance dancing through whimsy and cutting political satire in their respective works *Sorry to Bother You* and *Random Acts of Flyness*, Lil Nas X bringing an overt brand of queerness and flamboyance to the Billboard charts, director Janicza Bravo and screenwriter Jeremy O. Harris animating a viral Twitter thread through *Zola* . . .

This is to say nothing of the cultural phenomena of the last few years that have been Beyoncé's *Homecoming*, Jordan Peele's *Get Out*, Ryan Coogler's *Black Panther*, Kendrick Lamar's *DAMN.*, Cardi B and Megan Thee Stallion's "WAP" . . .

What a time to be alive, and Black.

But to be alive and Black also means to acknowledge cultural cachet and power, in the so-called mainstream at least, can be tenuous in myriad ways. There's the fickle nature of Hollywood, for one, where blackness has historically been treated as a fad—hot for a sec and then unceremoniously pushed aside. (See: the Blaxploitation movement, the robust era of 1990s Black sitcoms.) And there's the ongoing issue of cultural theft when it comes to Black artists and influencers, whose work is often bastardized and distilled by white artists and influencers on platforms like TikTok without proper credit and/or payout, a practice that predates social media by decades. (See: Perry Como's bland cover of Little Richard's "Tutti Frutti," Addison Rae's white-bread performance of dances choreographed by Black TikTokers on *The Tonight Show Starring Jimmy Fallon*.)

To be alive and Black means to acknowledge that not everything Black people create or have a hand in turns to gold, and that they can be just as complicit in engaging with insidious stereotypes about Black people as other races and ethnicities. Of course, before the industry can even get tired of any "fad," it first has to duplicate it ad nauseam, running it into the ground with a proliferation of uninspired and lazy knockoffs. (See: the Blaxploitation movement, our current post–*Get Out* era of "social thrillers" and their play cousins within the genre, Black-man-killed-by-cop plotlines.)

To be alive and Black means to acknowledge that progress is still incremental, and the work is nowhere near done, but that we're further along than we ever were before. (See: the empires of opportunity by creators like Shonda Rhimes and Ava DuVernay, the emergence and stardom of younger performers like Marsai Martin and Storm Reid.)

Arts and entertainment industries have come a long way, baby—that is, opportunities are more plentiful and varied, and bigwigs at least pay lip service to inclusivity—and the forums inviting us, the consumers, to weigh in are more democratic than they were before. Social media makes it so that anyone can share their opinion and find others who share those same opinions and disagree with those who share opposing opinions. And there are more people of color such as me working professionally as cultural observers to offer perspectives that aren't tied to the traditional, predominantly white and male world of criticism.

This has meant that our golden era of Black artistry is coinciding with a wild west of recorded feedback, much of it rooted in cultural landscapes of the past: evaluations based on preconceived standards of "positive" and "negative" representation (the definitions of which are very subjective depending upon whom you talk to), assumptions about people's blackness and political stances based on what they like or don't like, and, most troubling to me, the belief that all Black artists should be exempt from negativity (this often overlaps with standom).

One common refrain I've encountered as a critic, usually echoing from the corners of White Film Bro Twitter, goes something like, "I read your review of [*insert movie I probably said nice things about overall but critiqued for including some undeniably racist bullshit here*] and you're an idiot. So we should cancel [*X director*]??? Not everything is about race, RACIST." There are at least two things someone can do to convince me to never take them seriously: (a) engage in bad-faith arguments about people being "canceled" when what they're really referring to is people being called out and/or held accountable for their actions, and (b) accuse someone of "making everything about race" merely for pointing out something racist.

But there's a *different* verse I'm also all too familiar with, usually coming from a random one or two incensed Black people, who ask something along the lines of, "Why are you, a Black critic, dumping on [*insert mediocre Black movie here*]? You just like to feel superior or something?"

And when the call is coming from inside the house, sometimes I'll ask myself, "Did I actually like this movie, or am I just trying to be protective of it for the sake of Black art? Is this actually good, or does it merely say things about blackness I agree with, generally? Where do my identities as a Black person and a Black critic align and diverge?"

Black people have always sought out representation in art, but now we're living in an era where, regardless of your demographic makeup, art = your identity, your ideology, your personality. Or at least that's what the culture has taught us over the last couple of decades between Facebook groups, BuzzFeed quizzes, and social media prompts enticing users to filter their entire beings through a franchise, a pop star's fandom, or a cause.

When people offer opinions and critiques on popular culture these days, it's no longer just, like, your opinion, man. It says everything about your taste, your morals, your politics, and your activist bona fides.

Here's a real DM I received from a random dude who took the time to find me on Instagram after our *Pop Culture Happy Hour* episode reviewing the movie *King Richard* (lazy grammar and punctuation are his own):

Question, is you and the rest of the Pop Culture happy hour crew's job to zag on every popular opinion. Respect your work but . . . it feels like the more popular . . . a movie is the less likely you'll compliment it. Like it or not Will [Smith] is gonna win an Oscar.

Ah yes, an accusation that has plagued all critics everywhere since the beginning of time—being contrarian for contrarian's sake. Typical stuff, regardless of the critic's background or identity, because if they don't like something, it's because it was made for the *PEOPLE* (the lauded average Joes and Joannas who only ever want to *escape* into a movie and never have to think about what they're watching), not critics, those coastal elites of entertainment journalism. Critics *are not* the people, and also *they hate* the people. Never forget, of course, The Great Divide of 2021 when any critic who dared argue that *Don't Look Up*—Adam McKay's star-studded "satire" about terrible Americans ignoring a fast-approaching comet—is terribly unfunny, smug, and illogical (it really is!) was branded a climate change denier who just didn't "get it." (McKay himself tweeted that his movie might not "make any sense" if "you don't have at least a small ember of anxiety about the climate collapsing [or the US teetering].)"[1] Never mind that most movie critics probably *do* care about climate change a great deal.

But back to that rando in my mentions. The kicker from this *King Richard* stan is when he concluded, *Can't we just be happy that a majority Black cast made a great film. Always going against the grain isn't as trendy as you think.*

echoes *Can't we just be happy that a majority Black cast made a great film . . . made a great film . . . made a great film . . .*

As if greatness isn't subjective. As if *King Richard*, the movie about

Venus and Serena Williams's father, starring Will Smith doing a very peculiar accent, was some triumph of filmmaking instead of the just okay biopic that it is. (This is my opinion, man.)

. . . just be happy that a majority Black cast made a great film . . . great film . . . great . . .

No! I don't want to "just be happy" about *King Richard*. I want more than a pudgy Will Smith doing a weird accent in a movie that chooses to focus primarily on the man behind the two women giants of tennis. I want more than just a blandly "positive" uplifting story about overcoming adversity; I want interiority and surprise and characters who feel as though they have a reason to exist beyond retelling history. To encourage "settling" in our tastes is to act as if no or very few examples of great Black films and shows don't already exist, when they do. To rattle off just a few from the last few years: the achingly beautiful *If Beale Street Could Talk*; the poignant and topical melodrama *Queen Sugar*; the haunting examination of race, identity, class, and attraction that is *Passing*; the very funny and weird love letter to Chicago, *South Side*; the lovely bildungsroman about a Muslim mother and daughter, *Jinn*.

I want more than to operate strictly from a scarcity mindset. Black art isn't a package of long-stemmed wineglasses that must be handled with care. Black art isn't fragile.

There was a lot of Discourse™ when it came to *Queen & Slim* and the *Bonnie and Clyde*–meets–Black Lives Matter drama from director Melina Matsoukas and screenwriter Lena Waithe. It's a movie almost programmatically calibrated to set fingers a-tapping on Black Twitter: Two beautiful Black people (played by Jodie Turner-Smith and Daniel Kaluuya) go on the run after shooting a racist white cop in self-defense during a traffic stop? Check. A radicalized Black teen shoots a cop in the face during a protest supporting the fugitives? Check. The fugitives become martyrs, dying gloriously in a hail of bullets at the end? Heavy, *heavy* check.

I didn't review the film myself, but a few Black critics responded negatively to it, like *Vulture*'s Angelica Jade Bastién, who deemed the movie "beautiful" but ultimately "a hollow narrative to consider," and *Shadow & Act*'s Brooke Obie, who balked at the movie's violent and fatalistic ending. (I agree with these critiques, for what it's worth.) They and others were targeted online for "putting down another sister's art publicly," being an "Uncle Tom," and other "sins" in the name of blackness; the furor and backlash were strong enough to spark multiple articles about the dynamic between Black critics and Black viewers and how years of scarcity in Black representation in both filmmaking and criticism feed into these extremely charged responses. "There is an expectation that you must support Black art unilaterally with no regard for quality," Bastién told *The Guardian*. "I find this both condescending and patronizing for Black art and Black critics."[2]

Indeed. Again, Black art isn't fragile.

This is something I've had to learn for myself while honing my skills as a critic and figuring out what kind of writer and consumer I want to be. In my earliest days, I could occasionally lean hard into the "representation for representation's sake" frame of mind, in large part because I was operating primarily from that same scarcity mindset that those *King Richard* and *Queen & Slim* defenders were—a concern that if I didn't support Black artists, by either not buying a ticket or an album or giving a lukewarm or negative review, I was dooming opportunities for Black artists everywhere.

One of the very first pieces I ever had published, at the start of my career, was a blog post examining a minor cultural debate that had sprung up in the wake of the release of the movie *Red Tails* in 2012. Now there's a strong chance you'd long forgotten about *Red Tails* until this very moment, or that you have no recollection of this movie at all. It was only a modest success at the box office, making just under $50 million domestically,[3] and it didn't leave much of a cultural ripple in its wake, though many of its stars—like Terrence Howard, Michael B. Jordan, Leslie Odom Jr., and David Oyelowo—would soon go on to make bigger and more acclaimed things that you almost certainly remember better.

So as a brief refresher: *Red Tails* is a rollicking dramatic retelling of the famed Tuskegee Airmen, directed by Black filmmaker Anthony Hemingway and written by John Ridley and Aaron McGruder (of *Boondocks* fame). Executive producer George Lucas was very much the face of the publicity campaign, as it had been a passion project of his for decades. In fact, Lucas and the other creators were not shy about having envisioned this as a *Star Wars*–like take on history, with the visuals harkening back to Hollywood's 1940s- and 1950s-era war movies and an emphasis on the aviation action.

In an interview on *The Daily Show*, Lucas was blunt about why it took him so long to get the movie made—it wasn't "green" enough for investors, i.e., a majority-Black cast action movie made for a medium-size budget was considered a huge risk because Black casts are not seen as "bankable" abroad. He stressed the importance of telling a story like this, one that was about "real heroes" that could inspire Black teenage boys, and revealed he already had a prequel and sequel in mind.[4] (This man can only imagine art in terms of trilogies, it seems.)

The catch, of course, was that audiences needed to come out in droves to see this movie first.

Reviews were not too enthusiastic about the movie, though—the *New York Times* called it a "mildly entertaining classroom instructional,"[5] hardly a ringing endorsement. And while the majority of the reviews at major publications came from white critics, I can say that the few Black people I know who actually saw the movie also had some not-so-great reactions to it. (A "stupid, stupid movie," was the summation of one of my friends at the time.)

It was, it seemed, an example of "progress" (an action film about real-life Black heroes actually getting made and released widely in theaters) conflicting with the matter of art.

And that was the issue central to the conversation around *Red Tails*: whether or not to reward mediocrity for the sake of showing "support" and convincing Hollywood to make more movies by and about Black people.

"Is it my duty to see *Red Tails*?" I wondered in my *Slate* article. That's what Lucas and the rest of the publicity campaign seemed to be telling me, as if my purchase of a ticket would function as a civic service that would help stave off another prolonged dry spell for Black storytelling. Kind of like a stern guilt trip, to be honest.

I wasn't the only one who felt the call to duty. Some news articles from that time profiled several loosely organized efforts in cities across the country by ordinary people who wanted to get the word out about *Red Tails* and set up special group outings to see the film. There was a lot of talk about how this was a "positive" image to show young Black people, and everyone needed to mobilize behind it. One of those articles reported that an organizer expressed exhaustion over hearing people complain about there not being enough Black people in movies: "The only way to see more films with Black actors," he says, "is to support the films that are made."[6]

I mean, yes, sure, sounds logical, but what about the *quality* of the film? (These same organizers weren't quoted as having commented on the performances, the action sequences, or whether or not they even found it, at the bare minimum, entertaining . . .)

After wrestling with the art vs. progress conundrum of it all, at the end of my *Slate* piece, I pretty much echoed those organizers and concluded, proudly, yes, I would see *Red Tails* in theaters. "Moviegoers who want to see such stories told *do* need to support these films," I wrote. "Not because we'll lose our hypothetical 'Black card' if we don't, but because it's the only way those stories will be told again—and maybe, the next time, a little better."

Cut to 2018, spring: I struggled with how to write my review of *A Wrinkle in Time*, Ava DuVernay's adaptation of Madeleine L'Engle's classic sci-fi/fantasy novel. I'd read the book in grade school, like plenty of other kids, though I didn't have a particularly strong attachment to it nor had I really thought about it since then. (I hadn't even been aware of the reportedly not-good 2003 TV adaptation.)

But by then I was all-in for whatever project DuVernay had her fingerprints on, in awe of her visual and narrative crafting in features like *Middle of Nowhere* and the documentary *13th*. I was excited to see what she'd do with her biggest budget to date—$100 million, a first for a woman of color at the time—and intrigued by the cast, which included Oprah, Reese Witherspoon, Mindy Kaling, and, as the main protagonist Meg, Storm Reid.

A major studio sci-fi/fantasy film about a young Black girl, and it's directed by a Black woman? Sign. Me. Up.

But as I left the theater of the press screening, I knew processing the movie and writing about it was going to be a particular challenge because unfortunately, I'd come away feeling *meh* on the whole thing. The story's world-building felt half-baked, and the dialogue too often veered into overly earnest and rote territory.

But how could I feel good about being less than enthusiastic about this, a groundbreaking movie from one of the most powerful and influential filmmakers of the last decade? If *A Wrinkle in Time* received tepid reviews from critics like myself and/or underperformed at the box office, it could be decades before another studio handed a movie of this stature to a woman of color, I thought.

(It wasn't—since then, Chloé Zhao has helmed Marvel's *The Eternals*, reportedly on a $200 million budget.[7] But that movie's "underwhelming" box office inevitably stirred up the same tired conversations about women filmmakers' box office pull even when other pretty huge factors were in play, namely the ongoing pandemic.)

I know that women and minority filmmakers are held to a different standard, constantly forced to jump through hoops to fund their projects, while comparatively "unproven" white dude directors make the leap from indie darling to franchise directors with relative ease and much less pressure. White guys are allowed to fail again and again; the rest of us are not.

My one review might not make or break a big budget movie like DuVernay's, but I felt a sense of personal responsibility to not tear down this movie out of fear of what it might mean for The Culture, writ large.

You can sense my hesitation to come down too hard on *A Wrinkle in Time* all throughout the final review that was published. After carefully laying out DuVernay's bona fides as a character-driven director based on her previous films, I revealed, "I take no pleasure in reporting that her latest feature . . . stumbles in its world building and can't quite find its groove." Throughout the piece, I'm quite obviously walking the tightrope between a pan and a lukewarm review, sprinkling in caveats (maybe I'm just too old to really appreciate this?, I wondered) alongside more pointed commentary (Meg's romantic interest was "generically handsome" and "Ansel Elgort-lite," a descriptor I still stand by wholeheartedly). I pointed to a couple of specific moments in the movie that did feel emotionally resonant to me, and I made it a point to note that DuVernay was not credited with the script, so it was hard to weigh how much of the murkiness was the result of her vision versus the screenwriters'.

In the end, I think I was true to my own reactions to the movie without being scathing. It wasn't like I hated the movie; I was mostly disappointed. But my agony bugged me. My job as a critic was, and is, to parse through my responses to media thoughtfully and honestly and then distill them through writing or conversation thoughtfully and honestly. Why did I feel such a responsibility to conceal or downplay those feelings? I knew better than to fear a hypothetical loss of future opportunities for more stories like this to be told by people like DuVernay; one little review wasn't going to change the industry, because that's not how it works.

I've got to place my anxieties (and the anxieties of others) within the context of history, the hundreds of years' worth of anti-Black stereotypes: blackface, Stepin Fetchits and mammies, butlers and jezebels, *Birth of a*

Nation, Gone with the Wind, and so on. Their tail of influence is long, and the repercussions live on in the many examples of modern-day black-face in *30 Rock, Tropic Thunder*, and other shows that were scrubbed by streaming services during the post–George Floyd "racial reckoning" of 2020 and the gross caricatures of Black men and women strewn throughout reality TV.

And of course, the dearth. There was a time when *Jet* magazine would publish nearly every Black appearance on TV for that given week, and they'd have trouble filling the page.[8] If you've ever seen a copy of *Jet* out in the wild on your grandmother's coffee table or at the beauty salon or on a rack in the bathroom for your *ahem* longer trips to the toilet, you're aware it's smaller than your average magazine, closer to the size of a tourist guide pamphlet than, say, a full-size publication like *EBONY* or *TIME*. Which is all to say, for decades there were barely any Black people on TV!

I also have a deep awareness of how white critics and viewers misinterpret, dismiss, and denigrate Black artistry. A classic example of this is *Do the Right Thing*, which prompted some astoundingly alarmist and tone-deaf reviews, like David Denby's in *New York*. Of the climactic uprising that occurs after the police strangle Radio Raheem to death, the critic wrote of how Spike Lee was "endorsing the outcome" by having Mookie (played by Lee himself) hurl the garbage can through Sal's pizzeria, and that he was "prim(ing) Black people to cheer" on the destruction. "It's his fiction," said Denby, incredibly. "It's not life."[9]

Time has not looked kindly upon that Denby review—at this point, *Do the Right Thing* is considered to be as close to an unassailable work of popular art as one can get—but the effects can and do still linger.

For more recent examples, see also: former *New York Times* critic Alessandra Stanley suggesting Shonda Rhimes's hypothetical autobiography be titled "How to Get Away with Being an Angry Black Woman"[10] (the article was apparently supposed to be an "appraisal" of Rhimes); and *Variety*'s Peter Debruge's cringey review of *Girls Trip*, where he lazily compares it to Tyler Perry (aside from Spike Lee, maybe that's the only Black director he's aware of?) and singles out Tiffany Haddish's Dina, the silliest and most bombastic character in the cast, as "uniquely Black."[11]

And so, my instinct can be to want to resist the white gaze and not go too hard on Black artists whose work I don't connect with. I want to give Black creators the same chances, freedoms, and benefits of the doubt that are so frequently afforded to white men (just think of the many, many times Hollywood kept trying to make Ryan Reynolds happen before he finally became a star; then recognize how quickly Halle Berry was discarded following her historic Oscar win).

To be clear, there's nothing wrong with being thoughtful and deliberate in critiquing Black art—to consider the history, the context, and the efforts while engaging with it. It's also natural to grant some grace when the art is not up to our standards or doesn't exactly align with our sensibilities, in certain circumstances.

If there's one moment from *Queen & Slim* that rings true, it's when Kaluuya's character bemoans the idea of "Black excellence": "Why can't we just be ourselves?" I concur! It's why I find it refreshing to watch Lil Nas X's rise, because it's been so groundbreaking, exhilarating, beautiful, and imperfect. It can be a tricky thing to assess someone like him because so much of his image is crafted in the glow of progress, and the urge to protect him is so strong. But he hardly came to us fully formed or polished as a musician and performer—his stage presence early on left much to be desired—and it's okay to acknowledge that, too. (He continues to improve and continues to be someone to root for.)

But that impulse to protect, and do so blindly, sits uncomfortably right at that friction-filled intersection of art and progress. In her essay "Artistic Integrity," bell hooks wrote about this conflict while citing Stan Brakhage's theory of aesthetic ecology and how political aims and impulses can come to overwhelm artistic expression for the worst. In response to white supremacist structures, hooks wrote, many Black filmmakers "feel compelled to assume responsibility for producing re-sisting images." Striking a balance can be difficult to do and creates "limitations on those artists who allow it to overdetermine everything they do."[12]

This is easily applied to certain creators working presently, whose entire brand could be boiled down to the character Dead Mike wear-ing a kufi cap while rapping militantly about being "blackety-Black and I'm Black y'all" over and over in the gangster rap satire *CB4*. Their politics are loud, but the artistry is lacking—that is to say, there is an overemphasis on presenting Issues and Messages while coherent storytelling or sharp craft fall by the wayside.

This is what happens so often with supposedly "uplifting" projects like *King Richard* or most things Lena "unapologetically Black" Waithe touches. (*Them*, the anthology horror series she executive produced about a Black family integrating a white suburb in the 1950s, is unre-lentingly brutal and devoid of any soul or characterization.) Ditto most things involving Common and/or John Legend. (Ava DuVernay's *Selma* is one of the best movies ever made about the Civil Rights Movement because it avoids so many clichés, which is why I will forever clown its theme song "Glory," the sappy, cliché-ridden Oscar-winner by Common and Legend.)

Yet I've felt this way about my own approach to criticism as well. How limiting, how constricting is it for me to always be starting from a point of resistance and defensiveness; to constantly evaluate movies, shows, or music as if I've got a sheet of paper on a clipboard holding "representation boxes" that need to be checked off in column A ("positive") or column B ("negative")?

Again, it seems crucial to look back to understand the roots of these urges. There's an article from the *Philadelphia Inquirer* in 1972 that I stumbled upon a few years ago while doing research for a piece. It was written by the paper's entertainment writer at the time, William B. Collins, and it says a lot about the state of Black people in Hollywood during that era. Or, more specifically, reactions to Black people in Hollywood during that era.

"By simply breaking the pattern set by Black exploitation movies, *Sounder* has been rewarded with an impressive show of gratitude," he began, referring to the quiet drama starring Cicely Tyson and Paul Winfield as the heads of a Depression-era sharecropping family living in Louisiana. Jesse Jackson was among the Black civil rights leaders at the time championing the film, and Black kids were being "herded downtown" to the local theater to see it. *Sounder*, he observed, was benefiting greatly from being the antithesis of another recent release, *Super Fly*, a crude flick featuring a drug dealer as the antihero audiences are meant to cheer on. "It features dope and sex and violence. Its language is shocking. And," Collins concedes, "the awful truth is that *Super Fly* is the better movie."

Throughout the rest of the article, Collins makes a case for how the ostensibly more dignified movie is not as progressive in its depiction of Black characters as its creators and supporters would have you think because its approach to racial adversity is decidedly whitewashed. Yes, it's a movie about "real people" and devoid of stereotypes, but it's also an "honest lie, because it de-emphasizes everything that might in real life bedevil its people more than they are here." *Super Fly*, on the other hand, for all its broadness and unseemly characters, feels more "true," because the cocaine-pushing ladies' man Priest feels forced into his lot in life by The Man (aka white supremacy). It has a "recognizably real ghetto type (the successful businessman) making a hard choice based on the way things are, not the way they ought to be."[13]

Collins, for what it's worth, was a white guy commenting bluntly on the "authenticity" of blackness on film, which, you know . . . is *a choice*. But his analysis echoes a notorious *New York Times* essay about Sidney Poitier's celebrity and artistry by Black playwright, actor, and critic Clifford Mason that was published a few years earlier, in 1967. That was the year Poitier became the biggest box office star in Hollywood—besting other performers of any race—with the social issue movie trifecta of *Guess Who's Coming to Dinner*, *In the Heat of the Night*, and *To Sir, with Love*.

The headline of the piece was "Why Does White America Love Sidney Poitier So?" And you can probably guess the answer to this query without reading it in full if you know anything about Poitier's journey as one of a handful of Black leading men working in the movie industry in the 1950s and 1960s. Mason was much more scathing than Collins in his own critique—in the newspaper of record, he referred to Poitier as both a "showcase n———" and a "good n———" eager to take roles where he solves white people's problems—and questioned the star's public statements disparaging the two roles he *had* been ashamed to have taken: the crippled beggar Porgy in the musical *Porgy and Bess* and the antagonist king Aly Mansuh in *The Long Ships*.

How could Poitier dismiss those two roles and yet feel satisfied with his other career choices, playing bland characters meant to appease white folks in movies like *Lilies of the Field* and *To Sir, with Love*? he wondered. Porgy, Mason assessed, was an undignified stereotype to be sure, but "at least we have a man, a real man, fighting [for] his woman and willing to follow her into the great unknown." And Aly, villainy aside, "was nobody's eunuch or Black mammy busting his gut for white folks as if their problems were all that's important in the world."[14]

What Collins and Mason were both getting at were conundrums that have haunted the creation, critique, and reception of Black art for well over a century: Who benefits the most from Black performance, especially the kind that entertains a widely mixed-race audience? And under what circumstances can and does Black artistry truly thrive?

The "answers," insomuch as there might be any at all, have varied with time and on an individual basis, as they should. There's certainly no blanket assessment to be made about such queries, nor is there a hard and fast formula for calculating how much Poitier or *Sounder* contributed to Hollywood's becoming a little less racist and a little more welcoming to Black performers in their wake. They each inarguably changed the course of the movie industry in their own unique, non-linear ways.

Poitier and *Sounder* challenged notions about imagery and what audiences, especially Black ones, could and did want from Black performance. After years of barely existing at all outside of roles as maids, butlers, or buffoons with a handful of lines or showing up only to perform a musical number that could be easily excised for Southern theater exhibitioners, opportunities had gotten a little bit better, depending upon who you asked. In James Baldwin's "The Devil Finds Work," he recalled the anguish he felt encountering Stepin Fetchit, Willie Best, and Mantan Moreland as a kid: ". . . certainly I did not know anybody like them—as far as I could tell; for it is also possible that their comic, bug-eyed terror contained the truth concerning a terror by which I hoped never to be engulfed."[15] Yet in that same book-length essay, Baldwin had some choice words for *The Defiant Ones*, a movie with fantastical aims on racial reconciliation, starring Poitier and Tony Curtis as prisoners, one of whom is an outright racist—guess which one—who escape while chained together. What Black audiences resented about that movie, he wrote, was this: "That Sidney was in company far beneath him, and that the unmistakable truth of his performance was being placed at the mercy of a lie."[16] White liberals cheered when Poitier jumped off the train at the end of the movie so as not to leave Curtis's character behind, he wrote. But Black audiences in Harlem were pissed.

And so you get this tension between those who overemphasize a perceived "positive" image and those who are asking, "Is that all there is?"

That friction hasn't disappeared. Even as the landscape has changed significantly over the last twenty or so years, and Black creativity has reached new echelons of expression and marketability, the discourse around audiences for Black art and fulfillment through it remains, if in slightly different modes than the likes of Collins and Mason. It's striking to see people refer to Lizzo as a "mammy" who makes music for white people simply because she's a fat Black woman whose music just so happens to be embraced wholeheartedly by non-Black people. More than one hundred years later, that stereotype's effects cling so tightly as to exist within the imaginations of some, where no such stereotyping is in actuality occurring. That, and too many people throw words around without any understanding of their historical context.

And it's frustrating to see Kenya Barris, in an episode of his short-lived and redundant Netflix series *#blackAF* (seriously, this show was just a less funny retread of Barris's other family sitcom *Black-ish*), agonizing over Black tastes and criticisms of Black art. In one scene, the fictionalized version of Barris asks Tyler Perry, guest starring as himself, about how he deals with harsh criticism, to which Perry responds that his focus is to "serve my niche" and that he's "talking to us," not "white folks"—as if Black critics of Perry don't even exist. He echoes the many times I've seen people complain about there being "no Black critics" who've reviewed "*X* Black movie" with a not-great Rotten Tomatoes score, when our reviews are so easily searchable. (Also, as I've already proven, just because we're Black doesn't mean we're going to review that movie favorably. Sorrynotsorry!)

We're still having debates over good and bad representation, and a scarcity mindset still lingers in critiques—that fear that this moment of influence may be snatched away at any moment. One hundred-plus years of mammies, coons, jezebels, and buffoons don't just evaporate. Racism's wounds don't just heal without leaving a scar.

But Black art isn't fragile, and I refuse to treat it as such. For one thing, years of scholarship and financial support of Black film history by the likes of Jacqueline Stewart, Maya Cade, and DuVernay have allowed for the rediscovery and redistribution of little-seen films from the past. A movie like Horace B. Jenkins's *Cane River*, which initially premiered in 1982 and then went mostly unseen for nearly forty years afterward, demonstrates how Black filmmakers were still able to tell powerful stories even when opportunities were incredibly scarce. It's a modest movie set in Louisiana about a young man from a storied family who returns home and winds up falling in love; against the backdrop of this compelling romance are conflicts involving the legacy of slavery and colorism. When people complain about the lack of good, complex Black stories, I want to point to a movie like this, to show how Black creators have always found a way, even if us viewers have had to search harder to get to them.

Representation alone isn't going to save us and cannot override a clumsily executed story. As bell hooks said, "Just because writers and directors are Black, does not exempt them from scrutiny."[17] (She said this in regard to *Waiting to Exhale*, a movie I happen to really like; nevertheless, I appreciate her scathing critique of its depiction of Black femininity, because lo and behold, it's possible to disagree with someone while also respecting them! What a concept!)

Progress should be measured not just in the lack of stereotypes but in the ability to critique mediocre or flat-out terrible Black art without fear of outsize retribution. Black art deserves to be taken seriously, not coddled.

I *want* to always be asking: Is that all there is?

I'm not naïve; I recognize that a huge part of the reason I feel comfortable asking this question is because the landscape has shifted. There's less of a drought than there was in the era of Poitier, *Sounder*, or even ten, fifteen years ago, and thus—in my view—less of a scarcity concern. Just before *Insecure* ended after five seasons, other shows like *Abbott*

Elementary and *Grand Crew* (created by an *Insecure* writers' room alum, no less) premiered and scratched a different kind of itch for Black comedic storytelling.

And just weeks before the release of *A Wrinkle in Time*, *Black Panther* became a huge success, proof we are living in a unique time where two major studio releases of sci-fi/fantasy movies by Black filmmakers could just so happen to arrive around the same time. DuVernay's career hasn't been hurt by the middling reviews for *A Wrinkle in Time*—I was far from the only one who was underwhelmed!—and in fact, more recently she's developed *Naomi*, a CW series based on the DC comic book series about a Black woman superhero.

But that's the benefit of being alive and Black right now—our predecessors fought hard to expand representation, to push beyond mere "positive" and "negative" markers of progress, the better that we could immerse ourselves in the artistry of it all in the present day. That's freeing and a sign of progress—one that should be embraced.

Oh, and spoiler alert: To this day, I still have not seen *Red Tails*, not in a theater nor at home. I'm okay with that. I have no guilt. I feel liberated.

3

I'M A COOL GIRL

The video begins in the bathroom, with a shower, a plop on the toilet, then into the bedroom for a shot of alcohol and a snort of coke, all from "your" point of view. Like a first-person video game, the frenetic camera acts as the window to debauchery, carrying you through a chaotic and truly reckless evening that includes sexually assaulting several women in a bar, instigating a fight on the dance floor (clobbering the DJ while you're at it), puking and shooting up drugs in a bathroom, heading to a strip club, and taking one of the women home with you for a woozy, intoxicating lay. You are an unstoppable hurricane of brazen, violent id, the Tasmanian Devil in an NC-17 world.

"Change my pitch up! Smack my bitch up!" an aggressive voice repeats over an aggressive electronic beat several times over the course of this bender. This is, as the lyrics say, "Smack My Bitch Up" by EDM group The Prodigy. When it was released in 1997, many radio stations refused to play it, and the accompanying video only played on MTV in the wee hours of the morning for a few days.[1] The National Organization for Women (NOW) publicly denounced it as misogynist.

For all the video's perversions—it channels the lurid energy of the movie *Trainspotting*, released a year earlier, while anticipating *Requiem for a Dream* a few years later—the most memorable aspect of it might not be the central character's antics but the fact that it's revealed at the very end that the central character is . . . *a woman*.

Didn't see that coming, did ya? A woman acting like a man. Or at least, the way we've been conditioned to believe some men naturally behave—boorishly, angrily, violently. The subversion is jarring because it upends so many of our expectations about the construct of gender and who gets to be at the center of such a depraved story. Maybe. Or is that a stretch?

The vice president of NOW at the time, Elizabeth Toledo, didn't find anything subversive about the video, only offensive. "Just because it's a woman doesn't alter anything," she told *The Washington Post*. The brunt of the violence was still "directed at women."[2]

Fair enough. For their part, the members of Prodigy refuted accusations of sexism in the song and shrugged at the criticism, with Liam Howlett calling it "probably the most pointless song I've ever written."[3] The video's director Jonas Åkerlund would later recount how the events of the story were inspired by his own wild rager one night in Copenhagen; he's admitted the decision to make the character a woman was something he "didn't think much about . . . other than it would be an unexpected twist if this crazy party person was a woman and not a man."[4]

Åkerlund may not have considered it too deeply, but he was employing a common cinematic trope I'll dub, "He's *gasp* . . . a *she*!"

How many times have you watched a fight scene where the badass adversary/assassin is covered from head to toe or strategically obscured off-screen, just so the other characters can be surprised when said assassin dramatically removes their head covering with a toss of their long luscious locks?

Girl power! This trope blurts out with more fervor than a Spice Girl. Anything men can do, women can do, too—or even better. It can also scream: *Ha, gotcha! Broaden your horizons, you plebeian. How DARE you assume this character is a man? Sexist!*

The "Smack My Bitch Up" twist isn't particularly edgy, just tacked on merely to be provocative. But even the most tossed-off artistic decisions have influence and reflect the real world.

And when you're a tween who comes of age at the turn of the twenty-first century, watching a lot of MTV before graduating to *Sex and the City* and many other cultural references reinforcing traditional roles between men and women, the twist of "the brute is actually a woman" might seem alluring and even kind of cool and transgressive. You may not have any desire to assault anyone or shoot up drugs in a nightclub bathroom, but you can get on board with women "acting like men" in other ways. Because that's equality, right? And who doesn't want power?

What follows is the story of a girl who sought power through exception and various posturings of masculinity.

Or how I learned to stop wanting to be "the cool girl."

• • •

I'm eight, you see, and there's something about Kristy Thomas. She's the founder of *The Baby-Sitters Club*, my current literary obsession—

seriously, I've read every single book in the series that's been released so far, including the "Super Special" and "Mystery" offshoots—and I'm drawn to Kristy's knack for leadership and assertiveness. But most of all, I'm into her self-identification as a full-throated, unapologetic tomboy. She loves baseball, hates dresses, and (mostly) doesn't have time for worrying about boys in a *like-like* way.

Ughhhhh, I wish I could care less about liking boys, but those other traits—yeah, I can totally relate to. I did intramural softball for a season and turned out to be a pretty good hitter, and it's always fun when summer comes along and Dad takes me to a New Haven Ravens minor league game. I love sitting in the stands, getting that buttery, salty, overly processed popcorn, a giant soda, and settling in to watch them play. Rally the Raven, their mascot, is pretty cool, too.

And I, too, despise dresses and would much rather be wearing pants or shorts. I'd prefer it if I could resemble Kristy's look in *The Baby-Sitters Club* movie (killer soundtrack, BTW): loose jeans, a tucked-in tee—but only in the front, allowing the rest of the shirt to billow over the top—and a baseball cap. I don't want to look too "girlie." Ick! Being girlie's dumb. It's weak. There's a reason the boys in gym class are always kicking the ball way harder and further than the rest of us girls; they're just better at sports than we are. And I hate that. I'm a much better dancer than an athlete, and nothing makes me feel as good as when I'm learning choreography and dancing, but it feels so *typical*. *Of course* I do ballet, jazz, and tap—I'm a girl, and everyone on my dance competition team is a girl.

I don't want to kick like a girl.

Or dress like a girl.

Or cry like a girl.

I want to be different from other girls.

I want the boys to think I'm cool.

I want power.

I want the power that comes with being seen as strong—being like a boy. It's not that I want to change my body; my body is fine. I do like how I can slide down into a full split and pirouette and leap and tap my feet fiercely and how sometimes someone, usually an old person, will look at me admiringly and say I'm cute or pretty, even if I don't quite feel that way about myself.

But I've only existed on this Earth for less than a decade so far, and already I can tell these things won't translate to real power. I still feel small whenever the boys make some crack about something being "girlie" or "girl's stuff," their lips curled in the shape of a judgy sneer. The description drips with such disdain and dismissiveness. I may wear a t-shirt that reads "Girls Rule" in pink and purple glitter, but it's more an aspirational statement than a real, tangible fact.

And so I look to Kristy for my style inspiration. I gravitate toward the spunky boyishness of Ashley Spinelli in the cartoon *Recess*, even though her interactions with other schoolkids can be kinda bully-ish sometimes. Ditto *To Kill a Mockingbird*'s Scout Finch with that scrappy, don't-care approach to play and the way she can hold her own alongside her brother Jem. Give me those girls who are girls without the "girlie"—the ones who can hang and whom the boys respect and treat equally.

(I'll only process this later in life, but it seems like no coincidence that these tomboys tend to be the central protagonists in their stories. See also: Harriet in *Harriet the Spy* and Troy in *Crooklyn*. The girlie girls more often follow the Smurfette Principle, serving as the lone representative of their gender in a narrative teeming with boys. As Katha Pollitt, who coined the trope in a 1991 *New York Times* magazine essay, explained it: "Boys are the norm, girls the variation; boys are central, girls peripheral; boys are individuals, girls types. Boys define the group, its story, and its code of values. Girls exist only in relation to boys."[5] Thus, the less "girlie" a character is drawn, the more powerful their narrative.)

And again, power is what I want. Which is why I tuck my shirt in halfway and only wear dresses and skirts when my parents make me (on those very rare occasions we go to church, for example) and join in when everyone teases another classmate, regardless of their gender, for "throwing/kicking/hitting like a girl" during gym. No, it doesn't make sense; it's harmful, and it's screwed-up thinking. But I'm eight, and it's the 1990s. What do you expect?

• • •

Can't get my mind off you. I think I might be obsessed.
The very thought of you makes me want to get undressed.

—Toni Braxton

In the video for "You're Makin' Me High," Toni Braxton's voluptuous figure is poured neatly into a sexy white catsuit and she's donning a slick shoulder-length bob framing her angelic face as she saunters and sways and poses seductively for the camera, crooning in that sultry signature tone of hers about the man who gets her off—er, high. In other scenes, she's got a different look—a little less Bond girl, a little more night-out-on-the-town—and a penthouse suite, where she's invited her girlfriends over for a get-together. Said girlfriends are peak-1990s Black Hollywood royalty: Tisha Campbell, Erika Alexander, and Vivica A. Fox; all of them are treated to entertainment in the form of a cavalcade of hot men.

They sit in front of the penthouse elevator as the doors open and close to reveal a different guy on display each time—tall, short, Black, white, hot, not, nerd, hunk. There's even a ridiculous-looking cat daddy in a giant fur coat who's just chucking bills in the air like it ain't no thang. They rate each man with oversize playing cards, holding up tens for the hotties and lesser numbers for the notties, nodding their heads in approval or busting out into laughter at the weirder man candies. The women are in control here. They are the ones doing the looking at, the judging of, and the choosing of whichever man looks as if he stepped out of a Magic Mike production.

This is the era of women in R & B and hip-hop asserting their right to be the ones doing the objectifying—Salt-N-Pepa and En Vogue's "Whatta Man," Aaliyah's "One In a Million," most of the tracks on Janet Jackson's *Janet* and *Velvet Rope* albums. Ten-year-old me is probably too young to be listening to most of it, but I hear it anyway, either on the radio or when I'm sneaking views of MTV and VH1 in between reruns of *All That* and *The Powerpuff Girls*. (I've quickly learned the benefit of keeping my finger poised over the "return" button on the remote control in case one of my parents happens to walk into the room.) I've had "The Talk" with Mom about my changing body and the basics of sex, and I'm already acutely aware that I'm into boys, having had my first crush in preschool and at least one new crush every school year since. Also, Prince Eric in *The Little Mermaid* and Kel Mitchell have made me feel things.

This will only crystallize for me later in life, of course, but Toni and all the others are showing me a different kind of strength—one that straddles the line between tomboy and girlie girl. They speak of men not unlike men so often speak of women—lustfully, explicitly, bluntly. And yet they do all of this while still exuding femininity in crop tops and slinky catsuits and without it sounding abrasive or creepy. I hear these songs and watch these videos, barely having entered my double digits, and the seeds are planted. It's okay to want boys and express my desire for boys, though this is easier digested than it is enacted, as it should be when you're a fifth grader. And in reality, I barely know how to talk to boys, especially if I *like-like* them.

In sixth grade, I finally scrounge up a bit of boy-related courage. I decide I sort of like another kid in our class, who is not quite a social outcast but definitely isn't one of the popular kids, so we share that in common. He also doesn't tease me like some of the other kids do. He's kind of scrawny and seems nice enough, and because the stakes feel low, I go for it.

"So . . . I kind of like you."

"Oh . . . okay." I'm not sure he knows what to do with this information. "Cool."

We start "going out," which in elementary school just means we sit together during lunch and recess sometimes and write the other's initials, enclosed in heart shapes, on our notebook covers. We barely touch each other—maybe a hug here or there. Honestly, I don't actually want to kiss him or anything.

"Wait—you and J are *together*???" classmates comment, confused, probably, because he's white and I'm Black. Or because he and I have barely interacted before now.

Frankly, it's weird to me, too.

But whatever. I'm going for it! I like being "coupled" because all the cool kids are frequently "coupled" up, and now I, too, feel cool. But I also like it because I clearly have the upper hand in this elementary dynamic; I'm Toni and her girlfriends picking and choosing their men from an elevator, picking and choosing my "boyfriend" during recess.

After a short time, he seems to be really, really into me, and I don't think he'll ever break up with me, so that's a nice boost to my ego. The only time we see each other outside of normal school hours is at our sixth-grade dance in the gym, which is where I break up with him.

"I don't wanna go out with you anymore. Sorry," I say sheepishly. It devastates him. All I can do is avoid him the rest of the night.

I feel kind of bad, and I probably could've picked a more tactful time to "end things" than within close proximity of all our peers as *NSYNC's "(God Must Have Spent) A Little More Time on You" probably blares through the speakers in the background. But when you know, you know. And I'm just not feeling this kid and maybe never really was. Everyone finds out what happened pretty much immediately, because nothing stays under the radar for long among a bunch of gossipy hormonal tweens.

I instantly regret this dalliance, which probably lasts all of a couple of weeks, and how I started and ended it. I may or may not apologize to him later for being a little flippant with his feelings. But I also feel a twinge of satisfaction knowing that someone could like me more than I like them, and that I could have so much control over a boy. It's the sixth-grade, utterly naïve equivalent of donning a catsuit and rating guys on an elevator in a penthouse suite.

For a moment, at least, I've got the power.

• • •

There's that famous scene from *Sleepless in Seattle*—you know the one. It's probably the most memorable scene in the entire movie, and it doesn't even involve its central hetero destined-to-be couple, Sam (Tom Hanks) and Annie (Meg Ryan). No, this one involves Sam, Sam's son Jonah (Ross Malinger), and Sam's couple friends Greg (Victor Garber) and Suzy (Rita Wilson). Sam recounts how he's unwittingly become one of the country's most eligible bachelors after having opened up about missing his deceased wife to the host of a late-night talk radio program live and on-air. Now women from all over are sending letters for Sam to the show, and one in particular—Annie—has asked to meet him on the top of the Empire State Building on Valentine's Day.

Upon hearing about this cheesy romantic gesture, Suzy lights up with recognition, identifying it as a nod to the plot of the classic Cary Grant / Deborah Kerr romance drama *An Affair to Remember*. And then, of course, Suzy delivers a delectably committed monologue recapping the movie's premise to Greg, Sam, and Jonah and becomes so overwhelmed by just the thought of it, that by the end she's a sobbing mess. The guys trade glares as she descends into estrogen-induced hysterics, and when she's calmed down a bit, Sam swoops right in there with a sneering zinger: "That's a *chick's* movie."

Greg promptly joins in as they both mock her by recalling how they cried while watching *The Dirty Dozen*, one of the all-time white boomer dad movies.

This scene . . . *this scene*! Why does it hit teenage me so hard? It's familiar, the perfect distillation of "men are from Mars, women are from Venus," a million comedians' "men act like this, women act like that" routines, and every sitcom about a husband and wife ever. Of course the irony is this scene takes place in a "chick's movie," and Sam *does* wind up meeting Annie on the Empire State Building. Which is supposed to hit the viewer in the feels, just as Suzy gets about *An Affair to Remember*.

Then again, this is the tenor of many modern rom-coms, from the Rock Hudson / Doris Day movies of the 1950s and 1960s up through to the Apatow-verse era of the 2000s: Even in the cheesiest, gooiest, rom-commiest of movies, the gender lines are clearly drawn. The men only hang out with other men; the women only hang out with other women, unless there's a token gay best friend involved. The men are playboys (until, by the end of the movie, they're tamed by love); the women are uptight and probably haven't gotten laid in a long time (until, by the end of the movie, they find love). There are chick movies and then there are guy movies, and it's okay to laugh at women for liking the former and for being "too emotional" about a piece of work that's meant to move the viewer, for being too much of a girlie girl about feelings. (Brief aside here: We say "girlie girl" and "manly man," but never "boyish boy" or "womanly woman." What's up with that? I feel like I'm Gabrielle Union's character in *10 Things I Hate About You*, wondering if anyone can ever just be "whelmed.")

I'm haunted by the ways the genders can be so easily reduced to women liking Cary Grant romances and men liking rugged war movies.

Or women being either "high-maintenance" or "low-maintenance." I fear I might ever be perceived as Sally is in *When Harry Met Sally . . .*, the girl who's "high-maintenance but thinks they're low-maintenance," according to Harry (i.e., the worst kind of combination). After all, I, too, am the kind of diner who will frequently ask for modifications because I have this thing about certain foods and food accoutrements (keep most sauces, especially creamy ones like mayo, away from my plate, please!).

Oh, god. *Am I Sally?!*

• • •

So I'm in high school now, puberty in overdrive. I've long left the Kristy Thomas aesthetic behind and have taken to aspiring to shop at Abercrombie—the force of LFO's "Summer Girls" is strong with suburban Connecticut kids—and actually shopping at cheaper Abercrombie-adjacent stores like Weathervane, wearing tight, preppy, midriff-baring outfits that test the boundaries of what my dad and my school's officials might deem "inappropriate." But the fact remains, I don't want to be like other girls, at least not when it comes to how I deal with the opposite sex. I've heard the ways some boys talk about girls primarily as sex objects, commenting on our boobs, our asses, and who's got the best of both. This applies equally to famous girls they will never meet, like Britney and Christina (currently Xtina, as she's firmly in her "Dirrty" era). Are you hot, according to their standards? Then they will pay attention to you. Are you not, also according to their standards? They will pick on you or just ignore you.

I've started getting attention from boys, now that I've got decent-size boobs for my small frame and an even shapelier ass that many people, boys and girls, comment upon admiringly; comparisons to J. Lo abound, because we're in peak J. Lo-conquers-the-box-office-and-Billboard-and-Ben-Affleck-all-at-once times. Not gonna lie—I like the attention, because who in 2002 wouldn't want to have their ass compared to J. Lo's? I love dancing with it to "Hot in Herre" and "My Neck, My Back," the "WAP" of my youth. But it also frustrates me, because it just proves my point that boys only care about sex, and to them, girls are more or less disposable and at the mercy of their ever-fluctuating interests. I vow to harness the energy of "Girl Power"—*in my horrible faux-British accent, fingers splayed in a peace sign*—and say no to being any boy's little plaything.

No scrubs. I'm an independent woman who just wants to get dirrrrty like Lady Marmalade, gitchie-gitchie ya-ya . . . where's all my soul sistas?

I let my guard down anyway, though. The kid who will become my first real-ish boyfriend, sophomore year, is the first boy to make me truly feel wanted, and we meet while both performing in the ensemble of our fall musical, *Kiss Me, Kate*. He's cute; skinny and much taller than me—which I like—and a total goofball/charmer in that Will Smith-as-the-Fresh Prince, pre–The Slap way. His complexion is a little lighter than mine, and he's constantly carrying a huge brush in one of the ginormous pockets of his baggy jeans so he can brush out the waves in his hair whenever he wants, which is often.

At the cast party, we dance to Nelly and Kelly Rowland's "Dilemma," a great love duet for our times. (This is actually a song about a guy plotting to become the sidepiece to a woman with a husband and kid, but I'm fourteen, so I don't listen to actual lyrics.) He asks me to homecoming, he meets my parents and I meet his dad, and we take pictures together and we're so cute together, and it feels like heaven to experience this magnet of mutual attraction. We're like Cory and Topanga, so in sync and all in.

We talk on the phone nightly, and I'm floating on air because I have a boyfriend now, and he says nice things about me, and we get along great. He writes me love notes in his scraggly, nearly illegible handwriting. I'm flattered, though, I tell him that while I do like him *a lot*, perhaps more than any boy ever before him, I'm not sure if I *love* him, in part because I recognize that I'm all of fourteen-going-on-fifteen, and what the hell do I know about love? But also because to say "I love you" would be to make myself vulnerable and open to getting hurt. And girls, I think, are much more likely to be the overly lovey-dovey ones and the ones who usually say "I love you" first or try to rush into things, and that will never be me.

We break up after a year and a half because, as I've said, when you're in high school, what the hell do you know about love? I enter my senior year a single gal and try to pretend it doesn't bother me as much as my not-so-subtly cryptic AIM away messages indicate.

And as this is all happening, my parents' marriage of nineteen years is crumbling, and there are a lot of arguments and tears and slammed doors. My sister and I are stuck in the middle, forced to shuffle back and forth once my dad moves out and into an apartment nearby and hear from each parent about how the other one did this or said that. Even before I could sense they were unhappy, I'd already begun to suspect that I might not get to have a solid, compatible love of my own. Now, I'm certain that if they couldn't make it work, there's no use in my even trying.

Now I can't escape from my "poor provincial town" fast enough. I want the freedom to meet new guys and make out with new guys and start anew, without heartache. I haven't had sex yet, but I have been watching the Charlotte-esque, prudish versions of *Sex and the City* reruns on TBS (my parents aren't paying for HBO, sorry to me), so of course I fancy myself a potent combination of Miranda and Samantha: cynical about love, horny AF. I ultimately decide that falling in love is definitely not for me, and when it comes to the opposite sex, I'm just going to act like a dude and date like a dude because caring and baring your soul is for the weak.

• • •

I find new ways to express my Samantha-like inclinations and to avoid ever being labeled high-maintenance. I'm in college now nearly a thousand miles away from home in the Midwest at Northwestern where the weather is truly crappy eight months out of the year, but they have one of the top musical theater programs in the country.

I lose my virginity before the first quarter of freshman year is over, in part because I like the guy, who's a sophomore, but mainly because I want to get it over with, to see what it's all about, and not have to obsess over it happening anymore. He's way taller than I am (what can I say—I have a type), premed, and has a Southern swagger and twang in his voice I've never really encountered before.

After it happens, clandestine late-night booty calls in our respective dorm rooms become routine; luckily, neither of us have roommates.

> **HIM:** yo—what's up?
> **ME:** just finishing up a paper—pulling another all-nighter.
> **HIM:** want company?

ME: sure. gimme like … 30?
HIM: k cool

But I know he's also probably hooking up with at least one other girl, and I'm not trying to get into a relationship my first year of college anyway. I flirt with and hook up with other guys throughout the year, proudly trading sexcapade stories with my new college buddies—complaining about bad sex, bragging about the good sex and the in-between, generally just pleased with the fact that I'm having any sex at all fairly regularly.

I don't attribute any real feelings to these sexcapades; I like these guys fine enough, but I can't say I'd actually want to date any of them. Except for the guy who took my virginity, who has started seriously dating that other girl, out in the open, while still flirting with me and intimating that he likes me even as he's tied up with this other actual, real relationship. I didn't want him to be my man until he kept saying things like "I really like you" and "You're so talented" and spewing the kind of sweet nothings people usually only reserve for their significant others.

And now suddenly, I'm wondering why he would rather be with her than me and why every time they break up—which is often—he keeps coming back to *me* after a month or two, hitting me up on text or AIM around midnight while I'm studying, with the classic "Hey" or "I miss you" or "Can I come through?" and then wondering why the hell I let him, even though I feel like I'm doing the exact opposite of what I've always said I would do. I've wrapped myself up in a guy and made myself the vulnerable one, the one waiting up for his messages, and hating myself every time.

And now I realize that in this dynamic, I'm not Samantha Jones, the confident badass who just wants to have fun and doesn't get attached (at least not until season four when she, too, succumbs to the romantic gestures and sweet nothings of smarmy Richard Wright). Instead I've become—ugh, it pains me to even think of this—*Carrie Bradshaw*. And this guy's my own Mr. Big—perpetually unavailable, constantly playing games, and always popping up just when you've finally forgotten about him and moved on, roping you back in, kicking and screaming, under his spell.

I've said it before, and I'll say it again: Carrie is the worst. No one aspires to be Carrie in relationships—"insecure" and "needy" and making plans around someone who only thinks of you when all their more desired options have dried up. This is bad.

It takes me until the end of my sophomore year to exorcise him from my soul—though believe me, I never stop flirting or hooking up with other people during this period; a college gal's got needs—and ultimately tell him he needs to leave me alone, for good. That I like him too much, and I can't keep entertaining him anymore, for my own sanity. The severing isn't nearly as dramatic as that time in season two where Big breaks the news he's engaged to a twenty-something he's only been dating for five months after stringing Carrie along for multiple years, and Carrie explodes on him in the middle of the restaurant and tips over her chair and trips over the stairs on the way out.

No, my severing is done the succinct millennial way, circa the late 2000s, via, yes, AIM. I've failed at being the dude here, unable to cut and run and ghost of my own accord before I'm in too deep. I chalk it up to being young and naïve and maybe even karma for the way I treated my elementary school beau when I was even younger and more naïve.

And so I hit the reset button and recalibrate my inner Miss Independent woman. I'm the girl who can quote that Judd Apatow-verse movie right back to you, you cute frat boy you, while openly admiring that *Scarface* poster on your wall—I've seen it once, and I don't get the hype, but I won't bother admitting this to you—and indulging your desire to watch *Any Given Sunday* on DVD for what is probably your one hundredth time.

(Meanwhile, in class, I'm exposed for the first time to feminist writers and thinkers like bell hooks, people who don't hang their feminism on how they can be more like the boys; instead, they critique how the power structures are designed to convince women to want to play that game so they can get ahead, therefore upholding those power structures. "Feminism, or for that matter, women's liberation, was never about trying to gain the right to be dicks in drag," hooks argued.[6] I hear them, but it hasn't quite sunk in yet how this could apply to my own way of moving through the world at this time.)

I'm just having fun, living my life, not falling too hard. A couple of other relationships edge toward something that could be called serious, or at least a little more involved than just hooking up after hours, but it's still college, and most romantic bonds at this time are going to be ephemeral stepping stones toward (ideally) greater emotional maturity.

There's the slightly older guy whom I meet at a bar (hooray, fake ID!) and says he might be falling for me after two dates. He won't sleep with me until we commit to being exclusive, so I say, sure, let's be exclusive; then he gets jealous when our cast party for my student production of *Hair* is cast members only, no plus-ones allowed (his last girlfriend cheated on him and broke his heart, so he's convinced I will do the same). I go to the party anyway, have an amazing time—but don't cheat, because I wouldn't, but also because it's theater and pretty much all the boys are gay—and the next morning he breaks up with me because I went to said party without him, and he now realizes I'm not at all interested in staying in Chicago after I graduate or being his shut-in wife and eventual mother of his future children. I'm shook up about it for a couple of weeks, though it's more from the sting of being The One Who Was Dumped rather than The Dumper. Deep down, I knew we were never going to work.

This is why I don't do relationships.

• • •

There's power in not caring. Not caring *is* power. When you don't care, or care less than others around you do, you can control the situation, because the outcome doesn't really matter. As a woman, the world expects you to care a lot about everything and everyone other than yourself. Fashion and appearances, being the only person your significant other will have sex with until the day you die, being married, being a mother—those are the things you're supposed to care about.

But being carefree is the dream. Being carefree, unbothered, calm, cool, and collected is the sign of a progressive woman. Just ask Samantha Jones.

Or Nola Darling. Nola is the sexually liberated twenty-something in Spike Lee's 1986 feature debut *She's Gotta Have It*, who loves sex and loves it in a variety of flavors on a rotating basis: Mars, an immature, perpetually unemployed sneakerhead; Greer, a vain supermodel who would definitely think this essay is about him; and Jamie, an insecure romantic who simmers with unsettling intensity. Nola woos all three men at once, and openly, though much to their chagrin. Greer calls her a "sex addict"; Mars suggests Nola's only a "freak" because of a poor relationship with her dad. (Lee cleverly undercuts this assertion by featuring Nola's dad in a documentary-style interview, where he recounts providing her with a happy childhood and various modes for expression. Embracing sexuality as an adult does not instantly equal daddy issues!)

Yet even as these men disparage her, Nola commands their attention and their interactions with her. When one calls her late at night while she's entwined in bed with another, she's got the upper hand. When Jamie comes by to take care of her while she's sick, he's threatened by her friend Opal, a lesbian who is eager to entice the very straight Nola. (Nola is so hot, so magnetic, so in control that even women want her!) This woman even convinces all three of these poor, pathetic dudes to join her for a joint Thanksgiving dinner, where through catty barbs and snide put-downs, they each attempt to be the victor who gets to spend the night. These men want her, and only her—or, more superficially, they want to lay sole claim to her attentions and affections. Meanwhile, for most of the movie, she couldn't be bothered to commit to one of them.

Nola's the blueprint. I'm drawn to her because she's emanating domination and superiority, wielding the quintessential Brooklyn artist life in the kind of vast, chic, exposed-brick Fort Greene loft that no twenty-something could afford today without self-identifying as a trust-fund baby, influencer, or both. I love how by the end of the movie, after briefly questioning whether or not she can make monogamy work with Jamie, she ultimately decides that she cannot and will not be "tamed" by any man. She's too independent for that, too interested in her own happiness to be bothered with settling down with one man. "He wanted a wife, that mythic old-fashioned girl next door," she says, but that's not her.

And that's not me, either. By now, I'm in my early twenties, a recent college grad slowly losing interest in being a starving artist for the rest of my life. My future is in limbo, but I know two things for certain about myself: I'm never having kids (I don't particularly enjoy being around children for long periods of time), and I give zero fucks about getting married. I highly doubt it will even be possible for me to handle being in a long-term relationship, since people get bored and compatibility is hard to come by.

I see myself in Nola Darling because her dating style butts up against conventional wisdom of female sexuality; isn't it men who have been historically accepted and championed as players in the game of love? Like Sam Malone, the dim-witted *Cheers* bartender (and clear forebear of *How I Met Your Mother*'s Barney Stinson) whose exploits as a womanizer account for most of his charm. At least 75 percent of his exploits qualify as workplace harassment. Upon a rewatch, you will almost certainly lose count of the number of times he asks Rebecca Howe, *his boss* for part of the series's run, to sleep with him. But that's just what guys do, amirite?

So when a woman in fiction acts more like Sam Malone—more emotionally closed off, looking to scratch only the surface of intimacy or something like it—and less like his uptight on-again-off-again paramour Diane Chambers, that's progress. That's power. (Or at least it's supposed to be. Never forget that *Sex and the City*'s Samantha gets slut-shamed by her neighbors for inadvertently letting a burglar into her apartment building because he snuck in behind her gentleman caller in the wee small hours of the morning. They shame her so badly she moves to another part of town! And in the third act of *She's Gotta Have It*, Jamie rapes Nola, but it's treated like a justified response to his frustrations with her noncommittal sensibilities. Thankfully, Spike Lee would go on to express regret for depicting that shocking instance of brutal misogyny in this way and left it out of his TV adaptation of the movie years later.)

But the great thing about living the Nola-Sam kinda life in your twenties, and not having a biological clock tick-tick-ticking away, is that you don't take your dates seriously and can presumably have more fun. Or at least, not get too bummed if your date is boring and there's no chemistry or he decides to ghost you.

My evolving circumstances make it easy to avoid emotional attachments. While trying to figure out what to do with an expensive degree in theater in 2009—it's never a great time to graduate with an expensive theater degree unless your family is wealthy, but it's *spectacularly* shitty timing to be released out in the world during a recession—I work in a couple of restaurants, as a host and server, and discover firsthand that the service industry is not unlike working in theater. You work odd hours in close quarters, and in between performances (i.e., waiting on customers), there's ample time to flirt with your colleagues.

Meanwhile, I remain on the dating sites with a profile that nods to my cool-girl attitude—the better to stand out among all these girlie girls who are probably listing *Eat, Pray, Love* as their favorite movie AND book.

About me: Went to Northwestern for undergrad, applying to grad school for film studies. Looking to explore the city, have fun, and meet cool people. *smiley face emoji*

Also, Tina Fey is my heroine. And by heroine, I mean lady hero. I don't want to ingest her and listen to jazz.

Interests: Movies (I'm a nerd), dancing, trivia bar nights, traveling.

Favorite movies and TV shows: *Do the Right Thing, Some Like It Hot, Superbad, Community, Mad Men, Goodfellas, 30 Rock, It's Always Sunny in Philadelphia.*

This surely makes guys who click on my profile think, "Oh wow, she seems *different*. Like she can hang. A cute Black girl who's into all this stuff? Score!"

Score indeed. "I'm a cool girl, I'm a, I'm a cool girl," sings Tove Lo, who in turn is interpolating the famous, scathing inner monologue of Amy Dunne in Gillian Flynn's *Gone Girl*. Except unlike Amy, you could never pay me enough money to pretend to like football for a guy—you mean to tell me, the players run a few feet, get tackled, the game pauses to reset, and then . . . they run away only to get tackled *again* . . . over and over? *That's* the game you all go crazy over?—and I don't know how to play poker.

Okay, honestly, I'm not like Flynn's cool girl at all, because I don't attempt to like everything he likes at all; I'm much too opinionated for that. And again, I don't want anything serious, y'all! We've only got to have enough in common for me to not get bored during a date or two.

But I do pride myself on being able to adapt a veneer of cool and utter detachment in my dating language. I keep conversations surface-level and mostly focused on movies and TV, and I let him send the after-date texts first before even thinking about sending my own. And I ghost like nobody's business. Because I'd rather end it with me promising to "hit you up next week," knowing good and well I'm not going to do that, than by having a potentially uncomfortable text exchange where I make it clear I'm no longer interested.

If the guy hits *me* up after that week's gone by with no word from me to say hi or try to set up another date, I simply block and forget. In my twisted way of thinking, this is kind of empowering.

I'll admit it—every once in a while, I lose my cool when I find myself on the receiving end of this schtick. I'm wondering why someone I thought was cute and chill to hang with hasn't followed up after our last date. At one point we were texting back and forth like cray, and we had a good, flirtatious rapport going there. I'm checking my phone now, and . . . nothing.

Did he forget about me? Do I write him off as a full-on specter now? Seriously though, why can't you just text back, "Hey, it was nice meeting you, but I don't see another date in our future" or just make up some fake excuse? Anything is better than nothing.

I refuse to be that girl who sends an angry text (or any text, for that matter) days later, making it known I'm still thinking about him and still interested. But I'd be lying if I said my ego didn't take a hit. Is doing this really an act of empowerment or just asshole behavior?

There's no one Keyser Söze moment but an accumulation of little moments that begin to chip away at the armor hiding my insecurity. I've seen one too many movies where the female action hero has to wear a crop top (impractical!) or demonstrate some forced caretaker trait while kicking ass. I think Beyoncé's "Run the World (Girls)" slaps—those Afrobeats, that intricate choreography—but know deep down that anthem is more representative of the billionaire Queen herself than it is the average woman who doesn't have access to a full-time nanny and must fight for equal pay. I start questioning the true power of all those cultural signifiers of "girl power" as I watch what goes down in the real world— high-profile women who are unfairly targeted and mocked for asserting their dominance in ways their male counterparts never are (*ahem* Janet Jackson); the exclusionary artifice of the white and wealthy #girlboss era (*Lean In*, The Wing); the persistent fandom and public defense of terrible men like R. Kelly and Bill Cosby.

And I begin to understand how the personality traits typically attributed to and prided in men—narcissism, dickish behavior, overconfidence—are not great personality traits to begin with and in their most extreme forms translate into bad bosses, bad romantic partners, and genuinely just bad people to be around. How the sexist dismissal of women's and girls' interests and tastes pervades every facet of American culture, and how deeply unfair and harmful the double standards are for women. It finally sinks in, years later, that bell hooks is right, and I've been falling for a lie about what I perceived to be the only thing worth striving for: "Some of us were tempted and began to think that if we could not really have our freedom, then the next best thing would be to have the right to be dicks in drag, phallocentric girls doing everything the boys do—only better."[7]

Her words are a shear through my being and my ego. She's absolutely talking about me.

• • •

A couple months before starting grad school at NYU, I meet B while I'm still living in DC. B works a kind of boring governmental-type job, and he and his crew are wayyy fratty (football games, Natty Lights, regular games of cornhole), but he's cute, and we get along great and share a sarcastic, dark sense of humor. Because we both know I'm leaving soon, we're never exclusive, but I wouldn't call what we have entirely casual either; we take trips together, text and G-chat pretty much every day, and visit one another once a month even after I've moved to New York.

We often discuss our experiences dating other people and what we're looking for.

> **ME:** Yeah, I just can't see myself having kids or doing the married thing, ever.

> **B:** Really? I hear you on the kid front, but you're probably gonna have a harder time finding a guy who'll want to be with you and not have some sort of commitment.

> **ME:** I mean, I just can't see myself finding someone I'd want to be committed to like that. But also, you can be committed without marriage—it's just a piece of paper. Also also, as a

woman, I think it'll actually be pretty easy. Plenty of guys would be happy to find a woman who's not looking for anything too serious.

B: Eh . . . more guys are looking for that than you'd think.

Honestly, if I hadn't left DC when I did, I'd have wanted to try being serious with him, and he feels the same way about me. This is new and strange to me; I've never felt this close to a guy and certainly never mutually so. We have deep conversations about our families, our lives prior to meeting each other. I like this feeling of being vulnerable and open, even as it terrifies me. Maybe it's not so "weak" of a thing to be.

After about a year of being long-distance friends with benefits, I decide he should probably cancel his next upcoming trip to visit me. This isn't going anywhere; I never want to live in DC again, and he has no intention of moving to New York. I'm concerned I've been unconsciously keeping myself from being serious with someone because he was a constant, and our arrangement conveniently kept me in the mindset of feeling like a freewheeling baddie.

There'd been one guy I'd started seeing during grad school who had potential to turn into something serious. After a few dates, we'd hit it off, and he was cute, smart, and seemed really nice. When he surprised me with a Christmas present (a basic scarf, nothing fancy, but a present nonetheless), I knew I had the upper hand in this dynamic, and it felt good. But I also freaked out internally, still fearful of forming a real, substantial attachment to someone. So I did what I'd done many times before and ghosted him. Real asshole behavior.

This time, though, I feel bad afterward. And I also feel a tinge of regret, wondering what it might have been like if I'd tried being a little less guarded with the guys who actually live a subway ride away rather than a Megabus away.

As I contemplate my personal life and bell hooks's wisdom and all those surface-level symbols of female empowerment, I start putting less stock in the copying and pasting of so-called male traits. I've begun re-framing my idea of what constitutes power and strength and recognize that it can also be found in vulnerability. So much of what makes Judy Garland, for one, so magnetic is her ostensible fragility and her funda-mental inability to mask it in her own work—"The Man That Got Away" hits so hard because she's *lived* that feeling and isn't afraid to tap into it. That's what her fans are connecting with and can identify with, and that's why her spirit endures fifty-plus years after her death. Ditto so many of our other tragic female icons like Amy Winehouse or Billie Holiday.

Of course, there's a danger, too, in glorifying the suffering of women in order to find strength, but there's a balance to be struck. And there are other types of power to discover in women: the messiness and persever-ance of characters like Fleabag, Rebecca Bunch in *Crazy Ex-Girlfriend*, Issa Dee in *Insecure*, Eve and Villanelle on *Killing Eve*—all characters who occupy varying parts of the antihero spectrum. The DGAF attitude of pop stars like Rihanna and Megan Thee Stallion, who have the likes of Toni and Janet and countless other women to thank for leading the way.

And then, just shy of my twenty-fifth birthday and only a couple of weeks after B and I end things, I go out with a guy I've been messaging with on OkCupid. He's—wait for it—much taller than me, in his early thirties, works at a nonprofit, cute. Our first date, at a swanky hipster bar serving grilled cheese sandwiches in Bushwick, is kind of perfect.

HIM: How do you feel about kids?

ME: Don't want them, not interested.

HIM: Wait, really? Not at all?

ME: Not even a tiny bit.

HIM: Wow, okay. Same! That's rare; I've had to end my last few relationships because they wanted kids.

ME: Yeah nope, never been me!

Banter, banter, banter. Maybe an hour later . . .

HIM: Did you grow up religious?

ME: I was raised more or less agnostic and turned out atheist.

HIM: That's awesome. I grew up super religious, but I'm atheist, too.

Banter, banter, banter. Another hour later . . .

ME: Yeah, my parents are divorced, and I'm not sure how I feel about marriage, either. Like, I would be fine never getting married. It's really just a contract, right? And there's no guarantee it's going to last.

HIM: Absolutely. I'm the same way. Don't care about it at all. So many people I know who are married seem unhappy.

This is huge. I'm physically attracted to him. We're on the same page on many of the important things. And he lives a subway ride away! (Though he's still technically long-distance, because Harlem is an hour away from Bushwick on a good day.)

I'm still wary at first but more open to the possibilities of a relationship than ever before. This person helps break down my apprehensions about relationships and being open and being in love. When he tells me he loves me after only dating a couple of months—during a night out of drunken karaoke—I'm confused and chalk it up to him being inebriated. But soon enough, I accept that he's for real. And maybe this is for real. And I can let my guard down a bit. I can let it be and see where it goes and see how he shows up for me in ways that we're used to seeing women do in movies and TV, and yes, real life—doing most of the cooking, being supportive of my career and workaholic tendencies, worrying about how little I'm sleeping and how happy or unhappy I am at any given moment. He's not perfect, I'm not perfect, we're not perfect, but it works. We make each other happy.

We do eventually get married, but only after a minor health scare makes us consider our rights in the case of a true emergency later down the line. We want to be there for one another.

I don't completely ditch everything I learned from the sexually assertive women figures of my youth. I still think we should be able to date and play around freely like Nola Darling if that's what feels good and if we're considerate of those we're playing around with. But even

Samantha fell for Smith Jerrod. And even Alanis Morissette could go from angrily kissing off Uncle Joey from *Full House* (rumor has it) to giving in to love, admitting she's "never felt this healthy before," and she's "never wanted something rational."

"I am aware now."

That's power.

I still don't want kids, though.

4

KENNY G GETS IT

While I recognize that present-day Dave Chappelle suffers from transphobic diarrhea of the mouth and has morphed into a crotchety old dude who will be dragged into the future kicking and screaming while complaining about "wokeness" run amok, I cannot pretend as though some of his old jokes no longer slap.

For one, a very funny and astute bit from his 2004 stand-up special *For What It's Worth*. The story goes more or less like this: Sometime in the immediate aftermath of the 9/11 attacks, the comedian recalls he was watching MTV. At one point, an anchor cut to, of all people, Ja Rule (*"It's Murdaaaaaaa"*) for comment. Chappelle is indignant: "Who gives a fuck what Ja Rule thinks at a time like this, nigga?! This is ridiculous. I don't wanna dance; I'm scared to death!"

Chappelle performs exaggerated shock and disgust, stomping around in a circle on the stage, emphasizing the ridiculousness of this media moment by playing out the thought process that would lead to someone turning to Ja Rule, of all people, for guidance in times of trouble. "Can somebody *please . . .* [*pause for effect*] *. . .* FIND Ja Rule, get a hold of this motherfucker so I can *make sense of all this*! *WHERE IS JA???*" he asks, feigning concern.

The bit is taking aim at the cult of celebrity and the media's obsession with turning to it in the most inappropriate of ways. Some two decades later, this obsession has only grown more pronounced, and in ways Chappelle probably couldn't have even predicted.

Going back decades, scholarship and analysis of star-audience relationships have been framed around how the latter looks up to or is inspired by the former. In 1974 for instance, film and sociology scholar Andrew Tudor, drawing from the audience research of movie producer Leo A. Handel, unpacked four increasingly intense degrees of this dynamic:

> **emotional affinity**—"the audience feels a loose attachment to a particular protagonist deriving jointly from star, narrative, and the individual personality of the audience member"

> **self-identification**—the audience member imagines themselves as the star persona on-screen

> **imitation**—mimicry of style and/or affectation of the star

> **(and most extremely) projection**—the star as "a receptacle for the projected desires, frustrations, and pleasures of the fan"[1]

These days, though, it's tough to ignore that the power scales have tipped, to a certain extent, between artist and consumer—how *the stars* are directly responding to and/or being influenced by *their audiences*.

Social media has personalized the public personas of celebrities, many of whom let us in on their private lives and thoughts more than they ever did or could in the pre-Twitter, pre-Instagram age. Instead of only communicating with us at arm's length through splashy magazine cover story puff pieces and primetime Diane Sawyer interviews, many celebrities (or their assistants/interns/nepotism babies/whatever) speak "directly" to their fans. I grew up when Britney Spears was in her prime, and still I don't think I'd ever seen her dance half as much as I do now whenever her Instagram posts show up on my feed. She likes to prance around alone in her house a lot, it seems.

This kind of unprecedented access has coincided with a confluence of events over the years—Obama's election, Trump's election, far too many mass shootings, the ascendance of Black Lives Matter, #MeToo, and the pandemic, just to name a few—that have helped reimagine celebrity culture and how artists and entertainers brand themselves. For those of us who care about such things—and I'd argue a lot of people *do* care, more than some might like to admit—it can be a letdown to learn an artist we've admired has done or said questionable things. (Me, anytime I see an up-and-coming pop star like Normani or H.E.R. collaborate with the repeat abuser and stalker Chris Brown: *Ugh! WHY, SWAY???*) And unlike previous generations, the internet has leveled the playing field to an extent, so traditionally underrepresented groups have a larger and more effective platform for voicing their perspectives on cultural and political issues.

In its most succinct form, this exchange can look like the time when Lizzo and Beyoncé were called out by fans for using the word "spaz" (considered an ableist slur by some) in their songs "Grrrls" and "Heated" within mere weeks of one another. Both responded to the critiques swiftly and rerecorded new lyrics to replace the word. They weren't the first artists to do something like this; in the early 1990s, Disney changed offensive lyrics on the original *Aladdin* soundtrack and in the movie after Arab-American organizations protested. But the digital age, plus our heightened attunement to cultural sensitivity, makes the pop stars' actions notable. "Let me make one thing clear: I never want to promote derogatory language," Lizzo announced at the time. "As a fat Black woman in America, I've had many hurtful words used against me, so I understand the power words can have (whether intentionally or, in my case, unintentionally)."[2]

And so, pop culture and politics—never strangers to one another—have become even more inextricable in the twenty-first century. Increasingly, celebrities manage their images by speaking out about politics and engaging in (or appearing to engage in) activism both through their craft and IRL. Many seem to recognize that the higher their status (and the younger their primary audience), the less silent or "neutral" they can afford to remain.

This has played out in many different ways in recent years. Beyoncé performed her song "Formation," evoking Black Panther iconography at the Super Bowl Halftime Show in 2016, and subsequently released the *Lemonade* visual album, which includes an excerpt from a Malcolm X speech where he declared the Black woman to be "the most disrespected person in America." This marked a turning point for a superstar who had largely avoided the subject of social justice up to that point. In the eyes of many, it transformed her from music legend to music legend-activist, catapulting her legacy into another dimension.

Two years later, Taylor Swift publicly endorsed Democrats Phil Bredesen and Jim Cooper in the 2018 midterm elections in her home state of Tennessee and later donated funds to LGBTQ organizations. ("In the past I've been reluctant to publicly voice my political opinions," she admitted in an Instagram post, "but due to several events in my life and in the world in the past two years, I feel very differently about that now.")[3]

Even Drake, who's probably the only superstar in these times besides Bruno Mars who's been able to get away with staying mostly mum on politics, reportedly donated $100,000 to the Black-led social justice organization National Bail Out Collective in the wake of the George Floyd protests in 2020. Granted, this was only after another artist named Mustafa the Poet called out him and The Weeknd on Instagram, imploring them to match and exceed his own donation to the org. But hey, it still happened; nothing quite like feeling the pressure from another celebrity to kick-start social change. (The Weeknd also reportedly took up the challenge and made donations.)[4]

Cultural activism among artists and celebrities isn't new, of course. (Hi there, Paul Robeson, Marlon Brando, Harry Belafonte, Jane Fonda . . .) But the degree of *expectation* for it from fans and consumers—liberal ones in particular, though certainly not exclusively—has definitely escalated into something unprecedented as people have become more tethered to the internet. There's now an implicit expectation that artists exhibit political and social awareness in their personal and professional lives—ideally, an awareness with a point of view that aligns with the fan's own core values. There's cultural cachet to attain in calling out and calling upon the ones who create the art we consume to prove their moral and sociopolitical bona fides. *WHERE IS JA???* the progressive public now calls out whenever another Black person's death at the hands of police reaches national attention, another powerful person is accused of sexual assault, or another national election season is upon us. Except what they're really asking—because even today no one's checking for Ja, especially not after that Fyre Fest debacle—is, *Does X famous person care about the same issues I do? And what are they saying/doing about it?*

As a consumer, caring about the political and social implications of art and the artists who make it is responsible; it's wise to consider what it means to support and engage with pop culture and ultimately decide, maybe, that you'd rather not ever listen to another R. Kelly song again.

But sometimes, the expectations of political messaging and noble behavior from celebrities veer into absurdity and, ultimately, bombastic discourse. For instance, the 2022 Super Bowl Halftime Show, where the headliners included a mishmash of generational and municipal representation—Snoop Dogg, Kendrick Lamar, Mary J. Blige, 50 Cent, and Eminem—all converging under the generalized banner of celebrating Dr. Dre, the superproducer himself. A long shadow hung over this show, cast by Dre's well-documented history of physically assaulting women and the NFL's own long icky history (domestic violence, concussions, and a Black former head coach who was suing the organization for racial discrimination at the time).

The performance itself was underwhelming, but what was perhaps most striking about this trip down nostalgia lane was the public's debate about something Eminem, the only white headliner among the group, did. It was that kneel—that nearly forty-second-long kneel, which came right after he concluded his performance of "Lose Yourself" and just as the concert transitioned back to focusing on Dr. Dre, who was plunking out notes from Tupac's DeBarge-sampling track "I Ain't Mad at Cha." The first time I watched that kneel, I didn't think much of it. Soon after it aired, however, a heated debate was well underway. Some people had interpreted the kneel as a gesture of respect in memory of Tupac. But many more people interpreted it as a defiant political protest on the sports world's largest stage.[5] "The move was an apparent nod to the former San Francisco quarterback Colin Kaepernick," wrote one reporter for the *New York Times*.[6] "Eminem taking a knee for Kaepernick?" tweeted *The Recount*, a digital news magazine.[7] This inference was layered with greater meaning because of a rumor that had begun circulating earlier in the day before the game, with some—apparently working off of zero evidence or sources, only vibes—claiming Em was told by the NFL not to kneel beforehand but did it anyway. ("Eminem the Goat" for this, read one tweet.)

At least one aspect of these interpretations was debunked; NFL spokesperson Brian McCarthy would respond to the claim about Eminem's so-called rebellion against the league by stating they were aware he'd be kneeling based on the dress rehearsals, and the act was "not an area of concern."[8] (Though considering this is the NFL, they also could've been trying to save face by claiming to have known about it all along.)

Whether or not Eminem, who has voiced his support for Kaepernick in the past, was actually nodding to Kaepernick was unclear. None of the artists involved, including Eminem, weighed in in the immediate aftermath of the performance. But that didn't matter; plenty of people were all too eager to turn the Halftime Show into a demonstration of integrity on the part of Eminem (again, the only white headliner of the bunch), perhaps in an effort to counter all the other issues surrounding the league's reputation.

One of the most egregiously desperate responses to this moment came from left-wing media outlet Occupy Democrats, which tweeted the night of the performance:

> Rap superstar Eminem takes a knee during his Super Bowl Halftime performance in support of Black athletes like Colin Kaepernick protesting police brutality—even though the NFL demanded that he not do it. RT IF YOU SUPPORT EMINEM'S BRAVE STAND![9]

In the case of Eminem and The Ambiguous Kneel, viewers didn't even have to ask *WHERE'S JA???* They just conjured "Ja" up out of thin air based on a whole lot of assumptions.

This episode reveals how it often isn't just about a desire for celebrities to do better; it's about wanting to *feel* better about liking a celebrity (or, in this case, to feel better about watching the Super Bowl). No matter how massive a piece of pop culture gets, the individual's connection to it is deeply personal. It can become a prism through which we view ourselves or wish to view ourselves, a medium often tied to nostalgia and sense memory.

It's also a language used to communicate and grow closer with others, especially online, where people are encouraged to express their personalities and tastes in the most public ways imaginable. It's easy, and even cool, to wear our cultural fixations on our sleeves, bodies, avatars, Twitter profiles (#rihannanavy, #beyhive, "Betty White Stan Account"), streaming/podcast/Substack subscriptions, algorithms, and everything in between.

This kind of identity tagging can create the broad perception that people are what they enjoy; that there's a strong correlation between taste and who someone is as a person. In this mindset, people may perceive criticism of something they've enjoyed as a slight, a ding at the very core of their being.

Kenny G, the man whose smoothly pestilential saxophone sounds warmed the hearts of millions of boomers for reasons I'll never fully understand, put it perfectly in *Listening to Kenny G*, a documentary exploring his polarizing appeal: "When you love a piece of music, you're basically exposing something about you. 'I like this, don't you?' 'No, I hate that.' They're basically saying to you they hate something about you."

(There was a period in my youth when my mom would play Kenny G CDs on longish car rides, and not just during peak-G season, aka Christmas time. So naturally, I have long despised that man's catalog with all the fiery passion of a Kendrick Lamar verse. What kid enjoys listening to ersatz jazz for hours on end? Still, respect to Kenny G for being so admirably self-aware and spot-on in his understanding of how taste can work. He seems like a genuinely good dude who happens to make terrible music.)

The *Where is Ja?* of it all is only one adverse effect of this.

In some cases, the inverse occurs, and celebrity-audience dynamics rely upon huge swaths of fandom to adopt an unwavering obsession that flat-out ignores any complicated moral or ethical issues at play. And then, when others deign to point out those issues, the fans take grave offense.

But what it all boils down to is this: no matter who you are or what you believe in, everyone wants to feel validated by their tastes. That's not an inherently bad thing. But the ways that desire for validation sometimes manifests . . . well, that can get ugly.

"You"

But first, how did we arrive at this equation of peak "taste = identity" politics? The most obvious place to start with is—surprise!—the internet, everyone's favorite villain.

Way back in 1995 when I was a scrawny seven-year-old obsessed with her Skip-It and *American Girl* magazines, the Pew Research Center published a report which found that while the number of homes with modem-equipped computers had jumped from eleven million in the previous year to eighteen million, "just 20% of online users go online every day." They also concluded that CD-ROM drives were "seen by consumers as a more essential feature than online services,"[10] which feels accurate considering how much time I spent in those days playing *Carmen Sandiego. *Sigh.* We were all so innocent back then.

Not too long after that study, the *New York Times* observed what it declared to be a relatively new phenomenon in American culture: self-branding. Advertising execs, celebrity moguls like Michael Jordan and Martha Stewart, and various media were touting the power of "the personal brand," training a growing number of Americans to view themselves as products to be marketed, according to the paper of record. "Personal identities are being swapped for the attributes of consumer products, as individuals come to see themselves increasingly as brands."[11] This was in 1997, when Al Gore's internet was still relatively nascent and accessible via dial-up and before the era of first-person narrative essays in online blogs like *xoJane* and *Jezebel* and before Buzz-Feed personality quizzes. (Boomers and some Gen-Xers like to blame our current hellscape of Kardashian supremacy and influencer overload on millennials, but let's be real—my generation has only picked up the baton from our elders.)

Within a few years, of course, we would all be online. So online, in fact, that in 2006, *TIME*'s choice for Person of the Year was the stunt-tastic "You." Yes, *you*. Your mama and your cousin, too.

The cover of the mag had a picture of an iMac, the screen made from a reflective material to mimic a mirror effect. The pronouncement was sweeping, describing this new internet age as a "revolution" where the people were "seizing the reins of the global media" and "framing the new digital democracy."[12]

What *TIME* was reacting to, in part, was how this new reality allowed for the cultivation of a different personality from the one we might have in our physical day-to-day lives. Personal email, personal websites, personal blogs, personal gaming avatars . . . whether you were a student, professional, or just someone looking to hang out with others sans face-to-face contact, the web made it possible to advertise yourself however you wished. AOL Instant Messenger, Myspace, and LiveJournal laid the foundation for social media to become the haven and hell of my generation in the early 2000s, where adolescents could try out identities and personas while broadcasting the process to complete strangers, not just the friends and family they interacted with in school and at home. A typical LiveJournal post could include not only the post-diary, pre-Twitter era inner ramblings of an angsty teen (that was me; I was that angsty teen) but also details about their "current mood" ("indifferent," "bored") or "current music" (lots of John Mayer, because I was a fourteen-year-old girl, and *Room for Squares* was made for moody fourteen-year-old girls. Also, in keeping with the themes of this essay, I'd like to dutifully note that this was in the time *before* he gave that infamously horrifying interview where he referred to his own member as a "David Duke cock" and said "n———").

That LiveJournal-Myspace DNA made its way into "the Facebook," which in its earliest iterations served as a kind of digital version of the inside of a teenager's locker—a collage showcasing all our interests and obsessions.

And so, a love or hatred for cultural products becomes something like a performance, perhaps unconsciously. It's not just about mining one's personal history for clicks and validation, but also, in many cases, attaching one's identity *to* cultural products, absorbing celebrities and franchises and characters as a full-on personality.

"...and I took that personally."

... which helps explain the rise of stan culture, the other side of the taste = identity equation. A wave of cultish behavior has threatened to overtake pop music over the past few years, where stans—originally a pejorative reference to a crazed, violent fan like the one described in

Eminem's song "Stan" but now apparently a badge of pride—express a kind of unyielding devotion to artists which mirrors zealous followers of religious leaders or rabid sports team enthusiasts. This goes well beyond the casual supporter who can rattle off every lyric of an artist's deep cuts or the more intense fan who maintains a frequently updated Tumblr page dedication. These are acolytes whose obsession is a nonstop performance of allegiance, whether it's seeking to boost sales by streaming a song across multiple platforms so as to rack up the play count (and encouraging others to do the same) or swarming upon and doxing any critic, professional or not, who dares to say their lord and savior put out a mediocre record (and encouraging others to do the same).

In a 2020 *New York Times* article, music reporter Joe Coscarelli broke down this phenomenon of religiosity in music fandom, citing the likes of BTS, Taylor Swift, and Nicki Minaj, whose fan bases are among the most obsessive. He spoke to Nancy Baym, an expert in online fan behavior, who described the internet as a platform that magnifies fandom to levels previously unheard of; the attention and influence fans are able to draw for their antics—sometimes from the artists themselves—is a "commodity" they've learned how to wield and exploit.

For the piece, Coscarelli interviewed a Little Monster—aka a Lady Gaga follower—who gleefully trolled Ariana Grande's fans by sharing a link to a leak of her new tracks ahead of the release of her album *Positions* to prevent her sales from surpassing those of Gaga's most recent album. (Apparently, despite the fact Gaga and Grande collaborated on a song together and appear to be on fine terms, some of Gaga's fans see Grande's individual success as a threat to their queen. Why???) The Little Monster explained their bonkers level of fandom in this way: ". . . when someone insults your favorite artist, you take that as a personal insult, and then you find yourself spending hours trying to convince someone in China that *Born This Way* was [Gaga's] best album."[13]

One of the more egregious examples of standom in recent memory is related to none other than Kanye West, if you can believe it. (*Of course you can believe it.*)

July 2022, Rolling Loud music festival—the rapper Kid Cudi is performing as a last-minute headliner, replacing West, who'd dropped out just a few days earlier. Cudi's alone at the front of the stage doing his thing, but random objects are being hurled in his direction by audience members. He ignores them until a water bottle pelts him directly in the face; understandably, he loses his cool. "I will fucking leave," he warns. "If I get hit with one more fucking thing—if I see one more fucking thing on this fucking stage, I'm leaving," he says. "Don't fuck with me."[14]

Like clockwork, another object whizzes by him and onto the stage. Cudi turns around and makes the long walk off the stage, never looking back.

The utter disrespect from some audience members went deeper than the kind of drunken, amped-up asshole behavior one will almost certainly encounter at any giant music festival. At the time, Cudi was in the middle of a highly publicized beef with Kanye. Months earlier on Instagram, Ye made it clear he was upset with him for being friends with ex-wife Kim Kardashian's then-boyfriend Pete Davidson. Cudi responded by calling Ye a "dinosaur." These are both grown men in their thirties and forties, by the way.

Anyone with even a passing knowledge of Kanye's tumultuous presence in pop culture knows the Cult of Ye is strong; his defenders will go to bat for him *hard* no matter what horrible and troubling things he says ("slavery was a choice"; anti-Semitic rants) or does (stalking and publicly harassing Kardashian), because he's a "genius." One has to wonder whether Cudi, upon being offered the gig to replace his estranged friend/collaborator, had a moment where he contemplated the potential optics and said to himself, "That's bait" as if he were *Mad Max: Fury Road*'s Tom Hardy coming upon that lone woman screaming for help in the middle of the desert, only to shrug and just say, "Fuck it. Let's go."

Either way, he did it, and the Cult of Ye wasn't having it. The tool who threw the fateful water bottle that sent Cudi packing that night tweeted afterward: "We wanted @kanyewest anyway. . . . @KiDCuDi you soft."[15] A number of videos[16] from attendees in the crowd show that as the rapper left the stage, segments of the crowd began chanting Kanye's name alongside dueling chants of Cudi's name—a poetic encapsulation of online standom rendered appallingly visceral in real life.

It was the grossest kind of fandom made all the more gross by the fact that Cudi has openly struggled with depression and suicidal urges in the past. The Kanye stans were performing incivility in the name of their leader, who later that evening actually did show up at the festival to perform alongside Lil Durk. (To add insult to projectile water bottle injury, Ye, being the troll that he is, performed a song Cudi is featured on.)

Like pop music stans, TV and movie fanatics have also been known to wield their collective power, from the outcries over the terrifyingly uncanny CGI design of Sonic the Hedgehog (displeased fans quite literally sent the animators back to the drawing board for a makeover ahead of the movie's 2020 release)[17] to the fans who successfully campaigned for the release of the Zack Snyder cut of *Justice League* after the director left the production to tend to a family tragedy. A not-so-great outcome of this occasional capitulation to stans is that the worst of them are also emboldened to loudly air their prejudiced grievances over every little thing, like the misogynistic fanboys who spammed IMDb with negative ratings for the female-led *Ghostbusters* before the movie had even been released[18] and the racist harassment Kelly Marie Tran and John Boyega faced for bringing a little more color to the most recent *Star Wars* trilogy.

As irrational and just plain silly as a lot of this behavior is, at its root is that desire to belong. Corporations have picked up on this, obviously, and milk it for all they can, stoking the flames of consumer excitement to encourage widespread devotion of a sort that would've previously been reserved for the rare *Star Trek*–like franchise. (Think about how Comic-Con has expanded to entice not just comic book and sci-fi/fantasy nerds, but also enthusiastic fans of the likes of *SpongeBob SquarePants*, *Bob's Burgers*, and *Abbott Elementary*.) With the explosion of media platforms across movies and TV, there's just so much content now, and anything and everything is ripe for ardent fandom.

A consequence of this explosion, as plenty of others have pointed out, is that the monoculture—that murky concept of universal approbation typically characterized by phenomena like Michael Jackson's stardom in the 1980s or a juggernaut like *Seinfeld* in the 1990s—is all but dead, or at least much harder to come by. The occasional *Game of Thrones* aside, there can be a heightened sense that far fewer people within your orbit are on a cultural diet that aligns closely with yours, especially when it comes to TV ("Are you watching *Better Call Saul*?" "No, but that sounds familiar. What's it about again?"), or that if they do consume the same goods as you, they're doing so at a completely different pace on a completely different timeline ("I haven't caught up with the finale of *Watchmen* yet—no spoilers!"). And because we're all doing our own thing, and the urge to share one's latest binge-watch can be irresistible AF, the streaming era has encouraged "evangelism." As one Vox deep dive article into the effects of algorithms on the perceived monoculture suggests: "We all become the programming head of our own virtual TV network, deciding what gets airtime and what doesn't."[19]

"limiting in scope"

Once upon a time on Twitter, where little good ever happens, a film critic lamented their own misfortune of having liked movies considered bad by many other film critics for any number of reasons. They wrote: "Everyone talks about toxic fandom, but what about toxic criticism?"

The question was posed to no one, and everyone, in particular. "Apparently," they continued, "anyone who likes *Wonder Woman 1984*, *Bohemian Rhapsody*, *Green Book*, *Hillbilly Elegy*, *Dear Evan Hansen*, or *Joker* clearly couldn't appreciate or enjoy those films because the powers of film Twitter said so." They went on to bemoan critics' "bullying," which makes "people feel bad for liking something they didn't."

What this person was really asking was: Why do you hate this thing I love?

But what makes something "toxic"? I personally prefer to keep my usage of this word limited to conversations related to science or karaoke renditions of Britney's "Toxic," but if we're going to play along with this concept, a solid definition of it would encompass some blend of disingenuousness, closed-mindedness, and/or a fundamental lack of curiosity on the part of the critic.

Actual toxic criticism can look like a white male critic describing *Turning Red*—the Pixar movie about a Chinese-Canadian girl's disconnect with her overbearing mother and the hereditary curse that turns her into a giant red panda once she hits puberty—as "limiting in its scope" simply because it's "root[ed] . . . very specifically in the Asian community of Toronto."[20] The problem with this review isn't so simple as *white guy gives negative review to movie with a girl-of-color protagonist*; people are allowed to dislike what they dislike, and there could be valid, introspective, or aesthetic arguments made for why this movie left him cold. (Richard Roeper's review, for one, called the movie "underwhelming" yet managed to critique it without sounding xenophobic.) What makes it "toxic" is the criticism begins and ends with the author admitting he's "not the film's target audience" while demonstrating an utter unwillingness to still engage with the film in a meaningful way. It's a dull, one-note approach to reviewing and ends up othering and dismissing what are in fact a few very broad audience demographics that might find *Turning Red* appealing: immigrants of color, parents, adolescent girls, and adults who were once adolescent girls. And also plenty of other people who might not fall into any of those categories but found something about it to connect with anyway. (Seriously, it concludes with this clunker of sentences: ". . . when that audience finds the movie, I've no doubt they will celebrate it for the unique animal that it is. In my opinion, however, that audience is relatively small, and I'm not part of it." Cool story, bro!)

Assertions like *This doesn't reflect my identity, so it's not a good movie* are a consequence of white male-centered storytelling being the dominant force in Western pop culture since forever. But they're also inextricably linked to a culture that birthed "You" as *TIME*'s Person of the Year and encourages everyone to seek themselves out in the things they watch, read, and listen to: queer, millennial, Black, athletic, kinky, white and nerdy, Muslim, rural, immigrant, ex-military, broke, boomer, college student, introverted, Gemini, single parent, disabled, forty-year-old virgin, scammer, and so on.

The wonderful thing about living in the now is that pretty much everyone *can* find something that will appeal to a facet of their identity and sensibility. (Whether or not it's actually any good is a whole other story.) The frustrating part of it is that those who have traditionally seen themselves at the center of pop culture can often be dismissive in the face of those seeking the same levels of representation. And that's the kind of thinking that seems to put TV shows like Netflix's *The Baby-Sitters Club* and *One Day at a Time*—shows with only decent viewership numbers but strong, dedicated fan bases—on the chopping block before their time. It's this often unspoken belief that stories about, say, tween girls or Latine families don't have a "broad" enough appeal. Ditto *Batgirl*, the $90 million nearly completed superhero flick starring a Dominican-American performer that was shelved by Warner Bros. Discovery, reportedly so the corporation could treat it as a tax write-off. [21]

Meanwhile, *Joker*—a movie that practically begs its audience to sympathize with an incel—won multiple Oscars and made over a billion dollars in box offices worldwide.

In its own way, this kind of peer-pressured influence is connected to the "cancel culture" boogeyman. I must be clear here and state I in no way believe that cancel culture as it's defined by the likes of Tucker

Carlson, Bill Maher, and the "esteemed" intellectuals who signed the infamous Harper's open letter "A Letter on Justice and Open Debate" actually exists in any form other than one's imagination. If it did, Mel Gibson—he who once allegedly told the mother of his kid it'd be her fault if she were "raped by a pack of n———s"[22] and who, according to Winona Ryder, once asked the actress, who is Jewish, if she was an "oven dodger"[23]—wouldn't still be working steadily in Hollywood. If it did, the various "thinkers" who have willingly left highly coveted positions at prominent perches like the *New York Times* and Vox while complaining about being "bullied" for their backward and disingenuous views about race, gender, and politics wouldn't be able to continue spouting those opinions on platforms like Substack toward ever so lucrative ends.

But the mere notion of "cancel culture," which is really just callout culture, has infiltrated our discussions around art and reveals how potent the intersection of self-branding identity politics and online interactions can be.

#teampersonal

Callout culture, standom, and "toxic criticism" are all products of overpersonalization and its encouragement of narcissism-fueled algorithms warping the consumption of pop culture. It's turned into a spectator sport, where sides are taken and battle lines are drawn.

There can be disturbing costs to this phenomenon—for one thing, a world where pathological and hostile behavior is freewheeling and abetted. This became especially clear during the sickening media circus that was the Johnny Depp / Amber Heard defamation trial, which brought the post-MeToo discourse to a new low. For a refresher, in 2016, Heard filed for divorce from Depp and obtained a restraining order against him, accusing him of verbal and physical abuse. In 2018, she wrote a *Washington Post* op-ed in which she described herself as "a public figure representing domestic abuse," though she did not name Depp directly in the piece. Nevertheless, Depp sued Heard for defamation, and she countersued.

One thing the whole mess revealed was how easy it is for what should've been a reasonably private matter to become a cause célèbre of epic proportions. As the televised hearings went on for weeks in 2022, with depressing details of unflattering behavior revealed in testimony from both sides, the Depp stans and men's rights activists went HAM on Heard, accusing *her*, and her alone, of abuse—a woman crying wolf. The case turned onlookers into amateur sleuths and wannabe lawyers, claiming to poke holes in Heard's claims in many a social media thread and video. It turned them into rabid Depp defenders who produced hours upon hours of content dedicated to "JusticeforJohnny." Many of them wouldn't even have considered themselves Depp fans prior to the case, though through him they cynically seized upon an opportunity. NBC News interviewed several content creators who discussed pivoting to anti-Heard content as attention to the trial gained steam and reaping the benefits in the form of millions and millions of views. (They all claimed to believe Depp was indeed the victim.)[24]

During peak Heard-Depp discourse, algorithms were pushing pro-Depp content to the top, which in turn only fed the frenzy of pro-Depp appetites and seemingly reinforced a perception of his innocence, which then led to more pro-Depp content, which . . . well, it essentially became a hellish feedback loop.

It even seeped into the political realm with the official Twitter account of the Republican House Judiciary Committee tweeting a triumphant GIF of Depp as Captain Jack Sparrow staring off into the distance, his pirate dreads blowing delicately in the wind, following the verdict.[25] (Heard was found guilty of defamation while one of Depp's lawyers was found guilty of defaming Heard.) And Heard testified she received many threats in the wake of the trial. "People want to kill me, and they tell me so every day. People want to put my baby in the microwave, and they tell me that," she said on the stand.[26]

So many were able to glom on to the story in the ickiest of ways, injecting their preconceived biases about victims of domestic abuse into this tale of marital strife. This, even as the case revealed evidence that Depp said and did vile things throughout their relationship, like texting a friend to say he hoped her "rotting corpse is decomposing in the fucking trunk of a Honda Civic"[27] and another instance where he said he'd "smack the ugly cunt around."[28]

But beyond bringing out the absolute worst in people, it also reflected the limitations of callout culture. Right after the verdict was announced, BuzzFeed published a list of the many celebrities who'd "liked" Depp and Heard's respective Instagram posts in response to the verdict.[29] It laid bare the queasiest kind of popularity contest: Depp's famous supporters (Jennifer Aniston, Gabby Douglas, and Patti Smith among them) tallied far more numerous than Heard's (Melanie Lynskey, Selma Blair, and just a handful of others). The aim of the article, it seemed, was to present the list as a morality measuring stick, allowing readers to easily suss out which celebrities had taken which side and judge accordingly.

This was *Where is Ja?* in action, a succinct and damning distillation of what so often happens when celebrity, standom, and something as serious as domestic violence mix. Not only was Heard a woman caught up in a patriarchal and misogynistic system, she was also a smaller fish than Depp in that big ol' pond of public recognition. Decades' worth of audience familiarity and nostalgic memories tied to his work as a performer—i.e., the *emotional affinity* Andrew Tudor described in his taxonomy of star-audience dynamics—supersedes her comparatively smaller body of work and lower-wattage star power. Many, many people identify with Depp. Accusations against him are something they take very personally. (All of this to favor a dude who inarguably has been phoning it in on-screen for at least the better part of two decades.)

And Depp, in all his brazen glory, seemed to know exactly this, which would explain why his lawyer welcomed having the trial televised to begin with.[30] Despite the fact it revealed unsavory details about how he views women—details that probably would have been glossed over had the case not been so closely watched—he seemed to wager, correctly, that his fans and much of the public wouldn't care. Like other troubling celebrities who understand the power they wield over their most ardent fans (see also: Kanye, Nicki Minaj, and, of course, Donald Trump), he was able to play off his position in the spotlight to get the outcome he desired and shield himself from accountability.

"Why do you hate this thing I love?"

Becoming too attached to an artist's image can obscure their bad behavior. But it's not just about how we process the private lives of stars.

An additional consequence of all this overpersonalization is a loss of pure enjoyment of the art for enjoyment's sake. I speak from a place of understanding—I've had to talk myself down off that ledge of despair plenty of times. Take Jeremy O. Harris's Broadway debut *Slave Play*, which was highly controversial from the moment it arrived on the scene, particularly among Black audiences and critics. I find it challenging and provocative (in a good way), even if it occasionally veers into didacticism and doesn't quite stick the landing in the final act. Others have disagreed, and fervently so.

In act 1, three interracial Black-white couples role-play sexual fantasies involving antebellum iconography and stereotypes (i.e., the mammy and the master); in act 2, we learn that the couples are part of a sociological experiment run by another interracial couple to help break through their relationship hurdles as they relate to race (the white partners are dismissive or ignorant of the Black partners' experiences and concerns); the final act turns its attention to only one of the couples, Keneisha and Jim, who are still reeling from the group therapy session, with Keneisha recalling a traumatic childhood memory of taking a school field trip to a plantation with her mostly white classmates.

Obviously, this show is a full Bingo card of "taboo" subject matters. Harris touches on so many hot topics—miscegenation, slavery, sex, queerness, microaggressions, violence—and stirs them all up in a confessional pot of bombastic, unfiltered gumbo (Harris is Black and gay, and some of his work has touched on his relationships with white men and under the white gaze). Perhaps in part because of my personal connection with much of the material—I dated a lot of white guys in my past and had, or wanted to have, similar conversations about our interpersonal dynamics when it came to race—I see value in and appreciate the way Harris attempts to unpack this country's greatest sin in such a provocative way. But I've seen critiques that not only review the play harshly for trafficking in gross stereotypes, but also suggest that any Black person who likes *Slave Play* is self-hating or akin to a Black Republican or a Van Jones.

Now, I *could* take this characterization personally, and I did at first. I was disheartened and felt as if my blackness was being attacked. I wondered if something was wrong with me for liking this show. Could I possibly be put up for the racial draft—to borrow from yet another classic Chappelle bit from the before times, #sorrynotsorry—and traded by my people for some random white self-identifying progressive who would've voted for Obama a third time?

Of course not. But I came to understand the strong negative reactions it invoked and accept the fact that there are those who might question my own taste knowing I liked *Slave Play*. Their critiques have in fact challenged me to think more deeply about *why*, exactly, I enjoyed it in the first place—its blunt humor, its scathing observation of white passivity, and again, my own personal connection—and I've wound up feeling ever more secure in my appreciation for the play. My enjoyment of it shouldn't be threatened by others' feeling vastly differently about them, because it's *my* experience to own.

Nor can I be defined solely by how I received the play. Some of those same critics I saw subtweeting us *Slave Play* appreciators had previously aligned with my own reactions to other pop culture sticking points (like Nate Parker's overblown *The Birth of a Nation*), which proves a painfully obvious point—we're never all going to agree all of the time—that nevertheless can't be reiterated enough. Taste, as in what appeals to your senses, and identity, as in who you are and how you see the world, can certainly overlap with one another, but they don't always. More important, they don't *have to*.

This is what's been lost in conversations about taste and debates about art; people are all too eager to turn what they love (or hate) into an entire personality and in turn get extra-sensitive about their shit. They perceive a bunch of critics panning an album or a movie (or just merely giving a less than glowing review) as being an attack on them as an individual. It could be helpful to turn to the ethos of the late film critic Pauline Kael, who mused that a movie can be "stupid and empty" but still contain something a viewer can find worthy: a captivating performance, an exchange of good dialogue. If it speaks to you, it speaks to you.

The overpersonalization of pop culture begets acrimony and pathological obsession. It also encourages oversimplification, though it's never that simple. By all means, let's have spirited debates about the things we like or don't like or the questionable politics or behaviors of artists. Participate in any healthy fan-culture behavior that brings you joy. But let's not lose ourselves in the muck of performative fandom and animosity.

Contrary to what the internet has told us, everything is not personal, and what *is* personal is exactly that.

5

EBONY & IVORY

Katie Darlingson (Gabrielle Union) in *She's All That**: *Ugh, I'm over it. This time, Taylor's gone WAY too far. She was a total jerk for throwing that drink on Laney Boggs at the party, and I'm not dealing with her bullshit and prom-queen drama anymore.*

Taylor and I have been BFFs since, like, fourth grade when my folks and I moved to town so Dad could take that job refereeing for the Lakers. I wasn't crazy about being around all these white people I didn't know at first—making new friends at a new school is already hard; just imagine being one of three Black kids in your entire grade!—but I was gorgeous, and Taylor was cute too, so we just hit it off one day while sitting on the sidelines during gym class, and it turned out we were both faking having cramps so we didn't have to subject ourselves to kickball.

Taylor seemed to get most of the attention from the boys. She was always voted Best Dressed, Best Smile, AND Best Hair. She hooked up with all the hottest guys, who barely noticed I existed until she lost interest in them or they broke up with her. It never really bothered me too much—most of these boys aren't really my type anyway. But I'm, like, WAY prettier than Taylor. What was their deal?

I've put up with her antics for years because we mostly got along, and being besties with her made my social life as a Black girl in this lily-white school way easier. I tried to warn her about losing focus, but she wouldn't listen, even though me and Chandler spent countless hours helping her write that prom-queen speech.

Laney Boggs is actually kinda cool, in that mousy, pathetic kind of way. So I guess that's why I've decided to switch teams and help her win prom queen instead. (Even though we all know it really should be ME competing against Taylor, because, duh. Still, I don't really get her appeal, either. I mean, I heard those two random Black dudes rapping about how "She's all that" in front of everyone in the courtyard the other day. Bland white girls really get all the shine around here . . .)

Truthfully, I'll be so glad when high school is DONE and I can leave all these immature losers behind. On the plus side, I think I've discovered my calling, after years of managing Taylor's tantrums and self-absorbed bitch seshes: high-powered celebrity publicist. At least then, I'll get paid.

———————

*If Katie from She's All That were written as the ascendant prom queen she truly is.

• • •

In *She's All That*, Laney Boggs (Rachel Leigh Cook) is a quiet, unpopular girl at school who suddenly finds herself entangled in the drama between the popular couple, Zack (Freddie Prinze Jr.) and Taylor (Jodi Lyn O'Keefe). In the grand tradition of *Clueless*, the movie takes a literary classic—in this case, *Pygmalion*—and very loosely adapts it to the 1990s teen movie formula. When the couple breaks up after Taylor cheats on him with a reality TV star, a scorned Zack makes a bet with his friend that he can turn the dumpy, uncool Laney into prom queen.

Taylor, of course, is piiiiissed and determined to beat Laney with the help of her sidekick friends Chandler (Tamara Mello) and Katie (Gabrielle Union).

The world of *She's All That* is affluent and mostly white; Katie is one of the few Black people who inhabits it, and in the few minutes she appears on-screen throughout the movie, it's in service of either Taylor or Laney. The buddies and secondary characters in any teen movie are almost always thinly sketched to begin with, but when that character is Black, it just hits differently, especially in the era of *She's All That* when Black protagonists in teen movies were hard to come by. (And especially in a movie with *that* title, evidently jacked from queer Black slang . . .)[1]

Katie belongs to a long line of Black Friends who have peppered the universe of popular culture, a trope that becomes easy to spot if you watch enough teen movies or young adult sitcoms from the 1990s and on. My tween self understood it right away because I was simultaneously living that life.

It was the late 1990s, I was about ten years old, playing with my girlfriends, and it was time to bust out that *Spiceworld* CD and choreograph some musical numbers. Like many kids everywhere at that time, we had to sort out who would be which flavor of Spice, which presents an interesting conundrum when you're the only Black one there, and everyone else is white. You wannabe Ginger, because she's your fave and so cool, but they expect you to wannabe Scary, because . . . well, duh. In my case, I sulked and dealt with it, but inwardly, I resented my skin tone taking precedence over my actual wants and desires.

This is why the "Posh" episode of the comedy series *PEN15* speaks to me. (To be fair, almost all of *PEN15* speaks to me deeply, as if my childhood memories had been extracted directly from my brain, dropped onto a petri dish, and examined under a telescope by scientists who also happened to be TV writers and who then turned their findings into an absurdist comedy series. The show was created, along with Sam Zvibleman, by Maya Erskine and Anna Konkle, two women who, like me, apparently had awkwardly god-awful tween experiences during the turn of the twenty-first century. The thirty-somethings play versions of their middle school selves alongside actors who are actually middle school age, tackling all the growing pains of adolescence against a backdrop of AOL Instant Messenger chats, gel pens, and landline phones.)

In "Posh," Maya, Anna, and their classmates are putting together a Spice Girls–themed video project. Maya wants to be the slinky, enigmatic Posh Spice, aka Victoria Beckham. Connie wants to be Posh, too, though. And Maya is overruled because, as Connie's twisted, seventh-grade logic goes, Maya looks "the most like Scary."

Here is where I'll pause to note that Maya is Japanese on her mother's side and white on her father's. Let that sink in.

And to make things even worse, while recording the video, the other girls except for Anna, who remains uncomfortably quiet, demote Maya from playing Scary Spice to being their servant, insisting she pretend she's a Mexican hunchback gardener named Guido because "you're, like, different from us, and you have a tan."

To be clear, again: Maya is a biracial Asian-American girl, explicitly told by her white peers that, for the purposes of their imaginary girl-group role-playing game, she resembles a brown-skinned biracial Black Brit (Mel B's father is West Indian; her mom is white). And *then* she's pressured into portraying a crass stereotype of a person of a completely *different* race. Or, in other words, Maya, Scary, and Guido are all the same race to Maya's classmates: not white.

Maya's on-screen experience is the extreme version of mine—at least being Black meant my friends weren't bending over backward and just bafflingly pulling excuses out of the air to justify appointing me Scary. And mercifully, they were never so ignorant as to have me pretend to be their gardener or housekeeper or whatever. But I kept Scary at arm's length. I liked that she existed, sort of—someone who looked like me, at least in complexion. Yet she also made life as The Black Friend challenging. Why was she called "Scary," I wondered? Everyone else had fun, playful names, like "Baby" and "Posh," and the one Black woman was . . . "Scary"? Even as a kid, that moniker never sat right with me.

I didn't like being forced to like her simply because I was Black. I resented the assumption that I had to identify with her personality or her style simply because we shared skin tones. I hated that she stood out because she was the only Black girl in the group, just like I was almost always the only Black girl among my friends. I wanted desperately to blend in and bury the inescapable self-awareness of being The Only One at a time in my life when existing as anyone already really, really sucks to begin with.

(I was also resisting the truth: Scary Spice is the best Spice, hands down. She sings the opening line of "Wannabe"! Her outfits are on point. She seems chill as hell. I wish I could've realized that then; I know it now. Maybe, just maybe, I was forcing the issue too much and not giving myself over to her awesomeness.)

I also agonized over this when it came to the fictional Black Friends I encountered elsewhere. Katie Darlingson, Lisa Turtle on *Saved by the Bell*, Dionne Davenport in *Clueless*, Jessi Ramsey in *The Baby-Sitters Club*—I was wary of them all. I was too young and unsophisticated to recognize that the industry's machinations were specifically designed to relegate many of these Black characters to the sidelines, a gesture of feigned inclusivity and the bare minimum in terms of character development. Funnily enough, these Black Friends represented me in a way I wasn't yet ready to acknowledge—they were a reminder of my isolation and the fact that I often felt as if I was a blip on the radar of the many white peers I attempted to befriend.

Who were these characters' families, I wondered? What were their aspirations? Did they have crushes? How did they feel about being The Black Friend? Did they really like that boy they were coupled up with, or did the uninspired casting just call for the one Black girl in the story to be linked up with the one Black guy? Did they have *any* friends of color outside of this core group of white people? Sometimes some of these questions were answered in the script. More often, you had to fill in the blanks on your own.

I knew I wasn't interested in being Scary Spice, even if she did get to belt out one of the most memorable opening lines in pop music history and actually seemed like she could be totally fun to hang out with.

What I really, really wanted was just to be The Friend, period, or, even in some cases, The Best Friend.

• • •

The Best Friend, period, is also known as the foil, the sidekick, the cheerleader, the supporting (and supportive) character. Sometimes, their presence is practically inconsequential to the driving plot except as an obligation to fulfill a narrative trope, because if you're a protagonist in a coming-of-age story, rom-com, or a buddy comedy, you absolutely must have a BFF who can thumbs-down that hideous outfit you're considering wearing on your first date. You know they're there, because they show up for a scene or two to offer some cheeky but real advice and words of encouragement or jokey comedic relief, but they probably won't show up in a scene unless our hero is in it, too.

Sometimes—more often in TV shows, where there's time to develop characters—The Best Friend has more to do. Sometimes they've got their own B-plotlines and occupy center stage for periods of time. We learn about their families, their quirks, their dating lives, and they influence the story line's dramatic events. Think of most ensemble shows involving a group of BFFs (*Living Single*, *Girlfriends*, *How I Met Your Mother*) or any number of bildungsroman shows (*Leave It to Beaver*, *Moesha*, *Lizzie McGuire*). Even then, there's no questioning who is still the center of the overall narrative, the one whose perspective we're supposed to align with most often. In the case of *Girlfriends*, for instance, it's Joan (Tracee Ellis Ross) who's the hub of the group. The best friends are the spokes.

The Best Friend shows up in some form or another across all genres and cultures because it's a useful storytelling device—you want another character who can complement and affirm the hero's status as the primary focus of the narrative. But the cross-racial friendship, especially when it's presented through a Black-white dynamic, is a very particular trope. Inherent to that relationship is a more complicated power imbalance, not just in terms of character development but for the obvious reason that Black people have to move in this world differently from their white friends. Depending upon the era in which the story was conceived, and/or when it is set, this unevenness might be acknowledged or even serve as the central conflict. Or—and this has frequently been the case in interracial friendship stories of the last thirty-plus years or so—race doesn't even come up, at least not explicitly.

The Black Friend as an abstract concept has existed in the public imagination for at least a couple hundred years, when pro-slavery advocates such as George Fitzhugh trotted out the baffling argument that the white Southerner was "the Negro's friend, his only friend."[2] This disingenuous posit was an attempt to counter the imagery of slavery as an inherently brutal and inhumane practice by creating the perception of a benevolent, mutual partnership. (You can trace a direct line from this era right up to Donald Trump and every other modern-day white person who claims to have "Black friends" after being caught saying or doing something racist.)

From whence did The Black Friend arise? Black sidekicks have long existed in literary fiction and travelogues, often appearing as some version of the noble savage—that innocent-to-the-point-of-infantile character upon which white writers projected their curiosities, neuroses, and, occasionally, critiques of white supremacy.

Huckleberry Finn's Jim is a quintessential early example of The Black Friend. Jim is a runaway slave who encounters the title character while he, too, is on the run. Huck's not a fan of his guardian, Widow Douglas, or his mostly absentee alcoholic father, so he fakes his own death and escapes, and Jim forms a bond with Huck that is deeply rooted in their unequal power dynamic. Jim is unwaveringly faithful to Huck, showing unadulterated affection for and dependence on his traveling companion; at one point, when they're reunited after being briefly separated in a fog while making their way down the Mississippi River, Jim expresses relief, claiming that his heart "mos' broke" and he "didn't k'yer no mo' what become er me en de raft."[3]

Much of *Huckleberry Finn* is an exercise in white awakening, to some extent. Huck is reluctantly sympathetic to Jim's plight, casually referring to him as a n—— (one of the primary reasons Mark Twain's story is frequently among the most banned books in schools) and chastising himself for aiding in Jim's escape. ("People would call me a low-down abolitionist," Huck notes, while admitting he's going to do it anyway.[4]) As Huck wrestles with the expectations and social mores of his race, he evolves, somewhat, over the course of the novel to become even more defiant in the face of white supremacy.

Yet that obstinance arguably stems as much—if not more so—from his personality as a petulant fourteen-year-old determined to stick it to The Man as it does an acknowledgment of Jim's humanity. Huck never sways from viewing Jim as inferior. He begrudgingly concedes that Jim might care for and love his own family in the same way "white folks does for their'n." And Twain's ludicrous third act sees Tom Sawyer and Huck going through deliberately obtuse and round-the-way machinations to make their act of freeing the newly recaptured Jim more "honorable" (and more exciting) instead of just . . . sneaking him out the easy way. Jim is the catalyst for the protagonist's heroism and maturity. As Toni Morrison notes in *Playing in the Dark: Whiteness and the Literary Imagination*, "there is no way, given the confines of the novel, for Huck to mature into a moral human being *in America* without Jim."[5]

Other earlier fictional Black Friends include Delilah and Annie in the 1934 and 1959 versions of *Imitation of Life*, who blur the line between employee and close confidante of the white protagonists; Mammy in *Gone with the Wind*, who strikes up an amiable rapport with Rhett Butler (he gifts her a red silk petticoat—what a guy!); and Rochester, the valet and sidekick on *The Jack Benny Show*.

I use the term "friend" here loosely and broadly, because many of these characters are products of white imagination, and it's fairly common for a white imagination to see a "friendship" where a Black person might see "a relationship I need to maintain in order to feed my family/not get killed/just live relatively peacefully."

But without them, you wouldn't have The Black Friend in its current iterations of the last thirty-ish years, unmistakable products of their predecessors that occasionally nod toward enlightenment or at least self-awareness. And within this trope are three key ways these friends function relative to their white counterparts:

1. To give

2. To side-eye, sweetly

3. To provide purpose

Let's return for a moment to poor Katie in *She's All That*. She devotes all her time to trying to help Taylor win prom queen, so much so she forgets what it's like to do things she actually wants to do for herself. Katie is The Black Friend of the Mean Girl, which is on a lower tier than The Black Friend of the resident-pretty-protagonist-behind-the-glasses, Laney.

Katie is what I'd call the quintessential "Giver" for most of the movie. Every conversation with Taylor is about Taylor (prepping her prom speech, dumping Zack, dating the wild and creepy older guy).

The Giver is the best friend who gives their all but doesn't seem to receive any of that same energy back. IRL, it's a fairly common friendship predicament that knows no racial bounds. But why does it just *seem* as though Black Friends have traditionally fallen into this role so frequently in pop culture? The more obvious and cynical read on this is that Hollywood has needed to transfer the stock types of maids, butlers, and other service workers (paid and unpaid) to the more palatable, generic roles of "friend" in order to keep up with the changing times and not openly offend Black audiences. (Unless, of course, it's a period piece set firmly in the past, which is how we've gotten *Driving Miss Daisy* and its demon baby *Green Book* born nearly thirty years later.)

It also seems likely that the behind-the-scenes push for greater and better representation that's always existed—to varying degrees of success and failure at any given time—has something to do with it. The predominantly white and male gatekeepers in the industry were never going to make space so readily for more than a very select handful of Black superstars and protagonists at a time. One way to slot in "diversity" in the least disruptive way possible since as far back as the silent movie era has been to cast Black people in sidekick roles. A study presented in

1989 looked at a small sample size of hours of network TV, spread out across four months in 1987, and found that "nearly 40% of television's minorities have no contact with whites." When interactions did occur, it was common for minority child and teen characters to socialize in "positive" ways with their white peers outside of school settings. (On shows where adults of different races interacted with one another, they found it was usually in a professional setting, where mingling is more or less involuntary.)[6]

So what you get in pop culture is a hybrid of tropes: The Best Friend meets The Maid/Butler. Casting Black performers in the friend role was a way to demonstrate "progress" while keeping the leading roles white, an especially fruitful tactic in products targeted at kids/tweens, like the role of Lavender in the movie adaptation of *Matilda*. Instead of giving because they are employed (or enslaved) to do so, they are giving because . . . that's what friends are for, right?

Speaking as a person who has consumed many, many iterations of these white-friend-Black-friend stories, and also as someone with lifelong firsthand experience being friends (and friendly) with white people, I feel pretty confident saying that this evolution can rarely feel like true progress.

Consider Chenille (Kerry Washington) in *Save the Last Dance*, a movie my thirteen-year-old self was obsessed with at the time it came out, and that I now look back on with fond embarrassment. (Julia Stiles's herky-jerky intensity while learning to incorporate "hip-hop" into her ballet routine is Peak Whiteness. I love it.) Chenille is a single teenage mother who's managed to stay in school but doesn't seem to have any aspirations for the future outside of hoping her brilliant, ridiculously good-looking older brother Derek (Sean Patrick Thomas) gets into med school and leaves their violent, low-income Chicago neighborhood behind.

Then Stiles's Sara drops into this predominantly Black environment, all awkward and bearing daddy issues, and there's Chenille, ready to take her under her wing and school her in how to get by in the 'hood. *Save the Last Dance* is a particularly pointed entry in this genre because it's the white girl who's technically "the other" here, yet she still manages to be the protagonist with The Black Friend, not the other way around.

Sass, style, and advice? Chenille's got it in spades. She's a Giver.

But how does Sara help Chenille?

Well . . . Sara and Derek fall in love while ignoring the haters who criticize their interracial relationship, so in a way, seeing her brother happy is what Chenille gets out of knowing Sara, I guess.

Sara, like *She's All That*'s Taylor, is a Taker. While Sara is clueless in her self-absorption, popping and locking hard in her leotard and toe shoes while unassumingly making everything about her, Taylor is malicious and knows exactly what she's doing as she takes.

As frustratingly limiting as these portrayals are, they do in some ways reflect my own lived reality. In elementary and middle school, I found myself oscillating between friend groups, all of them predominantly, if not exclusively, white. (I have to admit that by middle school this was largely a choice of my own making, because there were plenty of Black students there I could have befriended but didn't, or at least didn't become close with. I was dealing with some internal racism that made me assume I wouldn't have anything in common with them.)

One of those cliques hovered closely to the so-called "popular" end of the social hierarchy and included a group of girls and boys who were frequently "dating" and fooling around with one another. (Or so they said. Kids that age talk a lot of shit and often don't actually do shit. Contrary to parents' nightmares, most of us were not out there living in Sam Levinson's *Euphoria*.) I was usually the sole Black person at these parties and hangs—when I was even invited—and spent many minutes and hours listening to these people gossip and opine about their various crushes, who felt up who, and which person was pissed off at the other on any given day.

I was there to listen and nod and inwardly rejoice when we could finally talk about something else, like the new Britney album or the latest episode of *The Real World*. It was like living in my very own *She's All That*, and I was Katie, looking in from the outside of the action, watching everything happen to everyone else around me. I had crushes on some of those boys, but I knew they weren't checking for me in that way. It didn't help that I could be quite shy and was painfully insecure about how I looked in comparison to the white girls around me. Summertime pool parties were especially anxiety-ridden because I couldn't just get my hair wet and forget about it like everyone else, and my mom made me wear a swimming cap, which is the exact opposite of cool when you're twelve.

I played the Giver role dutifully because I wanted desperately to be accepted by my white classmates, and it was stressful. (One time, a "friend" invited me to the movies but didn't mention her boyfriend was joining us, and they made out the whole time while I sat there uncomfortably watching the boring Disney flick *Dinosaur*. I quickly deduced I was there as cover because her mom wouldn't let her go to the movies with a boy by herself.) But until recently, this aspect of being in a cross-racial friendship as seen through the eyes of The Black Friend—

how alienating it can feel and what it can do to one's self-esteem—has rarely been depicted in pop culture. When it *is* explored, some interesting patterns emerge to reveal how creators have begun to think more deeply about this perspective . . . while still playing into some familiar dimensions of the trope.

• • •

Winston Bishop (Lamorne Morris) in *New Girl**: *Well THAT was a conversation I had zero interest in having. Actually, it's the kind of conversation I've been avoiding forever. Nick just doesn't get it, and let's face it, never will. Which I tried to explain to him, even throwing out the example of that one time when we were eleven and watching the Bronco chase live, and he had the nerve to wonder why the Bronco "had to be white." Really, man?*

I knew it then, and I know it now: Nick and I may go way back, but there are some things we just can't come together on. I've gotta compartmentalize. Because this whole mess with KC and me being dumb enough to hide the fact that I'm a cop from her during our very first date . . . Nick couldn't understand. There's too much going on right now with all the protests, and I get where KC's coming from, and I actually think it's kind of hot she's so into this social justice activist thing. Mayyyybe I need to reevaluate being a cop . . . ?

At least this chat wasn't as painful as when Schmidt mentioned Big Momma's House in front of Mom when she and sis came to visit. Or when Schmidt tried to "help" me be my "blackest self" by buying us Rasta hats—I'm not even Jamaican!—eating ribs, and being idiotic enough to fall for my joke about going to find some crack. I don't need a Jewish guy who claims to be "catnip to African American women" helping me find my blackness. I got Black friends! There's Coach, and . . . the two other Black guys on my basketball team back in Latvia (though I haven't seen them in a few years), and . . . KC!

KC is Black, and we're sort of dating!

We've been on one date.

And on that date I lied to her and told her I was a stripper cop because I didn't want her to know I'm a real, flesh-and-blood member of the LAPD. I've . . . seriously got to reevaluate this career choice. Does it even matter if I'm one of the "good ones" if the entire system is corrupt?

---

*If Winston from New Girl was able to express how he really felt about his white friends with his whole chest.

• • •

New Girl's Winston is a frustrating problem to consider in the long arc of pop culture's Black Friend. Unlike most incarnations that preceded him, he occasionally got to explicitly confront common issues that surface in Black and white friendships, yet the results left much to be desired.

The sitcom is about thirty-somethings living in LA, and throughout most of its seven-season run, Winston was the lone Black Friend of the group. Winston's personality shifted throughout the show; in early episodes he's an über-competitive alpha male, later he becomes sillier and a lover of elaborate pranks. While he dates some Black women and we get glimpses of his family life, Winston's interactions mostly revolve around the other white main characters in the show.

Which often isn't anything but sometimes is. Schmidt, who in *his* earliest incarnation is basically *Family Guy*'s lecherous, offensive Quagmire in the flesh (*giggity giggity*), is constantly making inappropriate comments about blackness. He reaches the apex of deluded whiteness when, after seeing Winston chatting up a group of Black strangers at the bar, he becomes concerned that Winston isn't being his "blackest self" around the rest of the crew: "Let's let Winston turn on his Black switch, and let his Black light shine," he tells Nick and Cece. Schmidt makes it his mission to do all of the "Black" things he thinks Winston would want to do, which, unsurprisingly, involves tons of projecting and stereotyping about Black culture—wearing Rastafarian hats, eating ribs. Winston sees what's up and plays along, side-eyeing and smiling as Schmidt digs himself deeper and deeper into a hole of tomfoolery.

Winston is deeply annoyed and insists he has Black friends, but Schmidt ignores him. (I'm reminded here of the scene in the 1959 *Imitation of Life* where Lana Turner's Lora is surprised to learn her live-in Black maid and bestie Annie Johnson, played by Juanita Moore, has friends who aren't her. "I have lots of friends. I belong to the Baptist church; several lodges, too." "I didn't know," says Lora. "Ms. Lora, you never asked." Sick burn.)

Once it gets to the point where Schmidt has agreed to go out and buy crack because Winston suggested it—Winston was very obviously being sarcastic—Winston calls him out. "Being Black is whatever I want it to mean," he tells a rightfully chastened Schmidt.

And in season four episode "Par 5" when Winston has a conversation about race with Nick, his friend since they were kids, it becomes clear Winston has been side-eyeing while smiling practically his entire life. Winston's reluctant to discuss the conundrum he's facing over the fact that he's keeping his job in the LAPD a secret from a social justice activist he just started dating, because Nick wouldn't understand. In a quick-gag flashback, the younger versions of themselves are shown watching OJ's white Bronco chase when kid Nick makes an eye-roll-worthy race-related comment. Cut back to today, and Nick is seemingly as ignorant as ever, doing terrible, blaccented impressions of Eddie Murphy, even after all these years.

The Sugar-Coated Side-Eye is a limiting self-preservation tactic. It's the act of letting casually racist or ignorant comments slide, making self-deprecating jokes about your blackness in order to play along and seem like you can hang. Sure, you may acknowledge what your friend just said is out of line ("Dude, not cool!"; "No, you can't say it even if Kanye tells you that you can"), but the sentiment is tempered with a laugh, a smirk, a side-eye, a smile. It can be a useful tool of avoidance, one which, if you practice it enough (by which I mean, befriend enough white people), can start to come so naturally as to not even require thought. The point is to never get *too* serious about race or racism so the friendship can stay intact, even if that means it remains, in some ways, superficial. It's just a different side of the Giver coin.

The Sugar-Coated Side-Eye is a favorite and, frankly, lazy approach plenty of creative writers have relied upon when writing for characters from marginalized groups they presumably do not belong to. In the case of TV, the episodes it shows up in don't have to be "very special." It can be as fleeting as Brad (Damon Wayans Jr.) on *Happy Endings* observing "You people are getting way too comfortable" after his friends imitate his "Black voice" at brunch. Or it can play an integral, ongoing role in an on-screen dynamic, like the one between best friends and colleagues JD (Zach Braff) and Turk (Donald Faison) on *Scrubs*; so much of their amiable relationship is reliant upon Turk shrugging off JD's cluelessness about race.

This move might "satisfy" the writers in TV land, but to deploy it in real life is to be eternally unfulfilled. I should know; as a hard-core conflict-avoidant person, I've used it more times than I'd like to admit.

• • •

I was sixteen when *Mean Girls* came out—meaning I was basically the movie's target audience—and was instantly obsessed with its sharp take on the horrors of high school, including the cliques, the pressure to be conventionally hot and popular, and overprotective parents. To this day, I will reply in the affirmative with "grool." (If you know, you know.)

For a teen comedy made nearly twenty years ago, *Mean Girls* holds up surprisingly well in its depiction of the thorniness of teen friendships. Even if the lack of a social media component makes this movie feel, in some ways, as though it's frozen in time, its observations about high school hierarchies and the unique ways girls make one another's lives a living hell still resonate. But this is a Tina Fey–penned script we're talking about here, and as much as I appreciate the lady for giving us "You go, Glen Coco" and "I want to go to there," among many, many gloriously ridiculous things, she's notoriously shitty when it comes to race humor. Technically, some of the evidence of this has been removed from the internet as part of our post–George Floyd "racial reckoning," but #neverforget there were multiple unnecessary instances of characters donning blackface on *30 Rock*.

And Jane Krakowski playing a Native American on *Unbreakable Kimmy Schmidt*.

And Tituss Burgess dressed up as a geisha, also on *Kimmy Schmidt*.

Likewise, every time I rewatch *Mean Girls*, I brace myself for the moment where, for reasons I may never know, the n-word is just casually thrown about by an Asian-American student character. The scene in question comes in the midst of the all-girls assembly organized following the leak of The Plastics' scathing, insult-ridden Burn Book, which causes everyone to attack one another in the school hallways. Accompanied by captions translated in English on-screen, one girl accuses another of trying to steal her boyfriend; the other replies that she's just jealous, to which the accuser responds, complete with a hand motion to the other girl's face: "Nigga, please."

Why is it there? What's the joke? That Asian people have appropriated Black culture? Not entirely untrue considering how hugely influential hip-hop music and dance has been in K-pop, but . . . really, that's the joke? Or is it just "edgy" and surprising if an Asian person does this versus if a white person did it, because, American history? Hmmm . . .

Really, it doesn't matter, because Tina Fey got "nigga" into *Mean Girls*. And it just so happens that among certain people of a certain age and predilection, *Mean Girls* is a highly quotable and, in present-day parlance, highly meme-able movie.

Which explains how one night, while hanging out with some of my core high school buddies—by sophomore year, I'd more or less finally found my people, a mix of mostly white and Asian friends, plus one Latino, and *moi*, The Black Friend—we all found ourselves boisterously quoting lines back and forth to one another, having just watched the newly released *Mean Girls* DVD together at one of our houses:

"Stop trying to make fetch happen!"

"Oh my god, Danny DeVito, I love your work!"

"Nigga, please!"

. . .

. . .

. . .

Ahem. 'Twas definitely not *I* who exclaimed that last quote. That was uttered, jointly, by two of my white friends in front of me, the only Black person in the group.

I'd never heard any of them use the word in front of me before. I was taken aback and instantly uncomfortable as they giggled and just carried on with the quotes as if it was nothing. I didn't say anything, in part because I was in shock, but also because at that point in my life, I still didn't know how to discuss race with my friends. In fact, I actively tried to avoid it coming up if I could.

Yet inside I was supremely irritated, annoyed that the dynamic I'd formed with them—i.e., one that didn't involve talking about race in any significant way—had apparently allowed them to feel comfortable enough to be so bold.

And in the most typical of Aisha moves at that time, I instead went the nonconfrontational-by-way-of-passive-aggression route and did a brief callout at the end of one of my LiveJournal posts the following day:

"Oh, and one other thing: you guys, the n-word is off-limits, whether you're joking or not. at least when i'm around. i didn't say anything last night because i was kind of shocked and disappointed you would keep repeating it over and over. so yeah, i'd appreciate that. no hard feelings, i swear," I sheepishly concluded in a bald attempt to cushion my critique by downplaying it. I didn't want to rock the boat *too much*; I still wanted desperately to be liked more than anything.

None of my friends left comments, unlike most of my other posts, which at that time were usually some combination of mindless recaps of the day's routines, the results of a quiz about old movies or musical theater, or some very pitiful, über-emo laments about my parents' contentious divorce and how I couldn't wait to break out of my suffocating, provincial hometown "full of little people" and live a fabulous meaningful life. (I was giving off true Belle from *Beauty and the Beast* energy then.) No one said anything to me in person, either; it just kind of lingered sadly in the ether, unacknowledged by everyone but me, who at least felt a little better having said *something*, even if it was in the most cowardly and millennial way possible. And at least I never heard them use it again.

I've spoken with Black friends who have had similarly frustrating experiences in their friendships with white people. One of them, who is now in his fifties, recalls an incident with a white friend after the two were pulled over for speeding by the police during a road trip about a decade ago. He was driving, and two officers approached the car, one on either side; the officer on his side had his gun drawn, while the officer on his friend's side did not. "They were nice to him, and they treated me like crap," he told me. Later, when he pointed out the disproportionate response, his white friend refused to believe race had anything to do with it.

"We argued about this, and it kind of ruined our little side trip that we were doing together," my friend said. "I noticed that this happens a lot—whenever I bring something up or mention something in passing like that, there's always an argument, there's always a 'but, but, but.' There's never a, '[I'll] take you at your word this was your experience.' And that's been kind of a lot of my experience with my white friends."

They're still friends and have even taken other road trips together since the incident, but he doesn't feel as if he would have maintained the relationship had the same thing occurred today; he's older now, plus the high-profile events of the last several years (the murder of George Floyd, etc.) have made him less tolerant of these kinds of exchanges with white people. "I was deluding myself a little bit," he said, "and I gave more benefit of the doubt than I should have in a lot of instances."

In my case of *Mean Girls*, I'd protected myself from drama with my friends, but it certainly didn't make me feel better about myself—only complicit. Clearly, it's nagged at me enough that I can still recall this memory vividly so many years later. These friends were not racist white people and certainly didn't mean to make me upset by saying the n-word. And anyways, this was the early 2000s; I wouldn't have called any of us, myself included, "woke" by the standards of today's teenagers. The concept of "microaggressions" wasn't yet part of the mainstream lexicon, and the pop culture aimed at us—like *Mean Girls* and *Can't Hardly Wait*—indulged in casual racism so often that it could be barely perceptible to a teenager who didn't know better.

But once in a while I'll wonder: Did they go on to say similar things in front of other Black friends because I didn't say anything beyond that measly LiveJournal post? After all, "Gold Digger" was mere months away from becoming an inescapable hit that invited white kids everywhere to scream "nigga" alongside their Black friends in dive bars and at house parties . . .

On *New Girl* and its ilk, relying on the Black character to show saintly, unyielding patience with their white peers ends up reinforcing a superficial kind of cross-racial friendship. The obtuse white friends may be made aware, briefly, of their obtuseness when it comes to race, only to be reassured it's water under the bridge and that the dynamic of their relationship hasn't fundamentally changed. It's The Black Friend who winds up doing all of the stressing in order to spark their white friend's epiphany. And then they live happily ever after, or until the show comes to an end.

When these moments happen in real life, though, the relationship *does* change, at least for the Black half of the friendship.

Interestingly, the *New Girl* episode where Winston feels conflicted about being a cop was the brainchild of the actor who played him, Lamorne Morris. In an interview published during the peak period of the George Floyd protests—several years after the show had ended—Morris reflected on having felt "really weird playing a police officer" on TV while high-profile police killings were becoming a recurring media fixture: "You felt like you were betraying your people; you're like, 'pick a side'—that's the thought process you're going through in your head."[7]

Morris said he was encouraged by *New Girl*'s creator Elizabeth Meriwether to cowrite the episode "Par 5," his sole writing credit on the show, and it's easy to empathize with his creative impulse. But the episode really demonstrates the limitations of tackling such heavy subject matter in one B-plot within a half-hour sitcom that otherwise never seemed all that interested in addressing race outside of comedic bits. That conversation between Winston and Nick about their different experiences doesn't go far enough in interrogating why Winston has never felt comfortable talking with him about race—it just devolves into a bunch of Eddie Murphy and Jerry Seinfeld impressions.

New Girl and *Scrubs* had a few credited Black writers throughout their runs, but as many a TV writer of color has told me in my reporting over the years, being in the room doesn't necessarily translate to being heard by your majority-white peers. Often it means feeling pressured to speak for the entire race or being shot down when a colleague suggests a line that might be just a little bit racist. Morris seemed content with how "Par 5" turned out, and he had a leg up from most TV writers in that he was writing for himself, the performer. And yet, I'm not surprised when I hear of workplace equivalents of the Sugar-Coated Side-Eye being thrown around in writers' rooms. Do the white colleagues even notice when it happens?

Maybe! Probably not, though. That's kind of the point of Sugar-Coated Side-Eye. It's meant more for the Black person giving it, for ease, and downplaying anxiety. Sometimes being a Black (work) friend is exhausting, and we don't want to have a teachable moment or feel the burden of being the catalyst for their self-discovery . . .

• • •

Molly Abrams (Gina Ravera) in *Showgirls**: *I'd just gotten done with work for the night—another grueling two-show day of Goddess— and I was exhausted. It had been a particularly shitty day because Penny's costume wasn't latching correctly, and she blew up at me* because it got stuck on stage, and she wasn't able to take it off during the number.

So that night I'm approaching the parking lot, and I see this girl about my age, with bleach-blond curls that look like they came from a dye box kit you'd get at CVS, banging the shit out of my car. She was tall, skinny, and had legs for days. Definitely looked like a dancer. And I'm like, "What the fuck is this chick doing to my car?" She was raging, disoriented. As I get closer, I hear her wailing something about a suitcase, and then—get this—she straight-up barfs right there on the pavement. As in, spewing chunks. It was nasty.

AND THEN she runs into the middle of the busy friggin' Vegas strip, flailing her arms furiously, and I just instinctually go after her and push her out of the way of oncoming traffic. I know some might call it heroic—and don't get me wrong; I'm glad the woman did not get crushed on the street—but that weirdo encounter was a red flag for me. Nomi Malone—that was her name, I learned—is a chaotic mess, and she will make your life a living hell.

I felt bad for the girl and bought her something to eat. She looked like a pathetic, kooky lost puppy, and when I asked her where she was from, all she could say was "Different places!" as she tossed her plate of fries in the air like a rag doll. For an instant, I considered inviting her back to my trailer to stay with me until she could find her own place, but I thought better of it, gave her a few bucks so she could check into a hotel for the night, and gave her my number in case she needed any advice/job leads. She could maybe get a job at Goddess. Cristal would probably be into her.

But I'm not a charity, and I really need to focus on making it through this production while I apply for a better-paying gig that might allow me *to be a bit more creative with my designs. I wish the girl well, but mama's gotta keep reaching for her dreams. Good luck, Nomi.*

———————

*If Molly from Showgirls was written by Janicza Bravo and Jeremy O. Harris.

I think about *Showgirls* a lot—more than any normal human being probably should—but hey, I'm a film nerd who loves Grade-A trash/camp, and it's allowed in those circles. I think about Elizabeth Berkley's admirable commitment to an ill-written character and her herky-jerky, now cultishly adored performance as Nomi Malone, a roustabout with a mysterious past who lands in Vegas and simultaneously attracts and confounds every stranger she encounters. I ponder Cristal and Nomi's erotic and at times nonsensical flirtations and the myriad ways the movie always seems at odds with seeing itself as a serious drama while being executed so utterly ridiculously it couldn't possibly be taken seriously.

But I also consider how Nomi's Black Best Friend in the movie, Molly (Gina Ravera), serves as the catalyst for our hero's twisted redemption arc.

Very little in this movie makes sense, and anyone who's seen it will tell you as much. That's no secret. But it's jarring to see Molly, who starts off as a cut-from-the-mold Giver at the beginning of the film (she literally saves Nomi from being run down on the Vegas strip, invites her to crash at her place, and eventually gets her a gig working for Cristal's headlining show), graduate to becoming a full-on Provider of Purpose. Her purpose? Give Nomi's life meaning and dramatic verve. This is another primary aspect of the Black-white friendship dyad I've come across frequently in these narrative scenarios: the purveyor of the meaning of life.

What is it, anyway? Why are we here? And how is The Black Friend going to make it all better for The White Friend?

In the final act of *Showgirls*, Molly is brutally gang-raped at a party by her idol, the musician Andrew Carver, and his bodyguards. It's the one scene in the entire movie that feels real and visceral without the campiness of Vegas-y sequins and neon lights that hover over the rest of the film. Her screams are piercing, Carver's hulking figure is menacing. Molly lands in the hospital, barely hanging on, and that's where she'll remain until the story ends.

Meanwhile, Nomi goes through that physical transformation common to movie protagonists who are about to set out and right a wrong experience: She slicks her blond hair back, paints her nails black, and throws on a sexy little leopard-print outfit, seducing Carver in his hotel suite. Once the trap has been laid, she gets her comeuppance and beats him up badly, in high heels and red pasties to boot.

It's so extra and so obviously supposed to be this "ra-ra!" moment of white femme empowerment, but it rings hollow, because (a) like many female revenge narratives, it thinks merely looking hot while kicking ass is "feminist," and (b) the movie's already underdeveloped Black Friend character is reduced to a source of pathos.

Molly barely has any context outside of Nomi and has to suffer in the most horrifying of ways so that Nomi can move on to what we can only presume will be her next wayward act in life. Molly is The Purpose Provider, a figure that has long existed in pop culture and real life.

Again, I return to Huck Finn and Tom Sawyer's challenge to free

Jim. They must perform the most elaborate escape plan because, as Tom reasons, "There's more honor in getting him out through a lot of difficulties and dangers."[8] Jim, Purpose Provider. (See also: *Green Book*, *The Help*, *American History X*.)

• • •

In reality, The Purpose Provider—a fiction born of the white imagination—is more complicated.

Summer, 2020: Those black squares were everywhere. Every company was posting about Black Lives Matter and donating to social justice causes. People you'd never seen out in the streets in response to previous Black-person-turned-hashtag events were out in the streets protesting, marching, mobilizing.

And some white friends—or those who may have name-checked a Black person as a "friend" to make themselves feel as though they had a "diverse" social network but were really just colleagues or acquaintances or a neighbor they'd spoken with maybe once since moving in—started texting and "checking in" on Black people, expressing remorse about "everything going on."

It became such a cliché that multiple articles were written about the awkward and exhausting influx of well-intentioned white guilt unburdened onto us Black Friends. One woman told *The Washington Post* she'd been embarrassed to receive an unsolicited Cash App payment from a co-worker she wasn't particularly close with.[9] While at the *New York Times*, I edited an opinion essay from a writer who felt weighed down by all of the "I'm sorrys" and "I love yous" he'd received from white friends in those early summer weeks.[10] (I, too, received a couple such notes from dear friends, who I know meant well—and were *not* looking to me to ease their conscience. I believe they genuinely cared about how I felt, though even they couldn't inspire me to muster up enough energy to respond. Everything seemed so heightened and especially bleak then.)

In real life, white people who view you as their Purpose Provider don't really look like Nomi or Ed Norton's Derek in *American History X* with smooth, unchecked character evolutions that involve becoming their best selves through their Black Friends. Instead, they look like Danielle,* my friend's sort-of/kind-of friend. Danielle has a tendency to latch on to Black people in her profession and assume the role of a mentor/buddy to uncomfortable results.

"She is constantly trying to get me to alleviate her guilt," my friend tells me. "She's either confiding something in me that's totally inappropriate, or . . . she wants me to say this [other] Black person's being ridiculous" about a perspective on race that she disagrees with.

"She has no clue about the basics of race in America, but she's very guilty and very defensive," she adds. "I think that's probably why we're not going to be really close friends, because she's not interested in growing in that realm."

The Purpose Provider is ingrained in the infamous cross-racial relationship between Elizabeth Eckford, one of the Little Rock Nine, and Hazel Bryan, the white girl who was enshrined in history by a photo showing her as one of the snarling, screaming harassers on the front line of anti-segregation protestors in 1957 Arkansas. Both women were

---

* Name has been changed for privacy.

teenagers at the time of the events, and Bryan would go on to express remorse for her actions, calling up Eckford out of the blue to apologize a few years later. When they were brought back together in person for the first time in the 1990s while appearing at an anniversary commemoration, the two became (briefly) close, as David Margolick would chronicle in magazine articles and a book, *Elizabeth and Hazel: Two Women of Little Rock.*

Their reconciliation and friendship wilted in short time, as Bryan frequently felt "on the defensive" because of a wary reception from others, including members of the Little Rock Nine who didn't fully trust that she had changed. For Eckford's part, she told Margolick she believed Bryan "wanted me to be cured and be over it and for this not to go on anymore. She wanted me to be less uncomfortable so that she wouldn't feel responsible."[11] From the trauma she experienced while integrating Little Rock High School, Eckford endured depression, intermittent employment, and multiple suicide attempts.

Those crucial details are less glamorous than the Hollywood portrayals. But that's the truth. It's exhausting being a Purpose Provider. Can't we just be friends?

• • •

My younger self was embarrassingly complicit in mimicking Hollywood's Black Friend identity. These days, I feel much more comfortable in my skin and in my ability to create healthy friendships across all races and ethnicities. I still probably have more white friends than the average Black person does (a study from several years ago conducted by Robert Jones, of the Public Religion Research Institute, found that most Black people counted eight white people as friends out of one hundred).[12] Regardless of background, I've learned how to pick better friends and be (I hope) a better friend.

I have zero qualms discussing race with any white person I consider a friend nowadays, and some enlightening and fruitful conversations have come out of this. The last few years of high-profile police killings and other acts of discrimination have made me, like so many others, reconsider who I want to interact with regularly, and I've been reclaiming my time, so to speak.

There have also been on-screen attempts to challenge the confining structure of The Black Friend trope, or counter it, and those have been a balm: the smart and self-preserving Brenda (Regina Hall) in the *Scary Movie* trilogy, nerdy and multifaceted characters Troy (Donald Glover) in *Community* and Chidi (William Jackson Harper) in *The Good Place*.

But the most biting and surreal deconstruction of the last few years is the social media–inspired *Zola*. For the uninitiated or forgetful, in 2015, A'Ziah "Zola" King, a Detroit waitress and erotic dancer, crafted what unwittingly turned out to be a movie spec script via a 148-tweet thread. Her story was a recount of a fateful encounter with Jessica, a white woman and fellow erotic dancer who persuaded Zola to take a road trip to Florida to make some money dancing . . . within just hours of meeting one another. Zola's description of all the wild events that followed, involving Jessica's menacing pimp and Jessica's hapless boyfriend, are the stuff of movie magic, and director and writer Janicza Bravo and writer Jeremy O. Harris turned it into just that.

Zola (Taylour Paige) is The Black Friend. At various points in the movie, she plays the role of the Giver and gives a Sugar-Coated Side-Eye. But this is *her* story. It's an extremely heightened cautionary tale, a Black-white "friendship" gone outrageously, horrifyingly bad. In the movie, Jessica is renamed Stefani (Riley Keough), and she's presented as a white girl who's fully appropriated Black culture as seen in music videos, from her thick blaccent to her laid baby hairs. So much of Zola's apprehension of this walking caricature is conveyed only through her eyes, yet that's enough; they're so expressive that you know exactly what she's thinking at all times.

Two moments in particular stand out. The first comes in the third act of the film, after so many things have gone sideways and Zola is fully aware she's been bamboozled by Stefani into facilitating sex work (Zola herself does not partake but reluctantly helps Stefani find clients). The two women arrive at a house full of men, who insist on a gang bang with Stefani. Just as she's about to oblige, we cut briefly to Stefani's point of view, where she breaks down her side of the story; it's *completely* different from Zola's. Stefani describes Zola as "very ratchet" and "very Black" (as this voice-over narration occurs, Zola is seen patting her weave and body rolling) and paints herself as an innocent, reformed Christian who got sucked into Zola's wild schemes.

The coded language and imagery of that sequence, which has hints of the opening dialogue from Sir Mix-a-Lot's "Baby Got Back" ("Oh my god, Becky, look at her butt . . . Look, she's so *BLACK*!") explicitly underlines how Black and white womanhood are perceived in contrast to one another. (Black femininity/sexuality = Jezebel; white femininity/sexuality = pure.) It also lays bare the fragility of this "friendship," one that is built on deceit, posturing, and assumptions about blackness.

The other moment occurs a little while later, when Stefani is held hostage by another potential client in a hotel room. Zola is able to flee and tells Stefani's pimp X (Colman Domingo) that they need to get her help. "You're supposed to be looking out for her, Zola!" X exclaims angrily.

"Who's looking out for me?" Zola quips back.

Zola's vulnerability as a Black woman is laid bare. She knows very well no one is looking out for her, and this is not the kind of friendship she needs in her life.

Okay, so most of us are not a Zola with a Stefani in our lives. But underneath this unusual story is a depiction of all the anxieties that can accompany even the most basic of Black friend / white friend dynamics: white appropriation of Black culture, white dismissiveness, white self-absorption. *Zola* shows a different way for The Black Friend to exist in popular culture: center stage, resisting fuckery, and thriving in any way they can. Just by having control of her narrative and showing how it threatens to break her, Zola is The Black Friend liberated.

6

THIS IS IP THAT
NEVER ENDS

t's summer. I'm six. My mom, dad, little sister, and I settle down for what has become an annual family tradition: an outing at the local multiplex to see the latest Disney animated feature. I've been anticipating this for what is probably only a couple of months but feels like years to my young brain. Commercials and preview segments aside, I hardly know what to expect beyond lions and songs.

We're in the theater with the microwaved Pop Secret popcorn my parents tucked into my Gymboree backpack (movie theater popcorn is expensive!), the screen goes black, a propulsive chant rings out, and that round, golden sun scrolls upward, breathtakingly, over the savanna. "From the day we arrive on this planet," a warm, soothing voice begins to sing while the rhinos, elephants, giraffes, and other animals assemble in front of a giant rock cliff thing and bow down as a monkey with a giant stick makes his way to the top of the rock cliff thing. He greets a lady and man lion and their baby lion and spreads some brown stuff—goo? jelly? anyway, it looks sticky—and some dirt on the baby's forehead.

He takes the baby in his arms and walks back to the edge of the rock cliff and raises it above his head with both hands as all the animals grunt and squeal in approval and reverence. The music swells, the baby looks bewildered, and the clouds part just wide enough for an ethereal spotlight to pour down on them.

". . . In the cirrrrrr-cuh-huh-ul, the circle of liiiiife," the warm voice concludes. *BOOM!* And then the title screen: *The Lion King*.

Oh. Yeah. This is my jam.

It's winter. I'm eleven. My mom, dad, little sister, and I—plus other extended family members—are at the New Amsterdam Theatre in New York City. The lights dim, and Rafiki appears, letting that chant ring out, proudly, powerfully. The golden sun scrolls upward, magnificently. The rhinos, elephants, and giraffes gracefully make their way through the aisles or from the side of the stage—they're right there, in the same room as me, towering and majestic!

It's so cool. I've watched this scene countless times before and know every word to the song, but I've never seen it look or sound quite like *this*. It's fantastic. I'm awed.

It's summer. I'm thirty-one. I'm in a multiplex in Times Square surrounded by movie journalists. Is this real life? Is this fantasy? I don't know, but it is almost certainly "Circle of Life" dubbed over an episode of *Planet Earth*. The golden sun scrolls upward. The elephants, rhinos, and giraffes make their way to Pride Rock, exactly as they always have. They do exactly what I expect them to do, appear at the exact moments as I expect—except, they are no longer lushly animated but photo realistically designed to such an extreme that I'm having flashbacks to the three-day Kenyan safari I went on five years earlier.

It's so weird. I've seen this millions of times before, but not quite like *this*.

It's a mishmash of feelings and moments I've accumulated over twenty-five years, mined and regurgitated back to me by a corporate entity—Disney—with which I've had a lifelong love-hate relationship. It feels surreal, as though it'll never leave me but will only keep morphing into something altered. That sensation of amazement and wonder I first felt in that theater in 1994 and my recollection of what it was like to be a kid at that time still remains, and that's what I cling to as I watch this warped imitation of the original.

Is this what nostalgia is supposed to feel like?

I'm six—no, I'm eleven—actually, I'm thirty-one. I love it, I love it, I hate it. *Hakuna matata* means "no worries": Mufasa will never stay dead for long. He'll be resurrected as an apparition in the sky as many times as you'd like, in as many forms as you'd like—2D animation, puppetry, CGI so real-looking it'll make you believe in ghosts.

Replace *The Lion King* with *Aladdin* or *Beauty and the Beast*, and the details change only slightly. This is Disney in the twenty-first century. But it's everything else, too, or so it seems. It's the reboot/revival of that

long-running show that went off the air decades ago: *Murphy Brown,
Roseanne, The Fresh Prince of Bel-Air, Will & Grace, Full House* . . .

Or it's the reboot/sequel to a movie originally released decades ago:
Coming to America, Ghostbusters, Bad Boys, Clerks, West Side Story . . .

The familiar characters from my childhood and yours, from my
teenage years and yours . . . heck, the familiar characters from just *a few
months ago* are back and will be back again after that. They may have
never left, really. Or you hadn't thought about them since they supposedly left, but here they are again.

Is this déjà vu?

Actually, it's the circle of life. But it's not the wheel of fortune; it's
the wheel of doom, as inevitable and meticulously calculated as the first
three phases of Marvel's Cinematic Universe.

. . .

In January 2020—the before times—Bong Joon-ho's *Parasite* was
building awards-season buzz and still playing to enthusiastic crowds
in theaters across the country when an HBO miniseries adaptation
was announced. Through his interpreter, Bong told *Variety,* "My goal
is to create a high quality and expanded version of *Parasite.*"[1]

An expanded version of *this,* this original movie not based on a pre-
existing intellectual property that achieves what too few movies are
able to execute—a tightly crafted beginning, middle, and profound
ending in just about two hours.

But . . . *why? Parasite,* the movie, is so good! And original! And . . .
my head spins. *Of course Parasite* will be expanded! How could I expect
otherwise?

How could I forget that in pop culture, a thing is never just A Thing anymore? Lots of things begin, but not much ends, and then you might not remember how it even began in the first place.

Remember the song that closed every episode of *Lamb Chop's Play-Along*? *This is the song that doesn't ennnnnnd! Yes it goes on and on, my friennnnd!*

Welp, *this is IP that doesn't ennnnnnd! Yes it goes on and on, my friennnnd!*

Here's season two of that show that was sold to us all (and won awards) as a "limited series" and featured a satisfying finale, but hey, the people loved it so much so why not keep it going? They loved the drama and trauma of those rich Monterey mommies, and like *Willy Wonka*'s Veruca Salt, they wanted more of it now, like, *right now*. Actually, yesterday.

Or so the creators and studio want us to believe. "What I used to say about *Big Little Lies* was that the only problem with it was that it's only one season," HBO's programming chief once said.[2] That was before season two actually materialized, of course. What *was* season two, anyway? How about more drama, more trauma (now with Meryl Streep being her Meryl Streep-iest!), but also an incoherent mess that never proved why it needed to exist and still never figured out what to do with Zoë Kravitz, who played its one main Black character.

Some people started making it not knowing when to pause—

The studios, networks, streaming services, creators, and actors involved in a soon-to-be-revived property: "Oh, you were super bummed about the unceremonious canceling of that irreverent but little-watched ahead-of-its-time sitcom?"

ME: Yeah, I was, actually!

THEM: Did you wish they could have gotten at least one more season and a proper send-off?

ME: Indeed.

THEM: Did you lie awake at night over the last several years wondering if the show would ever be resurrected and brought back to life?

ME: Um, I wouldn't say that—

THEM: What if we told you the entire original cast was willing to return, on a new network, for a brand-new season???

ME: I mean, yeah, I missed it, but the first three seasons were pretty perfect, and I actually don't mind that it went out on top instead of burning out. Plus, it's been . . . how many years???

THEM: Great! Here's a new season of *Arrested Development*! In fact, here's ANOTHER SEASON! *OPRAH YELL* *Have allllll the seasons*!

ME: Oh.

I watch. I cringe. I wish they'd stop. Sure, it's the same cast and characters, but it's like entering a strange dimension where everything is just a little off—the jokes, the pacing, the chemistry.

But they'll continue making it forever just because this is IP that never ends—

They—these studios and networks and streaming services and producers and creators and actors—have primed audiences to expect this, to demand continued stories and spin-offs. More, more, more. What was once the province of superhero fans and Trekkies and Star Wars obsessives is now open terrain for any fan of anything, no matter how niche.

It's how we get #sixseasonsandamovie, the rallying cry for the always-on-the-brink-of-cancellation *Community* (admittedly, I was once a part of this choir) and crowdfunded movie adaptations and Change.org petitions advocating for networks to bring shows back. It's how we get our favorite movies staged on Broadway, now with singing. (*Mean Girls, Tootsie, The Color Purple, Beetlejuice*.)

It's how we get a super-meta mockumentary called *High School Musical: The Musical: The Series*—yes, this is the actual full title—a scripted Disney+ show about a high school theater production of the Disney Channel original movie *High School Musical*, set at the same high school where the movie was shot. And then, as if to challenge *HSM: TM: TS* to a super-meta contest, there's *Lightyear*, a movie with a premise so convoluted, its star Chris Evans had to break it down for everyone on Twitter after the first teaser dropped:

"And just to be clear, this isn't Buzz Lightyear the toy. This is the origin story of the human Buzz Lightyear that the toy is based on."[3]

Thanks so much for clarifying, Chris!

The media plays its part, too. When an original movie is a hit, journalists ask the creators and stars some version of the same question: "What are the chances of a sequel?" Before a finale has *even aired*, journalists wonder: "Would you return for a reunion or a spin-off?"

Of course, hardly anyone answers in the negative. Which is how we wind up with news headlines like "This *Jane the Virgin* Star Would Definitely Do a Show Reunion."[4]

Even the creators and stars themselves are often eager to return to the well of familiarity, engaging in podcasts about their greatest claims to fame (*Scrubs* stars Zach Braff and Donald Faison's *Fake Doctors, Real Friends*; *The Office* stars Jenna Fischer and Angela Kinsey's *Office Ladies*) or stoking fan anticipation by teasing the idea of new projects related to their old projects.

I can't escape. It's like I'm Natasha Lyonne's Nadia in the brilliant show *Russian Doll* living and dying and reliving and then redying on the same day, over and over. I'm resurrected in that same bathroom each time, but instead of Harry Nilsson's "Gotta Get Up" on repeat, it's the *Lamb Chop* theme. We're all trapped in this loop because: *This is IP that never ends; yes, it goes on and on, my friend. Some people started making it not knowing when to halt, but they'll continue making it forever just because . . .*

Russian Doll has, of course, gotten a second season.

• • •

Because nothing "new" is ever actually new, how about a brief history of the film industry's recycling habit beginnings, shall we? It reaches allll the way back to the silent era, its earliest days.

In her book *Film Sequels: Theory and Practice from Hollywood to Bollywood*, Carolyn Jess-Cooke gets into the origins of movie serials (which, she writes, "concentrate on similar events occurring over a shortened period of time") and sequels ("medita[tions] upon the past and upon the gulf of time that has separated one event from another"). She notes that film serials like *The Perils of Pauline*, a melodrama about an adventurous heiress, made up the bulk of film production between 1906 and around 1936 and usually followed a narrative across twelve to sixteen episodes. (Essentially, TV before TV.)[5]

From the beginning, commercialism was the driving force for establishing ongoing properties and repetitive stories; exhibitors and filmmakers wanted to foster spectator investment and turn filmgoing into a habit. Jess-Cooke illustrates a source from 1926, which quotes a Biograph studio memo written in response to the encouraging sales of a movie called *Girl Climbing Apple Tree*: "I think we had better have some more of the Girl-Climbing-Apple-Tree kind," it read.[6] Marketers used the tactics we're so familiar with today to stoke and exploit audience familiarity, as she cites the ad description of a 1916 film called *The Sequel to the Diamond from the Sky*: "more dramatic—more powerful than the original."[7] And in the case of that serial, it originated as a public competition where $10,000 was offered for the best narrative outline. (This was apparently popular enough to garner a couple more competitions related to the series.)

Lest you think the serialization/sequelization of that era was only practiced by the long-forgotten filmmakers only the nerdiest of film buffs and historians would be able to name, some directors you might at least have heard of once were into the whole recycling thing, too. In 1911, D. W. Griffith (he of racist *Birth of a Nation* fame) released *His*

Trust and *His Trust Fulfilled*, which told the story of a faithful Black enslaved person (white actor Wilfred Lucas in blackface, because that's how Griffith rolled) taking care of his master's family while he's away at war. Cecil B. DeMille adapted a stage play called *The Squaw Man* three(!) separate times between 1914 and 1931.

Once "talkies" and Hollywood evolved, the tradition carried over from its scrappy origins pretty seamlessly. Take, for instance, the six-feature *Thin Man* series starring the delightful Myrna Loy and William Powell as a couple of married boozers who solve crimes (the first film, released in 1934, is a classic; the rest vary in quality) or Mickey Rooney's recurring Andy Hardy character (sixteen films in total were released between 1937 and 1958).

As early as the 1930s, rehash fatigue had already begun to set in for some, like the critic and eventual screenwriter Frank S. Nugent. (He went on to become a frequent John Ford collaborator and penned, among other things, *The Searchers*.) The sequel, as he described it wearily in a 1936 *New York Times* article, was a "form of ancestor-worship, tinged with honest reverence for the dollar, which deifies past cinema successes and urges producers to bullwhip their writing staffs into [its] creation."[8]

He name-checked a few recent returns to the well (*Bride of Frankenstein*, *After the Thin Man* included) and others that were reportedly on the horizon (*Public Enemy's Wife* and a remake of *The Hunchback of Notre-Dame*, which he cheekily imagined might be called *Son of The Hunchback of Notre-Dame*). And he observed that the serials of the day—"Wild West shows, cop and robber melodramas, harebrained tales of hidden treasure . . ."—were meant to appeal to "youngsters" rather than adults.

Yet notably, Nugent saw an amenable way forward with this Hollywood tactic. Pointing to popular literary series like John Galsworthy's *The Forsyte Saga*, he lamented "the misfortune of the filmgoer" who, unlike the avid reader with access to a library full of books they can enjoy again and again, could not easily return to their favorite on-screen characters and their adventures; once a feature completed its initial theatrical run, they usually lived on only as a memory. (This was, of course, the 1930s—before older movies could be broadcast on television, before the home video boom, and wayyyy before streaming.) The "only hope" then, Nugent wrote, was for studios to take a page from the literary world and bring back beloved casts to star in ongoing narratives that "carry them a few steps forward in a still-to-be-completed screen career."

Oh, Frank S. Nugent—if only you could see Hollywood now! Not only can we easily rewatch a bunch of movies from your era up until the present day, but we can all but guarantee our favorite still-living and still-working actors and casts will get the gang back together to put on another show. The majority of our biggest movie stars of today—if we're talking box office as well as pure cultural cachet—are that way in huge part because of the characters they've reprised on-screen multiple times: Robert Downey Jr., who spent the better part of a decade playing Tony Stark (really, I could just list most of the stars from the Marvel universe here, but I will sparc us all); Vin Diesel, who's played Dominic Toretto in a franchise that will soon celebrate a quarter of a century of fast cars, hot babes, and *Vin Diesel growl* "*family*"; Tom Hanks, who's been voicing Sheriff Woody for going on almost thirty years now. And somebody's definitely gonna have to pry the role of Ethan Hunt and the *Mission Impossible* franchise from Tom Cruise's dead, cold hands.

Nugent, we've gotten what you dreamed of and then some, though these are (in)arguably "serials" still meant to appeal primarily to "youngsters" and adults who are youngsters at heart. (Which is most people these days, myself included.)

We are a Nostalgia Nation—nay, Globe.

"Nostalgia" is from the Greek words *nóstos* (homecoming) and *álgos* (pain/ache), coined by the Swiss physician Johannes Hofer in a 1688 dissertation, though the phenomenon preexisted in various forms. He characterized it as a disease, observed in Swiss soldiers who were prone to an intense longing for home and their past lives which manifested itself in debilitating ways, especially, for some reason, come autumn. Symptoms included seeing ghosts, heart palpitations, and hunger.

Over time, nostalgia would show up in other ways, as Grafton Tanner, a writer whose work focuses on nostalgia, has noted. It's taken root as a defense mechanism of sorts, showing up in the era of Romanticism in the nineteenth century, an artistic and creative period that was in part a response to the increased rigidity of how time was scheduled—the introduction of the five-day work week, for one—and rapid industrialization.[9]

One prime example Tanner points to is Victor Hugo's novel *The Hunchback of Notre-Dame*, published in 1831. Hugo was an avid preservationist, and at that time, the cathedral was in a state of severe disrepair; with *Hunchback*, which he set nearly four hundred years earlier, he deliberately tapped into nostalgia for the building's better days. "There certainly are few finer architectural pages than this façade," Hugo wrote, a bit later describing its structure as "a vast symphony in stone, so to speak; the colossal work of one man and one people, all together one and complex, like the Iliads and the Romanceros . . ."[10]

Hugo's long passages expounding on the glories of its history and the danger it was in of falling to ruin helped lead to the start of the

Notre-Dame's restoration a few years later. But, as Tanner told the NPR podcast *Throughline*, the constant restoration of the cathedral over the years may have inadvertently led to the 2019 fire that destroyed the roof and spire. "It's kind of this lesson we can learn about trying to restore the past completely and fully and that it might actually end up in destruction of the thing that we long for," he said.[11]

It's easy to point to other examples of nostalgia for a past—either real or distorted by the imagination—taking hold in popular culture throughout the twentieth century: *Birth of a Nation*, *Gone with the Wind*, *The Wizard of Oz*, *Happy Days*, *The Godfather* all trafficked in it. But mining this sentiment from a marketing perspective in crude, explicit terms? Those bald, brazen attempts to cash in on and manipulate generations' wistfulness for their pasts didn't truly take hold until the mid-1970s, when a marketing professor named Donald W. Hendon coined the term "nostalgia tale."

Hendon advised the marketing industry to "take [nostalgia] seriously," Tanner told *Throughline*. "Instead of always trying to find something new to sell, we can sell something that people haven't seen in a while, and they're going to like it because they're going to feel nostalgia for it once we reintroduce it."

It's safe to say the industry took his advice. And then some.

There's this McDonald's ad from the early 1990s that literally references nostalgia, multiple times, to sell Happy Meals: "Parents LOVE to talk about when they were kids!" exclaims a wide-eyed, curly-headed blond girl. "It's called nostalgia!" says a wide-eyed blond boy, presumably meant to be the girl's brother, with a knowing glint in his eye. (Through this ad, the execs of this fast-food behemoth were full-on winking at parents as they blatantly exploited their childhood memories. Nostalgia!!!)

Cut to the dad reminiscing about playing with Tonka trucks and the mom remembering her love for Cabbage Patch dolls as they hold up the Mickey D's version of those toys. This Happy Meal "will give you that nostalgic feeling for just $1.99," the ad insists.[12] Who knew nostalgia could come so cheap? (If only visiting a Disney theme park these days were that cheap. *sighs in wistful nostalgia*)

By now, nostalgia is long past the point of being a disease, as Johannes Hofer deemed it in the seventeenth century, but something to be proud of and indulge in, at least according to the people who want to sell you stuff.

Like those moppets in the McDonald's ad, I was a 1990s kid regularly immersed in pop culture nostalgia I couldn't even possibly be nostalgic for, because I hadn't been alive the first time these things filtered their way through the culture. Nick at Nite, Nickelodeon's evening programming block dedicated to re-airing classic TV shows, was a cable staple; it's how I fell in love with shows like *I Love Lucy*, *The Dick Van Dyke Show*, and *The Jeffersons*, often watching them alongside my parents, who could look back on them fondly as shows they'd grown up watching when *they* were kids.

Once I found VH1 and MTV, I lived off a steady diet of *Pop-Up Video*, *Behind the Music*, and the entire *I Love the 70s/80s/90s* franchise, which was just a bunch of B- and C-list comedians and celebrities like Carrot Top quipping about weird cultural artifacts from whichever decade defined their youth. The Spice Girls and their disco-flavored outfits and songs ("Never Give Up on the Good Times" still slaps) made me briefly obsessed with everything 1970s; for my tenth birthday, I had a 1970s-themed sleepover, and my mom rented *Saturday Night Fever* from Blockbuster Video. (I *think* it was the edited PG-rated version of the movie that was made for TV, but I honestly can't recall. Either way, it was probably still inappropriate for a bunch of fifth graders to watch this movie, though I'm pretty sure it all went over our heads and my mom had forgotten all the details save for John Travolta dancing in that white suit, because it's doubtful she would've let that happen otherwise. In case you too have forgotten, the original version of this movie includes, among other things, a slew of racial slurs, nudity, and an explicit rape scene that's treated in the most matter-of-fact, perfunctory way. Eek.)

And then, of course, the internet exploded into the mainstream, and blogging and YouTube happened. Suddenly it got even easier to excavate and share things from the past, including, now, my own past—because apparently right around your midtwenties, when you really begin adulting, is when you start to miss your childhood. It doesn't take much to go down rabbit holes watching old commercials for the toys you once pined for or stumble upon a grainy copy of that random TV movie you remember watching a decade earlier. Have I tracked down an upload of *No One Would Tell*, the ripped-from-the-headlines TV movie about a teenager who's murdered by her abusive ex-boyfriend, which used to air on Lifetime all the time in the early 2000s and starred the actors who played DJ Tanner on *Full House* and Kevin Arnold on *The Wonder Years*? Who can say . . . ?

As Grafton Tanner succinctly put it in his book *The Circle of the Snake*: "We are only a click away from feeling instant nostalgia."

We can blame corporations, artists, and creators all we want (and they deserve so much of the blame!), but this only works because consumers find comfort in the familiar and always have. Even before everything under the sun was recycled, Norman Lear made a habit of introducing viewers to new characters on his TV sitcoms who then wound up starring in their own shows. (*The Jeffersons* and *Maude* were *All in the Family* spin-offs, for instance.) TV spin-offs continue to make up a sizable chunk of programming, especially on network TV: *Young Sheldon* from *Big Bang Theory*, *Schooled* from *The Goldbergs*, all the long-running law enforcement and medical franchises.

In the years 2016,[13] 2017,[14] 2018,[15] and 2019,[16] every single movie but one in the top ten for global box office returns was based on a pre-existing property as a reboot, remake, or adaptation; the sole outlier still relied heavily on familiarity, though—*Bohemian Rhapsody*, the biopic about rock band Queen. Even when assessing the weird and truncated pandemic years of 2020 and 2021, at least half of the movies in the top ten were familiar properties. And unsurprisingly, Marvel, Disney, and Harry Potter–related content made up the bulk of those movies. In a way, superheroes and Disney heroes have become the "classic" texts of our times. Just as every generation gets its version of a Jane Austen and Shakespeare reinterpretation, or yet *another* take on *Peter Pan* (*Hook* is a classic, and my seven-year-old self will stand by this 'til the day I die), so we are destined to see Batman's parents get murdered in that dark alley every couple of years or so. I told you—it's the circle of life.

Nostalgia isn't treated like a disease anymore, but maybe, in the case of our relationship to pop culture, it should be! (Also, in the case of Make America Great Again. And plantation weddings.) There are obvious reasons to support my very medical diagnosis here. For one, more often than not, the thing that's being remade or sequelized or rebooted just doesn't come close to the original—never mind being as good or better. And because nostalgia is crowding out more original ideas, entangling our favorite performers and filmmakers in franchises that often flatten their creative assets. As much as I enjoyed both *Creed* and

Black Panther, I'm more than a little bummed Ryan Coogler hasn't yet had a chance to flex his directing skills with an original property since his arresting debut *Fruitvale Station*.

Nostalgia also leads to some pretty god-awful attempts to "update" old properties and keep up with these changing times, which is how we wind up with Carrie, Miranda, and Charlotte getting Diversity Girl-friends of color on *And Just Like That* . . . (an obvious and grating attempt to atone for *Sex and the City*'s whiteness and racist tropes while wistfully resurfacing the show's happier memories) and Jasmine singing a bland (em)power(ment) ballad about not being silenced because of her gender in the 2019 live-action remake of *Aladdin*. We're getting a whole bunch of surface-level "progressive" takes all because studio execs want to resell us our childhoods.

Frankly, this nostalgic kick is unhealthy. Why can't we just let anything go?

. . .

I've described the side effects of this disease called nostalgia, but I'd be remiss if I didn't mention the benefits too, which do exist, if sparingly. Not all recycled ideas are inherently bad. Some are inoffensive. Others might even be good or very good. A very select few might even surpass their origins in crucial ways.

Here are several circumstances that can make for a worthy revisit:

1. **The approach is radically new or different.** This won't work all the time, or even a lot of the time. (*Bel-Air*, for instance, may be a "gritty" dramatic update far removed from *The Fresh*

175

Prince of Bel-Air, but it's trying so hard to hit its topical talking points it comes off like a series of woke Mad Libs.) But going in a completely different direction can go a long way toward making a familiar property feel newish enough to be worth it.

Better Call Saul is a prime example of this tactic. It's drawn from the same world as its predecessor *Breaking Bad* and incorporates some of the same key characters, and yet, it exists apart from it and as a compelling drama in its own right. The approach and scope feel different enough from *Breaking Bad* to justify its existence—less like a sweeping, action-heavy tragedy and more like a slow burn depicting the banalities and insidiousness of the corporate law world (so many long yet wholly engrossing scenes spent watching characters sift through files or use copy machines) and the crime world.

You don't need to know about or even remember anything that happened in *Breaking Bad* to appreciate the story it's trying to tell. There are so many new characters with deep and supremely fascinating relationships to Bob Odenkirk's huckster attorney Jimmy McGill: Kim Wexler, a fellow lawyer and sometime romantic interest who gets a thrill out of joining Jimmy in his compulsive scams; Jimmy's brother Chuck, who suffers from a debilitating psychological condition and with whom he shares an intricate, prickly dynamic. But if you come to *Saul* as a *Breaking Bad* fan, the experience of watching Jimmy evolve from a relatively harmless small-time conman to the amoral swindler Saul Goodman you love to hate is that much more rewarding.

Also crucial: *Better Call Saul* is very deliberate and judicious in bringing in other characters from the *Breaking Bad* world—the terrifying adversary Gus Fring doesn't enter into the equation until season three, and he does so in a way that feels organic to the show's narrative. This is a show that refuses to pander to fan service.

See also: *Creed, Little Women* (2019 version), *A Star Is Born* (1954 version), *Magic Mike XXL, Into the Spider-Verse*

2. **The original version is overwhelmingly agreed upon to have been BAD and/or problematic.** There have been compelling arguments made by Puerto Rican and Latine critics for why an updated movie adaptation of *West Side Story* isn't necessary; I'm inclined to defer to them the notion that continuing to breathe life into this dated musical through frequent restagings and reimaginings takes away from newer and more authentic stories about Latines that could be told instead.

And yet . . . Steven Spielberg and Tony Kushner's *West Side Story* is by far the best attempt of many to move the characters (and specifically the Puerto Rican characters) beyond stereotypes and into three-dimensional people. It doesn't solve all the problems with the original's script, but the power struggles and outside influences on the conflict between the Jets and the Sharks are more defined, and therefore the stakes and consequences feel much more visceral.

See also: *Dune, The Fly*

3. **The predecessor has established a compelling argument for having more story to tell.** *Toy Story* was a metaphor for an

existential crisis—Buzz Lightyear coming to terms with the epiphany that he's a toy. *Toy Story 2* was also about facing an existential crisis, but from a different angle—the fear of losing the love and affection of your best companion and how it affects your place in the world. *Toy Story 3*—yes, another existential crisis, but this time it's explicitly about death. (There was a fourth movie, but I forgot what it was about as soon as I left the theater. I prefer to consider this franchise a trilogy.) Taken together, these three films make for a natural arc around the themes of companionship, identity, memory, family, aging, and time. By the end of the third film, where Andy says goodbye to Woody and the gang before he leaves for college, I'm not gonna lie—I was sobbing in the theater as if I'd lost a family member.

See also: *The Godfather Part II* (duh), *A League of Their Own* (2022 version)

This is neither an exhaustive list nor does the presence of any of these elements inherently guarantee a recycle will be successful. The 2016 *Ghostbusters* remake with a fantastic all-female cast couldn't re-fresh a franchise that wasn't actually good to begin with. (I can hear the millennial fanboys coming with their pitchforks, and I don't care. Nostalgia will fog your memory!)

But they do point to how sparks of inspired creativity can be found even when the kernels of an idea are derivative. And after all, is anything ever truly new anymore? For hundreds of years we've been telling roughly the same stories and themes and just remixing and riffing off of them through different formats and storytellers.

Like Frank S. Nugent—recall he's the one who wrote in the *New York Times* about being kind of burnt out on movie sequels back in 1936—I've become somewhat resigned to Hollywood's formula and now ascribe to an "if you can't cure them of their nostalgia, hope they do something more interesting with it" attitude. I desire to be proven wrong with each "new" iteration of these same stories, to be pleasantly or even ecstatically surprised anew, as I was when I encountered *Mad Max: Fury Road* for the first time.

But remember—Nugent also suggested that if we must endure unoriginal ideas, the best-case scenario would be watching our favorite ensembles reunite to continue narratives across multiple films. He offered this vision for the future:

"... a hero and a heroine unmarried at a picture's end, still with some obstacles in the path of their romance and with a glint in their eyes betokening their willingness to set out upon some new adventures before consigning their characters into the limbo of shelved celluloid."

He practically anticipated the pattern for much of modern episodic television involving will-they-or-won't-they conundrums played out over the course of multiple episodes. But he could also have been anticipating one of the greatest examples of an exception to the rule that says derivative ideas are creatively bankrupt—a trilogy which, for so many reasons, shouldn't work (and wouldn't in lesser hands) but does.

How splendid and profound is Richard Linklater's trio of films meditating on love in so many of its forms—*Before Sunrise*, *Before Sunset*, and *Before Midnight*? Jesse (Ethan Hawke) and Céline (Julie Delpy) are that couple Nugent longed for—a pairing that avoids easy linearity in the way it so often does in real life. To watch a couple's evolution as individuals and as partners over the course of nearly two decades, each time dropping in on them for just a few mere hours of their lives, and yet feeling as if you, the viewer, can color in all that time and space that has passed in between.

What makes this series work are the pieces, linked by the same spirit (of searching for meaning in the big and small phases of life) yet unique in their own way. When Jesse and Céline first encounter each other on that train and the sparks are flying, they're young, curious, and overly intellectual in the way college-aged students and early twenty-somethings often are, but nevertheless, they're open to possibilities. It's the kind of curiosity and impulse that leads a stranger to suggest you hop off the train and spend a few hours with him before he returns to his home in the United States; the same kind that drives you to say yes and hop off that train with him.

As they flitter about Vienna's cobblestone streets over the course of a few hours, they say things like, "If there's any kind of magic in this world, it must be in the attempt in understanding someone, sharing something. I know, it's almost impossible to succeed, but—who cares, really? The answer must be in the attempt." That is, of course, what Jesse and Céline are doing throughout this evening, and it's so obvious they are the perfect couple for this moment, for this evening, at least. Totally into each other. Not yet jaded.

Nine years later, both in real time and in the context of the narrative, we get *Before Sunset*. And they encounter one another again, this time in a Paris bookstore where Jesse is doing a reading of his most recent novel. We learn they haven't seen each other since that fateful night in Vienna all that time ago, even though they'd made plans to reunite in the same location six months later. Jesse has to head to the airport in an hour, and they kill time walking and talking as they did before, except now they're older, more life has been lived. We can see how they've both changed and how they haven't, how Jesse seems unhappy in his marriage and Céline is struggling to "feel things" as she once did, and how both remain haunted by their dalliance and what could've been, constantly chasing after that rush and intensity they'd shared with one another.

It's a sequel that references its predecessor yet understands what the passage of time does to memory and passions, and it finds a whole new story nestled within the heart of that first story. Jesse and Céline's romance couldn't be over after that first night. We needed to understand how significant that night was for them, needed to hear them share their regrets about not keeping in touch. That final scene, where Céline bears her soul over the strum of her guitar, singing, *You meant for me much more / Than anyone I've met before.*

. . . how can you not wilt? These are the pangs and aches of nostalgia, maybe, but so what? Even if Jesse misses that plane and then it still didn't work out, they still had that evening, that moment of magic, as Céline once called it, where they attempted to understand one another, again.

And of course, nine more years later—*Before Midnight*. Fully jaded, or at least Céline is, now. Together, with kids (plus Jesse's son from his previous marriage). And while the setting, somehow, has never been more beautiful (the Peloponnese coast), their relationship has hit a snag. Jesse wants to move back to the States to be closer to his son; Céline worries about interrupting her career and being older and feeling as though they are no longer who they once were. Which is both true and not true at the same time. They have a cutting, awful, drag-out fight, speaking daggers we've never seen them launch at one another before.

The brilliance of this installment is how it calls back to all those years in between, the times we have seen and the times we've only heard about from their point of view. In the final scene, after that horrible argument, Jesse, in his charming, optimistic way, attempts to smooth things over by role-playing as Céline's future much-older self, writing a letter to her present self.

"I am sending you this young man—yes, young—and he will be your escort," he says. "God knows he has many problems and has struggled his whole life connecting and being present, even with those he loves the most. And for that he's deeply sorry. But you are his only hope."

It's so in tune with who Jesse was all those years earlier on the train, where, in *Before Sunrise*, he asked Céline to imagine what her life might look like if she didn't hop off with him in Vienna—that she could be stuck in an unfulfilling marriage, wondering about the other guys who'd passed through her life and what could have been. "I'm one of those guys. That's me. So think of this as time travel from then to now to find out what you're missing out on."

Jesse became the guy she feels unfulfilled by—at least for now. It's not a picture-perfect partnership, because none ever is. It's real, natural, and a perfect way to conclude the journey of these two. In the final moments of *Before Midnight*, Céline lets down her guard, and the ice seems to have begun to thaw. Maybe they'll make it work, and maybe it's run its course. Their fate is open to interpretation. But what matters is that they'd loved and been loved.

These characters feel lived in, and the added benefit is the deeply collaborative nature of the projects—Linklater wrote the screenplay for the first film alongside Kim Krizan, and Delpy and Hawke are credited with Linklater for the final two films. They drew from their personal lives and had a vision. It's a recycling that occurred under the best of circumstances, the kind of invention and reinvention that makes me soften on the idea of revisits in pop culture.

Even if this is a rarity, there can still be hope.

• • •

Just got back word from Sofia. She's booked for the next year developing a new Peter Pan from Wendy's point of view, and Rebecca's doing a limited series about the female ticket taker at the cinema where Batman's parents got shot.

—BoJack Horseman

Just because there are exceptions, though, doesn't mean we aren't fast approaching a nadir in this decades-long exercise of cyclical excavation.

In 1997, *The Onion* cheekily and presciently reported on a "warning" from the "U.S. Department of Retro": "We may be running out of past." Experts declared that culture was stuck in a "futurefied recursion loop." Where it had once been normal and sustainable for society to yearn for an era twenty years prior, the threat of nostalgia for the 1990s was real even before the 1990s had come to a close.

"We are talking about a potentially devastating crisis situation in which our society will express nostalgia for events which have yet to occur," the secretary of the Retro Department, Anson Williams, aka Potsie from *Happy Days*, announced.[17]

Indeed, we may actually be running out of past. Even before the pandemic grounded pop culture as we knew it to a halt, the crisis was dire. Newish things were being made newer: *American Idol.* (Canceled in 2016. Resurrected in 2018.) *Gossip Girl.* (Ended in 2012. Rebooted in 2021.) The *Spider-Man* franchise. (Ended in 2007. Rebooted in 2012. Rebooted *again* in 2017.) Things have been turning over so fast, in some cases there's barely any time to even arrive at the point of nostalgia.

Corporations and studios were also growing so desperate to mine fragments of the past they hadn't yet exploited that they were beginning to revive the long-dead with the help of hologram technology—"Whitney Houston" doing concerts in Vegas, "Tupac" making a cameo at Coachella alongside the very alive Dr. Dre and Snoop Dogg. In 2019, a ludicrous movie project was announced starring James Dean, who died in 1955 having completed only three films; in this case, he'd be resurrected via CGI to star in a film set during the Vietnam War—a conflict the real Dean never actually lived to see, of course.[18] Time is a flat circle, I guess. (Elvis Presley was reportedly the first choice, but his estate evidently had some dignity and turned them down.)

But the Covid-19 lockdown only made all of us—consumers, creators, and conglomerates alike—even more susceptible to falling down that pesky rabbit hole of nostalgia than before. Suddenly, a lot of us had a lot more free time on our hands, and how was that time spent? Among other things: Zoom calls, caretaking, developing new hobbies, and . . . revisiting our favorite shows, movies, and music wrapped in a comfy blanket of familiarity to distract from the despair. This is normal in times of crisis (9/11 had people looking back and basking in "happier" times, too), but with almost everything shut down, it presented an unprecedented issue—nothing new or old-as-new could even be produced, at least for a bit.

Into the past we dug, ever so deeper. Faced with production limitations in the early days of the pandemic, casts of beloved shows and movies were eager to reunite via staged Zoom chat readings of old episodes and one-off pandemic-themed ads, in the case of the dull and desperate *30 Rock* reunion. Meanwhile, the remake announcements for the eagerly anticipated "post-Covid" world—*Who's the Boss?*, *Dirty Dancing*, *Chicken Run*—hardly slowed, instead becoming more intense and threatening. Whoooo, exactly, was clamoring for a prequel to *The Sopranos*???

Was it ever this much, so fast, so out of control? Are the studios this risk-averse and money-hungry? Are we, the public, this easy to manipulate?

I wonder how much of this constant recycling is tied to a general human fear of death as represented by the unknown. Letting go of what you've already had is to accept the risk that what awaits might not live up to your expectations of whatever you think you need or want.

Faced with this existential crisis, I turn to, of all people, Friedrich Nietzsche. In *The Gay Science*, the philosopher wrestled over the doctrine of eternal recurrence, which frames life as an unending repetition of every detail (good, bad, mundane). He characterized eternal recurrence as "the greatest weight" and imagined a hypothetical scenario in which you're approached by a demon who informs you of your destiny to relive every single detail of your life until the end of time, in the same sequence. "The eternal hourglass of existence is turned upside down again and again, and you with it, speck of dust!"

Would you protest and lash out at the demon, he asks, or would you welcome this prospect with open arms? "The question in each and every thing, 'Do you desire this once more and innumerable times more?'"

The late philosopher Walter Kaufmann observed Nietzsche's perspective on this doctrine as being simultaneously appalled and enthusiastically challenged by it. "Evidently, he could endure it only by accepting it joyously, almost ecstatically," Kaufmann wrote in the introduction to his translation of *The Gay Science*.[19]

Of course, Nietzsche wasn't referring at all to our relatively insignificant state of being in a recurring loop of cultural reboots and recycles, but it can apply here, indirectly. We're reliving our cultural selves ad nauseam in some kind of sequence in one way or another.

And so the way forward, as we're faced with the demon—aka the giant corporations and entities so intent on selling back to us our cherished memories and connections to IP—might be just to succumb and embrace it. Indeed, many of us have already given in and find it utterly useless to resist at this point. Through ticket sales and streaming views, we've collectively accepted it, joyously.

But another part of me isn't entirely done with being supremely irritated by this plethora of easy cash grabs. I hate what it's turned so many consumers into—obsessed with IP and the Disney-Marvelification of nearly every corner of the culture, regardless of genre or scope. The delicate art of letting go is nonexistent these days and so is the ability to say farewell to characters and stories without the expectation of their eventual return, except in the form of rewatches and reruns. I don't actually believe any creator who claims their hit product is it, a one-and-done experiment to look back fondly on, appreciating the beginning, the middle, and, most important, the end. Phoebe Waller-Bridge *says* she has no intentions of doing another season of *Fleabag*. But I've been deceived before.

I understand, to some extent, why a lot of people find satisfaction in seeing the things they love milked in franchise-like fashion, especially now; there's comfort in the known. But I want endings. I crave them. And I crave the ones that truly last because they allow me to accept and appreciate what I've been given and to move on to discover new things. I don't want to become complacent in this endless feedback loop, nor do I want to exist in a permanent state of stasis, unable to move forward with my tastes and my life.

Let The Thing be The Thing. And then let it go.

• • •

It could be anytime, anyplace in the future. I'm settled into my seat in the theater with my $15 small bag of buttery, salty popcorn, prepared to make it through this remake of *Clueless* starring a Disney Channel kid and a TikTok teen I've never heard of before now as the modern-day Cher and Dionne. After no fewer than twelve trailers that include the newest *Spider-Man* (we're in the sixth phase of the franchise now), another installment of *Joker*, a gender-swapped *Moonlight* remake, and an adaptation of the board game Settlers of Catan, the movie begins. Sort of. Actually, it's just Cher and Dionne hanging out at Cher's house watching a remake of *Clueless*, not realizing they're watching a movie about themselves, but with different actors, set in the very far future when everyone rich lives on Mars—a movie-within-a-movie of sorts. And within *that* movie-within-a-movie, Mars Cher and Dionne are watching another remake of *Clueless*, just with different actors who are watching *another* remake...

> This is IP that doesn't end,
> Yes it goes on and on my friend
> Some people started making it not knowing when to halt
> But they'll continue making it forever just because...

7

ON THE PROCREATION EXPECTATION

'm in my thirties now, so, not infrequently, some version of this scenario has played out:

EXT. HIP RESTAURANT WITH OUTDOOR PATIO AND PRICEY SIGNATURE COCKTAILS

Two hetero DINK couples (dual income, no kids) in their thirties and/or forties meet for a dinner double date. Their day-to-day lives are busy enough that they haven't seen the other couple in a while—maybe two, three months—and so there's a lot of catching up to do. "How's the job been?" "Have you been watching [modern-day equivalent of a water-cooler TV show that's on one of the two or three top streaming sites]? Oh my god, how amazing is it?!" "So I was listening to this podcast, and . . ."

The apps are on the table, the drinks are flowing—well, for all but one member of the group, conspicuously—and for the first time since they all sat down, there's a brief lull in the banter.

WOMAN IN COUPLE 1

So, Dan and I have some news.

(She shifts in her seat a bit giddily.)

WOMAN IN COUPLE 2

Oh yeah?

MAN IN COUPLE 1

Yeah. We're pregnant!

WOMAN IN COUPLE 2

(Her eyes widen as she tries, but fails miserably, at cracking a big fake smile at the news. The disappointment flickers quite obviously across her face. Nevertheless . . .)

Oh wow. Cool. Congrats! That's exciting.

NARRATOR

It's not.

MAN IN COUPLE 2

(He doesn't even try to hide it. He's
visibly annoyed but resigned.)

Welp, good for you! Can't say we're surprised.
How much longer will we have you while
you're still child-free?

NARRATOR

Another DINK bites the dust.

WOMAN IN COUPLE 1

We're due in May.

NARRATOR

It's currently December.

WOMAN IN COUPLE 2

Ah, well we better get some additional hang
time in again ASAP!

(Chuckles sadly to herself.)

MAN IN COUPLE 1

Yes, absolutely! Gotta make the most of these
last months of freedom.

NARRATOR

The next time they hang out—in

September—there will be a whole newborn
baby accompanying them at brunch. The
fifty-person baby shower they attended in
April doesn't count as a "hang."

I'm the woman in Couple 2. The one who tries her hardest to be happy for her friends who decide to take the plunge into a lifelong commitment of being someone's parent but can't help but mourn the loss of The Way Things Were. The one who wishes everyone would just stop procreating because we have enough humans in this world already (the Earth is dying! So many children are waiting to be adopted!) but also because, selfishly, it means we'll now have to plan our hang times around naps and breast pumping and childcare. And because it might be years before I get to see you—just you, sans a tiny human—again.

This is very much a *me* problem. I still love my friends with kids and want them to be happy, if this is what makes them happy. But as soon as they drop this news on me, I know what that means: our friendship will never be the same, and I'll be seeing even less of them than I already do. (As every study or trendy article will reiterate, post-twenties adult friendships get harder to maintain with careers and significant others and whatnot, regardless of whether children are involved.) Plus, I've never "gotten" why anyone would make this decision in the first place. The concept of desiring to enter the realm of parenthood has long eluded me. When I look at what it entails and requires of people, all I can see is how much more difficult life becomes when you throw kids into the equation.

Because I'm a nerd who can't help but view pretty much all aspects of life through a pop cultural reference (if you couldn't tell by now), the practice of parenthood reminds me a bit of Cousin Oliver syndrome. Hear me out:

By 1973, *The Brady Bunch* was already running on fumes—having exhausted every possible iteration of "six rambunctious kids get into benign hijinks and learn a lesson or two within twenty-five minutes" at least thrice over. Toward the end of the fifth season, the show's writers introduced an entirely new character: Cousin Oliver, Carol's nephew. The excuse they provided for the sudden materialization of this child was that he'd come to live with the Bradys while his parents were living in South America.

Robbie Rist, the actor who played Oliver, wasn't even ten years old yet when he was cast, making him the youngest character on the show at the time. That was exactly the point, ostensibly; *The Brady Bunch* was on the brink of cancellation, and the Brady kids were no longer the adorable prepubescent kids and tweens they'd been at the start of the series's run. Oliver would hopefully inject some much-needed energy and youth into the dying production.

Famously, Oliver did no such thing. He was neither cute nor endearing; he was cloying and a total klutz who unwittingly caused destruction everywhere he went, whether it was knocking over Jan's art easel while she was trying to paint or accidentally squirting ketchup all over Greg, to the unending exasperation of everyone. (You can see why his parents ditched him for another continent—he was Steve Urkel before Steve Urkel.) Oliver lasted only six episodes—the last six, to be exact, because ABC finally canceled *The Brady Bunch*.

Cousin Oliver became a lambasted Hollywood trope, pop-culture-junkie shorthand for a TV series's painfully obvious and desperate ploy to keep the stalled train chugging along by bringing in a new cute kid. It became easy to identify when a show's writers had decided to go the "Cousin Oliver" route, and it rarely ever worked out any better for those productions than it did for *The Brady Bunch*, creatively or ratings-wise. *The Cosby Show* had Olivia and the slightly older cousin Pam, *Growing Pains* had Luke (an early Leonardo DiCaprio role), *Family Matters* had the orphan 3J, *Buffy the Vampire Slayer* had Buffy's little sister Dawn.

It's baffling that anyone would think throwing a new kid into the mix like that could attract new or long-lost viewers when your show's been on the decline for a while. And yet for decades, this is what TV writers have done. Maybe you see where I'm going with this—it's likewise baffling to me that so many people actively wish to throw a kid into the mix of *life*, regardless of the quality of their lives in that moment. And yet, people have been doing this for *eons*.

The odds of a kid actually improving someone's life are probably better than the odds were of Oliver saving *The Brady Bunch*, but it's still a total crapshoot. You and whomever you procreate with could be financially stable and by all accounts "good," attentive, and nurturing parents, and your kid could still end up depressive and/or a menace to society. As a Black woman, I run a greater risk than my white counterparts of dying or having serious complications during childbirth. And then, of course, there are so many people who probably shouldn't ever be parents at all (or maybe just not yet) and do it anyway; and then it's the kid who gets to suffer for it. (Am I . . . an anti-natalist? I'm still working that out, TBH.)

But still, parenthood, and especially motherhood, is treated as a given. Women who reach a certain age—usually their late twenties—begin to field questions from relatives, friends, and acquaintances about their plans for children regardless of their relationship status. Lucky for me, my family has always been fully supportive of my decision, even if, early on, they probably thought I might come around to the idea. But I'm of the age now where the assumption of eventual parenthood comes up when I meet new people and they learn I'm partnered up.

"... whenever you two decide to start a family ..."

LOL.

• • •

There are many forces at play when it comes to the Procreation Expectation. Religion is one facet, of course—rooting an individual's value in the having of children, "be fruitful and multiply and fill the Earth," etc. Anti-abortionism is only a relatively recent cornerstone of America's Christian religious right (in years prior to and immediately following the 1973 decision in *Roe v. Wade*, prominent evangelical leaders spoke out in favor of abortion on multiple occasions, including in 1971 when Southern Baptist Convention delegates called for its legalization[1]), though the loud opinions of a few have clearly placed a stranglehold on our government and ability to access preventative measures.

But that doesn't explain it fully, because far fewer people these days identify as religious; in 2019, a Pew Research study found that the number of adults who described themselves as atheist, agnostic, or "nothing in particular" had jumped from 17 percent to 26 percent in the past decade. (Those who identified as Christians had decreased by 12 percent over the same decade to 65 percent.)[2] Whether it's familial or peer pressures (i.e., same-age friends pairing off and/or becoming parents all around the same time), it's hard for us to shake loose the notion that having kids is just another square we must land upon on the board game of life.

This bleeds into pop culture, which both reflects and reinforces the Procreation Expectation. Think about how many people have cashed in on and become famous almost exclusively because of their identity as a parent, between TLC's factory farm of shows starring parents with too many kids (*Jon & Kate Plus 8*, *19 Kids & Counting*, *Doubling Down with the Derricos*, *Sweet Home Sextuplets*), MTV's *Teen Mom* franchise, the Kardashians (I'm convinced the primary reason the siblings have so many kids among them is because they need to keep their cash-cow industry flowing in perpetuity), and every product-hawking mommy and daddy blogger/influencer.

Scripted entertainment plays a part, too. It's rare to find a show with a twenty- or thirty-something protagonist on TV who doesn't contemplate and/or eventually wind up becoming a parent if the show goes on long enough. Hannah on *Girls* ends the series as a single mom; Mary Jane on *Being Mary Jane* has a traumatic experience freezing her eggs; Liz Lemon on *30 Rock* adopts two kids with her husband Criss after having trouble getting pregnant; Lawrence finds himself coparenting with Condola on *Insecure* with Issa becoming the stepmother at the end of the series. Had it not been unceremoniously canceled, the very last episode of *Happy Endings* season three suggests the show was heading in the direction of Brad and Jane trying to have a baby following three blissful seasons of child-free, youngish adult hijinks. Heck, even *Cheers*'s perpetual bachelor Sam Malone contemplates becoming a father with sometime paramour Rebecca Howe in the later seasons.

I can't tell you when it was exactly that I decided I wasn't going to have any children of my own, because there was no single event or "aha" moment that led me to this place. I *can* say with confidence that I've never been able to envision myself being a parent without also envisioning what I'd be losing in the process: the luxury to move about the world freely; the luxury to have my housing options dictated primarily by how much I earn and my desire to live in a bustling urban area rather than by which neighborhood is in the "best" school district; the luxury to not have to set aside money for another person's college tuition (at this time, I'm a decade removed from graduate school and still more than $60,000 in student loan debt); the luxury of not adding to a mountain of anxieties with concerns about whether or not my kid will, in fact, be alright.

That urge to bear a child and help mold it into an adult human being has never existed within me. I've never once felt compelled to be pregnant, give birth, or become a mother. Any "maternal instincts" within me have been directed toward my dogs, whom I love immensely and can't imagine my life without but who also haven't required 24/7 care at any point in their lives, unlike human children. This clearly makes me the pope's worst nightmare.

I realize this makes me unusual. Even those who ultimately choose not to have children often speak of having at least felt the urge at one point or another. But it's the rare area of my life where I have not budged from my position. In fact, the older I get, the more validated I feel in being child-free. For as much as pop culture presents parenthood as a near-inevitable stage of life, it also frequently makes parenting look like an exhausting, miserable slog.

In Judd Apatow's *Knocked Up*, there's a scene where Alison (Katherine Heigl) and Ben (Seth Rogen) are on a dinner double date with Alison's sister, Debbie (Leslie Mann), and her husband, Pete (Paul Rudd). Alison and Ben are still getting to know each other, trying out this whole relationship thing after getting pregnant from their one-night stand, and the chitchat soon turns to the exasperation of parenting.

"Isn't it weird, though, when you have a kid and all your dreams and hopes just go right out the window?" Pete suddenly blurts out, adding that if you're single and child-free and want to go to India for a year, you can just go and do it. Keep in mind, this is a wealthy white dude talking; with or without kids, the vast majority of us can't afford to just jet-set off and live abroad for shits and giggles for a full year. But you get the point—it's the *possibility* of doing it that's all but lost when raising kids comes into play.

The conversation then devolves into Ben likening his fear of impending fatherhood to O. J. Simpson trying to get away from the cops during the white Bronco chase ("I'm just hauling ass for Canada man . . . and I just bust through the border and I'm a free man"), and then he and Pete begin riffing on a ridiculous *Back to the Future* metaphor about traveling back in time to not have kids.

There are those who would find these flights of fancy to be *way harsh, Tai,* but it's quite obviously coming from a place of unbridled honesty. I've known enough parents to know that all of them have probably had these sorts of thoughts at some point, especially in the midst of one of their kid's very major public meltdowns. (Every now and again one

of my parents will chuckle while reminiscing about a particularly nu-
clear tantrum I exhibited in the middle of a Macy's when I was two,
though they most certainly weren't laughing at the time.) The moral of
this regret-tinged banter between Pete and Ben is that parenting often
sucks, man. Like, say goodbye to your freedom. And also, perhaps . . .
to your happiness?

Pete and Debbie are clearly unhappy, anyway. In the *Knocked Up*
spin-off, *This Is 40*, these characters take center stage, and as a consequence their familial discontent is far more pronounced and piercing.
Beset with the natural existential dread that comes with aging, questioning their commitment to one another, and wondering aloud if the
only reason they've stayed together this long is because of the kids . . . in
between comedic bits involving Megan Fox's hotness and Viagra, this
movie expresses a deep, lingering sadness about adulthood.

As in *Knocked Up*, there's the persistent question of whether parenting is actually worth it. Both Pete's and Debbie's dads were ambivalent
or inconsistent presences throughout their childhoods but have since
gotten a chance at a do-over of sorts with new, younger wives and new,
younger kids. In the case of Pete's dad, Larry, he maintains a whiff of
that meh-and-a-shrug attitude about his own young kids with his current wife: Larry'd assumed she couldn't get pregnant at forty-five, but
they "were very unlucky, and now we have these three beautiful children." A few moments later, as if trying to score points with his adult
son, Larry tells him that his mother wanted to abort him, but he convinced her to think about it over lunch first. (This is what I mean when
I say some people probably shouldn't have kids at all. Whether or not
it's true, why would anyone tell their kid this and in this way?!)

Pete and Debbie are less ambivalent in their own parenting than they are alternately anxious and resigned, depending on the day. One scene is several minutes of the two of them venting about their kids before ultimately concluding, with a heartfelt sigh, "Aw, I love them." When Debbie discovers she's pregnant again, at a time when they've only just begun to repair their relationship, they wonder if this is something they actually want to commit to. "What are we gonna do with a third baby?" Debbie says in the final scene. "I have no idea. We can't afford it," says Pete. They contemplate selling the house . . .

All I want to do as I watch this scene unfold is yell at the screen in my André 3000 voice: *Too soon! Don't do it! Reconsider! Read some literature on the subject—you sure?!* But the characters answer back: fuck it. And then moments later, they're laughing and seemingly in love again as the credits roll, because of course they're going to keep the baby and make it work. That's Hollywood, and that's life, I guess.

This perspective of "parenting sucks, but in the end it's worth it" in pop culture confounds me as a point of justification, but it does astutely capture the conundrum that is parenting.

Aside from peer pressure, yet another force driving the Procreation Expectation is the fact that, for those who can get pregnant, there's a timer ticking—and for those on the fence about parenthood, it's a factor they have to contend with and perhaps pushes them into parenthood out of fear of regret for not having done it. There's a unique sort of permanence to having a kid that doesn't exist in other major life choices—not romantic partnership, not friendship, not adopting a pet. And when a decision comes with such a daunting lifetime commitment, digging deep down to find optimism even in the darkest of moments is how you make the experience more bearable; it needs to be framed as a good, sacrificial part of life so that it can be worth it in the end.

But is that a good enough reason to bring new life into this world? There's very little room for regret or decision reversal; once you opt in, you can't just change your mind without courting condemnation and shame, especially if you're a woman. (This is why I can sympathize, to a point, with those who willingly became parents complaining about parenting. I've certainly regretted some of my own life choices. And of course, it's possible to hold more than one extreme feeling at a time whether you're a parent or not—to love and care for someone deeply while being intensely irritated by their presence in your life at any given moment.)

Much has been written on the impact having kids has on individuals and couples. In a 2010 *New York* magazine feature and a subsequent book, Jennifer Senior explored the notion that raising children is an exercise in "all joy and no fun." One study she cited, from a 2004 paper by behavioral economist Daniel Kahneman surveying more than nine hundred Texas women, found that childcare "ranked 16th in pleasurability out of 19 activities," behind exercise, napping, and cooking, to name a few. Another, which analyzed nearly one hundred studies over several decades, suggested married couples were less satisfied after kids entered into the picture. And Andrew Oswald, a British economist, told Senior that, in general, having kids doesn't "make you less happy; it's just that children don't make you *more* happy," either.

As Senior found in her reporting, it's extremely difficult to measure happiness across collective groups (after all, happiness means different things to everyone), though some minor generalizations could be inferred—namely that, as Pete and Debbie demonstrate throughout *This Is 40*, children can provide "unrivaled joy" as well as "unrivaled moments of frustration, tedium, anxiety, heartbreak . . . Loving one's children and loving the act of parenting are not the same thing."[3]

Something cool and liberating about the evolution of Western narrative storytelling is how more writers, Apatow included, have been able to explore this paradox of having children—the lulls and lows of it all right alongside the supposed pleasures. The FX series *Breeders* is one of those shows that has little sentimental or glowing to say about the adventures of parenting; its very title alerts the viewer to the central characters' at times austere, almost clinical attachment to the act. It's a very dark British comedy about a couple, Paul (Martin Freeman) and Ally (Daisy Haggard), who are raising their young children, Luke and Ava, while feeling emotionally depleted by nearly every moment of it.

In season one, Ally has to decide whether to take a huge promotion that would keep her away from the family for several days a week, for multiple years, which will put a strain on an already tense partnership. Paul especially finds it hard to control his exasperation with the kids and is prone to intimidating verbal outbursts as the small provocations build up. "No one has ever made me feel rage like they do," he confesses in the very first episode. In a different episode, he admits he sometimes has an impulse to discipline his son with corporal punishment but knows he can't, "so I hurt him in other ways, subconsciously." For instance: calling his kid a "waste of space" to his face. Eek.

The show isn't afraid of framing this troubled family unit as a series of stark negotiations and compromises, from something as life-altering as Ally taking that new role at work to Ally and Paul trying to decide whose turn it is to attend to the kids when they awaken in the middle of the night. Peppered in between these stressors are flashbacks to their child-free days, which are sometimes filtered through a notably soft glow of light and palpable nostalgia. They seemed happier then, or, bare minimum, significantly less anxious and angry.

It's not all gloom, and there are moments of good times with the kids depicted here and there, but *Breeders* really lays the anger and struggle on thick. Season two time-jumps several years ahead when the kids are now thirteen and ten, and the effects Paul's rage has on them are much more acute. (Things get so bad Luke punches his dad, and Paul decides to move out of the house.) *What were they thinking, having kids?* I wonder to myself. *That could never be me!* I see the nuance, I hear it, I understand it. I know not every parent is this extreme in their discontent, my own included, and that for plenty of them, it's more rewarding than not. Yet all my brain can process is "parenting sucks and doesn't seem worth it."

I slipped into a similar state of mind the first time I watched *The Lost Daughter*, Maggie Gyllenhaal's directorial debut and adaptation of an Elena Ferrante novella. Olivia Colman plays Leda, a college professor on holiday in the Greek islands. As the movie begins, Leda seems to be in pure bliss during her solo travels, driving along the roads contentedly, floating leisurely in the ocean, and peacefully reading on a beach chair with the whole beach pretty much to herself. At first, she reminds me of *Murder, She Wrote*'s Jessica Fletcher, a child-free middle-aged woman with the finances and free will to do whatever she wants, whenever she wants, living her best life.

Then, like the murderer who inevitably intrudes upon Jessica's best life in every *Murder, She Wrote* episode, a huge multigenerational family arrives, breaking Leda's peace, and the rays of annoyance dart out of her eyes as they boisterously descend upon the shore. They're the same rays of annoyance I've shot whenever someone decides to bring their rowdy kids to a bar on a weekend afternoon. The vibe is killed. Done. Gone, girl. When one of the group's members asks Leda to move her chair so they can have more space, she initially refuses, and a brief but uncomfortable confrontation occurs before they reach a truce. In Leda, I feel seen.

Eventually, Leda becomes intertwined with this family—in particular, Nina, a young mother of a three-year-old daughter—and their presence, and encounters bring up a wave of memories and intense, once-buried emotions for her. It turns out Leda has two adult daughters with whom she's had a tenuous and fraught relationship in the past; when they were little, Leda left them and her husband behind because she felt suffocated by the responsibilities of motherhood.

Via flashbacks, we see her younger self struggling to bear much of the burden of raising the children and pursuing her own career while her husband is often away for work. Like Paul in *Breeders*, her patience wears thin fast when faced with kids doing irritating things through no fault of their own, as kids are wont to do. She yells, ignores them, slams doors. Her husband seems oblivious or willfully obtuse to all of this, even as she tries to get him to understand that she's drowning.

Leda: "Sometimes I'm scared I can't take care of them. What if I pass out alone with them while you're in Arizona?"

Him: ". . . Oh honey, of course you can take care of them."

Ugh, this is such a gut punch—the presumption, the casual dismissiveness of it all. *Of course you'll take care of them. Of course.* That's what mothers do, right?

What's so refreshing about *The Lost Daughter* is how Leda's choices exist in gray, neither celebrated nor condemned but rather treated as a fact of her life that has had real emotional consequences. When she reveals to Nina that her daughters were five and seven years old when she left them for three years, Nina asks what it felt like to be without them.

"It felt amazing. It felt like I'd been trying not to explode, and then I exploded," Leda confesses, a glimmer of relief and liberation appearing to emanate from her memories of those solo years. Nina, who is also struggling with depression and exasperation in the midst of parenting, is clearly disturbed by this taboo admission. It "doesn't sound amazing," she observes, to which Leda responds matter-of-factly: "Okay."

Nina's judgment isn't the movie's judgment. Leda isn't depicted as deliberately cruel or uncaring, though she does admit what she did was "selfish." And quite obviously, the resurfacing of that period from her past brings with it feelings of dread and shame. But Leda also looks back fondly on her time away from her kids, and by the end of the movie, it's revealed she's managed to rebuild her relationship with her daughters when we see her call them from the beach following the movie's dark climax.

Leda doesn't have that "natural" mothering gene in her. She's unafraid to call children a "crushing responsibility." But unlike in, say, *Kramer vs. Kramer*, where Meryl Streep's Joanna leaves her young son behind not once, but *twice*, Leda's never the villain in this story. No one in *The Lost Daughter* really is, though some*thing* might be—and that's the unfair, unrealistic expectations that are hurled upon mothers. The movie's thesis could be summed up as "parenting sucks, and it's okay to say so without caveats."

Breeders and *The Lost Daughter* exist in a time when the stigma of questioning the idea of parenthood and its value is slowly but surely being chipped away. When the pope admonishes adults for choosing pets over children ("selfish," as he's put it, in response to declining birth rates), many people roll their eyes and admonish him right back for being so damn antiquated.[4] There's no shortage of first-person essays— like this one!—and reported pieces to be found on opting out of the whole kid thing. An article in the *New York Times* profiled a British photographer who created a portrait series, "We Are Childfree," featuring women like herself from across the globe. That same article cited a Pew Research Study that shows a slightly increased share of non-parents under the age of fifty who said they were "not at all likely" to have children in the future (23 percent in 2021, up from 21 percent in 2018).[5]

At the same time, parents seem to feel more comfortable expressing regrets, ambivalence, and sometimes envy with regards to their life choice, though usually anonymously on Reddit forums and the like. For instance, a Facebook page called "I Regret Having Children" has more than 40K followers and bills itself as "a support page for overwhelmed folks that need someone to talk to about the very real feelings they are having, that they feel they can't discuss openly with others."[6]

In a Substack post titled "The Things We Don't Discuss," journalist Jill Filipovic wrote about the lack of stories expounding on maternal regret and the vitriol and pushback she received after expressing a desire on social media to see more such stories represented in our culture. Many of the replies to her curiosity tweet, she writes, boiled down to labeling her as "sociopathic, abusive, someone with an empathy deficit on par with a serial killer."[7] One person compared regretful and ambivalent mothers to Andrea Yates. You know, the mentally ill woman who suffered from severe depression and drowned all five of her children in the bathtub in 2001. Um, dramatic much?

There remains a stigma against admitting that parenting is not just hard but can also be rife with sadness and longing and rage, too. And unsurprisingly, women tend to get the most hate and shame cast their way should they express as much, because we're supposed to be the nurturers and instinctual providers of care and love. It's worth noting *Breeders* star Martin Freeman is also the cocreator of the series and based the show in part on his own experience as a father, and that his character, Paul, is much more of an extreme manifestation of a taboo perspective on raising kids than Daisy Haggard's character, Ally. Yet Paul still feels more familiar as a character trope than Leda in *The Lost Daughter* does. And in so many sitcoms and movie comedies, the dad's ambivalence and/or ostensible distaste toward one or all of his children is treated as a joke (think *The Simpsons*, *Black-ish*, and the aforementioned *Knocked Up* and *This Is 40*).

But like Filipovic, I'm fascinated by stories that push back against or challenge the notion of "in the end, parenting is worth it." And it's not simply because I like to feel validation in my own choice via others' nightmarish scenarios. (Okay, fine—maybe it is, a little. I'm only human.) What I've found is that those stories have helped get me to a place where I can feel a certain level of empathy for anyone who's found themselves feeling less than enthused about having kids after they've already had them. Because there's so much intense pressure from our government, which has effectively struck down *Roe v. Wade*, and from family/friends/acquaintances/complete strangers on the internet to look at parenting as the only path to take on the road to adulthood, without any regard for how that pressure might churn out unhappy participants and unhappy children born from it. And there's a whole cottage industry dedicated to presenting a certain kind of bland, cookie-cutter brand of family life that finds "mommy bloggers" and the like crafting entire public personas around having kids and little else besides being the "CEO/founder" of some "lifestyle brand" on the side. (I'm leery of anyone who lists their parental stats in their social media bios. You have a kid? You go, Glen Coco, but I don't care.)

Our culture tries so hard to make parenting seem meaningful and fulfilling at all times, leaving little room for counterpoints and making it especially difficult for even the happiest of parents to feel comfortable venting about the worst parts of it all. This is one of many reasons I've made the choice that I've made. I'm almost certain that if I ever did have kids, I'd find myself exasperated and anxious all the time and in need of venting but feeling guilty about doing so. I easily spiral into anxiety attacks anytime I feel overwhelmed by work; I can hardly imagine what a screaming baby or an unruly toddler or a rebellious teenager would do to my psyche.

Maybe I'd lash out and say something horrible to my kid like Paul or slip into such a deep funk I'd contemplate leaving it all behind for a bit like Leda.

Maybe—nay, in all likelihood—I'd fight with my partner a lot over minor things like whose turn it is to take the kid to day care or big things like the best way to discipline them when they inevitably start getting sassy and whether or not to switch jobs/career goals so we can make more money to pay for the hundreds and hundreds of thousands of dollars it's going to cost us to raise the kid over the next twenty-two-ish years. Our relationship, which already takes effort and commitment and has had its ups and downs, would now become exponentially more difficult to preserve under the stress of child-rearing; our attention would be diverted from one another in favor of taking care of this little

208

human who would need us more than anyone has ever needed us. And then what?

Maybe we'd wind up like Sharon and Rob on the series *Catastrophe*—the show that proved to be the first instance in which I'd see so much of myself in a character who's also a parent and could really imagine what I might have been like if I'd had a kid. The bare-bones premise is not dissimilar to *Knocked Up*. Sharon and Rob meet at a bar in London while Rob, an American ad exec, is visiting for work, and they engage in a freewheeling one-week stand. Sharon finds out she's pregnant, and the two decide to make a go of it, both as parents and as a couple, with Rob making the move to London. Unlike *Knocked Up*, though, the series doesn't end after the baby arrives. And it gets *messy*.

To me, the choices they make defy logic. I can confidently say I would never try to make a go of it with a one-week stand who doesn't live in the same country as me, much less have a kid with them. (They briefly discuss abortion, but at forty-one, Sharon is worried this may be her only chance to have a kid. She also learns she has precancerous cervical dysplasia, and that childbirth could actually lower her risk of having cancer by "scrubbing" her cervix.) But the brilliant thing about *Catastrophe* is how Rob and Sharon are fully aware of the many mistakes and questionable decisions they are jumping into throughout their journey into building a life together and have a wry, cynical take on the whole situation.

"We're reasonably good people, so we could probably do this and not fuck the kid up too badly," Rob reasons while talking through their options after learning about the pregnancy. "I'm just saying a terrible thing has happened, so let's make the best of it."

Over the course of four seasons and some timeline jumps, that's exactly what they do—try to make the best of it. They fail a lot, because it turns out when you decide to get to know and start dating the one-week stand you got pregnant with, while simultaneously preparing to have a child with that person, and oh also, one of you suddenly uprooted your life to move to a completely different continent, the odds of it lasting and working out without a hitch are pretty much shot. Who knew? (Again, could never be me, but anyway . . .)

They suck at communicating; agreeing to compromise is neither one's strong suit; and as stressors pile up, be they work-, child-, or money-related, they buckle under the weight. Rob, a recovering alcoholic, relapses. Sharon develops a habit of swapping tags at retail stores in the spirit of a cheap thrill, often with her children in tow. They both lash out at one another often, pelting the most awful, cutting jabs and insults. Theirs could easily be defined as a dysfunctional, unsustainable partnership, one that only exists because they didn't use birth control during their weeklong sexcapades.

Now earlier, I noted how I could see myself in Rob and Sharon, and thus far, pretty much everything I've described about the dynamic of these two fictional characters is the complete opposite of what I have with my partner. But their general attitudes toward parenting—"A terrible thing has happened, so let's make the best of it"—is exactly how I would approach it were I to decide to keep an accidental baby. (Assuming I was still fortunate enough to have that choice, seeing as those who are able to give birth have lost a ton of autonomy over their own bodies in the recent past . . .) And as dysfunctional as their relationship is, they do seem well-suited to one another's tics and general outlook on life and still manage to find their way back to one another and rekindle that spark that attracted them in the first place. If a huge reason for this stems from feeling an obligation to keep the family together, it's also because underneath it all, they really do seem like a compatible match. Mostly.

At the beginning of season two, it's revealed they're pregnant with their second child. (Seriously, has any study ever found that having a second child makes parenting *easier*? I really don't understand what these two are thinking, Cousin Oliver-ing their lives, throwing another kid in to make things interesting. One more time for the back: Could. Not. Be. Me!) Sharon's mother offers them both a piece of advice: "After your brother was born, and your father and I had a bit of a rough patch, we decided that we had to put our love for each other above everything else, because we were man and wife before we were mother and father."

Sharon, of course, takes this revelation at face value—that her parents chose to love each other more than their kids. But her mom counters that she chose to love Sharon's dad "first," not more. (This prioritization of romantic love over maternal love sounds almost as if it could've come straight from the mouth of the writer Ayelet Waldman, who gained notoriety for proclaiming "I am in fact a bad mother. I love my husband more than I love my children" in a "Modern Love" essay.[8] For this bold declaration, she received widespread threats, condemnation, and, eventually, a book deal.[9])

It's a profound and—to many, probably—taboo statement that manages to capture the complexities of juggling relationships among children and romantic partners. There's this sense that children must always override everything, which is understandable, but not to the detriment of the emotional fulfillment of the parents. If the parents aren't happy together, the children suffer. Maybe trying to focus on your partner and making sure they're happy will benefit everyone in the long run?

Sharon scoffs at her mother's perspective, but this theme comes up constantly throughout *Catastrophe*, whether she's aware of it or not. Her and Rob's blunt conversations often touch on how out of sync they can feel with one another. At their wedding, right before their first baby is due, a flustered Sharon responds to Rob's insistence that he's trying to do the right thing by letting him know she'd rather be his "choice." After a particularly grueling day in another episode, Rob admits, "Sometimes I use up all my care units, and I don't have enough left for you."

The final episode of the series echoes that theme of choosing who and what to prioritize in the most thoughtful and aching of ways. There's a small detail in the first few minutes where they are arriving in Boston to visit his family, and at the airport, Rob and Sharon take a moment to embrace as their stroller begins to roll away. Rob sees it happening, but when a stranger expresses concern about the runaway stroller, an unbothered Rob counters back that he'll get it in a minute. This moment he's sharing with Sharon takes precedence.

Later, they have a blowout fight about Rob wanting to take a job in Boston, and it ends with a gut punch of him calling Sharon mean and telling her he doesn't like her. The next day they take a moment to stop at a beach on the side of the road while their children are asleep in the car some feet away. They have a heart-to-heart, with Rob apologizing for the mean things he said to her and Sharon apologizing for not appreciating him more. She tells him she's pregnant again, and they both seem ready to do it all over again. "If I met you right now," Rob says, beaming, "I'd still wanna fuck you for a week, and get you pregnant, and marry you, and mess it all up from there."

"Well let's do that, then."

In the very last moments, Sharon decides to take a dip in the ocean. Rob is uninterested in joining her at first but then glances back to notice a sign that warns of rip currents and clearly states "no swimming." He runs into the water after her, and the two of them swim out further and further. "I just didn't like seeing you adrift in there on your own," Rob says. As the camera pulls back in the final shot, it's clear that they are very far from shore, their kids still in the car. It's unclear whether they'll make it back. Sharon Horgan, the show's cocreator and costar, once said in an interview that the viewer's take on that ending "says what kind of a person you are. If you're a nihilist or a fatalist or an optimist."[10]

Perhaps this is a cop-out on my part, but I think I lie somewhere in the gray of all those things on this one. Regardless of whether they make it back, they do, in a way, live life as Sharon's parents did—choosing one another "first." And I think there's something kind of poetic and empathetic about that, even if the worst-case scenario were to end up happening and both Sharon and Rob left behind two young, traumatized kids. I know that probably sounds horrible—and this is probably the millionth reason I shouldn't have kids—but I get it. I can't fathom choosing to do half the things they decide to do with their lives, but to me, putting each other first and trying to make one another happy seems like a pretty good way to be a better parent.

I recognize I'm saying all of this as a child-free person. And I've never actually been faced with the possibility of having a child; I've consistently been on some form of birth control since before I'd even begun having sex, a privilege when access to birth control can be so difficult to find depending upon your circumstances. But what art like *Catastrophe*, *The Lost Daughter*, and *Breeders* has done is help me to better understand those who feel pulled, either by outside or internal forces, toward procreation; to realize that it's not so cut and dry for most people as it has been for me. And that, perhaps to the Ledas and Sharons of the world who make the choice to have kids despite having intense doubts and legitimate reasons not to, they didn't actually seem like choices in the moment, but instead, like coercion.

Maybe it's impossible for me to really speak on this because of my status. Yet while I'm not a parent, I have parents and am a daughter. While contemplating writing about any of this, I asked my mom a frank question I'd been nervous to ask her for years: *If you had a chance to do your life over again, would you have become a mom?* She was honest: probably not. She would've focused on a career, done more traveling. But my dad definitely wanted kids, and she was in love, and thirty-plus years ago, that was still something most people who could do it did, whether they were enthusiastic about it or not.

Her answer doesn't bother me in the least; in fact, it was a relief to hear. Truthfully, I'd long suspected this was how she'd felt. I have countless fond memories with my mom, who was a stay-at-home mother for the first three years of my life (until I was old enough to go to preschool) and who sacrificed many, many hours alongside my dad carting me from extracurricular activity to extracurricular activity and who was and still is a huge cheerleader for me in all my endeavors. But our relationship hasn't always been smooth. We can be very similar in terms of temperament and how we deal with conflict, which is to say, we tend to try to avoid it, sometimes for the worst. And I've sensed that there were things she always wanted to do with her life that she didn't get to, in part because she got married and had kids, and that it's affected her happiness.

I think some of that regret bled into her relationship with my dad, which ultimately led to their divorce when I was a high school senior. My parents wanted different things in life and drifted apart. They did so much for my sister and me, but for various reasons . . . they couldn't put each other first.

For a long time I resented my parents for their acrimonious split and wondered why and how they'd ever gotten together in the first place, not fully understanding how having kids changes people and changes relationships. My parents were not quite the same individuals they were before I and my sister were brought into this world, nor the same couple.

My heart still breaks a little every time I learn another friend is planning to go down that road to parenthood imminently, and I still think we don't really need to add more people to this world, especially considering how Covid has made being a parent exponentially more difficult, and climate change puts the future of this planet in serious question. But man, do I feel for the parents who found it harder than they ever imagined, and especially those who aren't afraid to convey it. Parenting's complicated, no matter how you slice it.

8

PARENTS JUST
DON'T UNDERSTAND

Today, A-list celebrities treat their Instagram feed like a glossy cover story, carefully curated to show themselves in the most flattering light possible. They may present their posts as though they're speaking directly to their audience, via first-person captions and intimate at-home selfies and videos, but in all likelihood, they've got a team working hard to help craft those posts for them.

This is not what Britney Spears's feed looks like. To her, Instagram is a public diary in which she can say whatever she wants, whenever she wants, for the entire world to see. It's stream-of-consciousness and freewheeling, with no discernibly cohesive theme other than, *It's Britney, bitch, and I'm all out of fucks to give.* Lo-res photos of herself striking poses in the nude, her hands cupping her breasts and a cheeky emoji covering the rest; videos of herself dancing around happily alone in her home; corny inspirational memes ("Don't let anyone treat you like free salsa. You are guacamole baby. You. Are. Guacamole."); long, rambling captions where she relays funny/silly recent occurrences in her life, like walking into a glass door[1] or telling no one in particular to "kiss [her] white ass!"

But Britney's not okay, and she wants everyone to know that, too. Amid the playful posts are the sadder ones where she unleashes her righteous anger upon her parents Jamie and Lynne and her siblings Bryan and Jamie Lynn. As the world is now well aware, following a mental health crisis, Britney was placed under a conservatorship controlled by Jamie, an arrangement that lasted thirteen years and screamed unethical in nearly every way. According to Britney's testimonies given when she petitioned to have the conservatorship removed, her finances and every waking moment were essentially dictated by her father—where she lived, who she dated, renovations on her home, even her birth control.[2] She's accused her conservatorship handlers of drugging her[3] and claimed she was forced to stay at a mental health facility after raising an objection during a rehearsal.[4] Yet at the same time she was deemed "unfit" to have any sort of independence, she was releasing albums and performing around the world, as Jamie—a reported alcoholic who's been estranged from his daughter for most of her life—and other members of her family lived off her payroll.

That's a hell of a lot of trauma to process. And so perhaps it's only natural that after years of mostly staying silent, she's clapped back in such a loud way, emboldened by the #FreeBritney movement and the intense media spotlight that brought awareness to her case. In one post from 2022, she shared a black-and-white photo of herself at age thirteen, her hair falling long and wavy along the side of her face. The look in her eyes suggests a hint of sadness. The caption beneath it (which I managed to screenshot before it was eventually edited out completely, maybe out of a twinge of regret for airing out too much "dirty laundry"?) was a long one, punctuated with a lot of emojis, and it read, in part:

"One thing the conservatorship did to me . . . and one of the things that hurt me the most . . . is that I was always being told I was fat and never good enough . . . My dad always made me feel like I had to try . . . try . . . try!!! BIG TIME!!! He ruined the deep seed of my existence . . . the seed that made me feel beautiful like when I was 13 . . . my confidence . . . my swag . . . my inner dialogue . . . and yes even my sex life . . . all completely ruined!"[5]

(Most of those ellipses are her own. There were a bunch of emojis sprinkled throughout, too.)

There have been many more public displays of Instagram venting. "Lord have mercy on my family's souls if I ever do an interview!";[6] "I was nothing more than a puppet to my family"; "I want justice and won't stop until something is done to those who harmed me . . . and YES I was harmed!!!"[7]

You get the gist. There's no artifice or publicity spin to be found here, just pure, unfiltered rage. It's an extremely famous person sharing thoughts and feelings usually reserved for an inner circle or therapist, not with the entire world, the kind of scathing callout that rarely finds its way into those glossy cover stories.

It's sad to witness Britney exposing her open wounds to the rest of us as a matter of trying to heal. There's also something that feels distinctly millennial and of-this-moment about it all. In recent years, the news and popular culture have transmitted a wave of stories from and about millennial minds wrestling with strained familial ties and intergenerational trauma. Aside from Britney, perhaps the biggest public rendering of a real-life umbilical cord cutting has been Prince Harry's estrangement from the royal family in the wake of his marriage to Meghan Markle (who is herself estranged from *her* father).

And on the entertainment front, the family pangs have been plentiful. Disney released *Encanto* and *Turning Red* less than six months apart, and both tell stories of a parent or grandparent whose trauma has been unwittingly passed on to the generations that came after. The Netflix series *Russian Doll* uses time travel to explore its protagonist's complicated relationship with her deceased mother, just before her fortieth birthday. *Everything Everywhere All at Once* uses the multiverse to depict a fractured relationship between an overbearing mother and her queer daughter. And on the semi-autobiographical front, comedian Jerrod Carmichael's HBO special *Rothaniel* and Michael R. Jackson's *A Strange Loop* resemble therapy sessions, where their messy family histories and the reactions to their coming out as gay are brought into unflinching focus.

Our elders might have dealt with such matters differently, if they dealt with them at all. Therapy might not have been a thing to even consider, much less seek. A cone of silence and a repetitive cycle of harmful behavior may have rippled down from generation to generation unchecked, which is how one can get to be not okay.

Younger generations seem fed up with and utterly exhausted by the crushing weight of this avoidance. It feels heavy. And so we're looking inward and backward.

Psychologist Peggy Drexler has dubbed millennials the "therapy generation," citing a 2017 study from Penn State University that found that "the number of students seeking mental-health help increased from 2011 to 2016 at five times the rate of new students starting college."[8] She also referenced a study from Blue Cross Blue Shield, which found that depression diagnoses among eighteen- to thirty-four-year-olds went up 47 percent between 2013 and 2016, likely because more people in that age range were going to therapy.

Meanwhile, *trauma* has become both a buzzy concept and genre of our times, trending on social media (the hashtag #trauma has billions of views on TikTok[9]), influencing how content is presented (trigger warnings, etc.), and frequently creeping into story lines and plot twists in pop culture. *The Body Keeps the Score*, psychiatrist Bessel van der Kolk's nonfiction guide on healing in the face of trauma, has spent years on the *New York Times* bestseller list since its initial release in 2014. Many other self-help books and memoirs targeting trauma continue to be published. Coinciding with all of this is the rise in self-care culture, which has its roots in medicine and evolved into a political act in the 1960s and 1970s as women and people of color fought to claim autonomy over their bodies in the face of governmental interference and failing institutions. Like trauma, self-care has been everywhere in recent years, from Solange's "Borderline (An Ode to Self Care)" to the highly lucrative "wellness" industry, which tries to convince people that buying its products is an act of self-care.

These phenomena gained prominence as millennials came of age and entered adulthood. The Iraq War, 9/11, the 2008 stock market crash, and other pivotal events of the last twenty-plus years have all served as reference points for understanding why this generation has turned to therapy, trauma-processing, and self-care. "It's forced a lot of millennials to look at, to be faced with where we are as a society and as a culture and say, 'Oh this isn't good enough for me,'" Jor-El Caraballo, a millennial and licensed therapist in New York City, told me. "And then exploring, how did we get here?"

Caraballo points out that most of the people considered millennials (those born between 1981 and 1996) are in their thirties now, a period in life when adults might be straddling the line between becoming parents and becoming caregivers for their own parents. This is likely one explanation for the wave of intergenerational trauma narratives in Hollywood, as our age cohort also finds ourselves in the stage of our careers where we are finally taking the reins in storytelling as creators and writers.

Millennials certainly don't have a monopoly on trauma in narrative storytelling; baby boomer creatives like Oliver Stone processed the turbulence of the 1960s and the Vietnam conflict for *years*. And the likes of Alice Walker, August Wilson, and Tennessee Williams have all written characters born specifically of intergenerational trauma. But unique, recognizable traits arise in these modern iterations, which tend to go deeper than the oft-pathologizing and villainizing notion of "mommy/daddy issues" (think *Psycho*'s Norman Bates). These contemporary trauma narratives typically reflect some combination of the following:

- a protagonist from a traditionally marginalized culture or identity (female, person of color, queer, etc.)
- multiple generations within one family who are affected by one or more traumatic experiences
- a fantastical element manifesting the trauma (family curse, metaphysical occurrences, etc.)
- a climax and/or conclusion that's rooted in forgiveness and redemption

Elder millennial Britney is an extreme real-life example, but my generation at large, and the ones coming up behind us, are not okay in many ways. And a lot of us are talking more openly and unashamedly about it, even if—or perhaps *especially* if—it means having to call out the people who helped raise us.

Trauma, Disneyfied

A running joke/observation about the monopolized world of Disney is how, for all the brand's squeaky-clean image-making, those animated movies many of us grew up on could be quite dark. Maybe not as dark as the Grimm's fairy tales or other original sources they were adapted from, but dark nonetheless. *Pinocchio*'s Pleasure Island sequence—that name alone is horny AF—where the bad young boys are lured to drink, gamble, and smoke before being turned into literal jackasses. The "Pink Elephants on Parade," a nightmarish scene where Dumbo and Timothy Mouse get "drunk." (Really, what they experience is a hallucination only something like LSD could cause, but they had to keep the illusion of being kid-friendly, I guess.) And, of course, the dead parents. Sooooo many dead parents.

Parents who are either dead by the time the movie begins or die as a part of the plot for the protagonist to deal with. That in and of itself is a kind of intergenerational trauma; just look at how Simba ran away, dropped out of life, and became a lion hippie for years after his dad died in that stampede because his evil Uncle Scar convinced him it was his fault. But it's one thing to process the devastating loss of a practically perfect parent like Mufasa. In more recent Disney trauma narratives

Turning Red and *Encanto*, the anxiety stems not from loss but from extremely overbearing parents. To process this particular kind of pain requires difficult conversations, arguments, and turning into a giant red panda or trying to figure out why no one in the family wants to talk about that one uncle of yours named Bruno.

What *Encanto* and *Turning Red* have signified is a larger trend within the current Disney-Pixar mold of doing away with the traditional villain character. In its place is a theme that's more complex than a simple "good" vs. "evil" conflict, though the outcome of this dynamic could arguably be considered on the neat side, depending on who you ask.

Even if these two movies hadn't been released so closely together, it would've been difficult not to notice the similarities they share, namely the teen girl protagonists who have a fraught relationship with the elder women in their lives and confront the consequences of long-held family secrets. In *Turning Red*, thirteen-year-old Meilin "Mei" Lee is a rambunctious, adventurous Chinese-Canadian girl living in Toronto in the early 2000s with a core group of friends and a totally healthy obsession with a boy band (and boys, generally speaking). As the movie's opening narration lays out plainly, Mei is conflicted about how her budding independence might affect her sense of loyalty to her parents, especially her mother.

"The number-one rule in my family: Honor thy parents!" she says, while also acknowledging that in doing so, "you might forget to honor yourself."

Her mother Ming is extremely overprotective and insists that Mei spend most of her free time either doing homework or helping out with the family business, an ancestral temple that also serves as a tourist attraction. The morning after a particularly extreme incident where

Ming irrationally embarrasses Mei in front of her crush and other classmates—try to watch this scene and not cringe while being transported to the memory of your own parents doing something similarly mortifying when you were a kid—Mei wakes up to discover she's morphed into a giant red panda. This transformation begins occurring whenever her emotions become much too much. (And as we all know, emotions becoming *much too much* is just what puberty is, basically all the time.) Eventually, Mei learns her transformation into a red panda is born of a hereditary curse that began with one of Mei's ancestors and has affected every girl in her family since.

Like Mei, *Encanto*'s Mirabel Madrigal fails to live up to the strict standards set within her family. She and her relatives live in a Colombian village in an enchanted house named Casita. Each member of the Madrigal lineage is bestowed a unique magical gift upon turning five years old (for instance: older sis Luisa has superhuman strength, her aunt Pepa's mood dictates the weather), Mirabel excepted. She's the odd one out who wasn't given a gift, and that feeds insecurities about her self-worth. It also breeds resentment between her and the highly demanding Abuela Alma, the matriarch of the family. When the Casita suddenly begins to fall apart and the Madrigal magic begins to falter, Mirabel sees it as an opportunity to prove her worth and figure out how to fix everything.

She tracks down her shunned Uncle Bruno—he's been in hiding, living in a secret passageway inside the Casita the whole time—and learns he disappeared because he had a vision of the future that revealed a potentially negative outcome for her and the Casita. "My gift wasn't helping the family, but I love my family," Bruno says sheepishly.

The drama in these films is driven by traumas left to fester, unacknowledged. What is *Encanto*'s "We Don't Talk About Bruno" but an extremely catchy song about ostracizing the black sheep of the family for dubious reasons and then pretending as if they no longer exist?

In another song, "Surface Pressure," Mirabel's sister Luisa reveals the physical and mental stress she's felt as one of the older siblings and the "strong" one who's forced to shoulder not just all the heavy objects but the burdens as well: *I'm pretty sure I'm worthless if I can't be of service.*

The number's conclusion is met with the only reasonable response to Luisa's truly relatable vent session: "I feel like you're carrying way too much," Mirabel observes. Um . . . yeah!

Many millennials have grown up amid a culture of silence and are now spending their adulthood acknowledging that they, too, may be carrying way too much; hence, an embrace of those therapy sessions. And ultimately in these intergenerational trauma stories, it's the kids who are the ones forcing the confrontation that leads to the processing. After learning that her mother, grandmother, and aunts chose to exorcise their inner red pandas via a one-time ritual, Mei ultimately decides to buck the tradition and embrace her own—which means embracing her more outgoing personality and being unafraid of her emotions, big or small. Mirabel finds Bruno and finally pushes back against Abuela's ongoing nitpicking and condescension toward her.

"I think we're now able to view our parents' generations and their parents' generations from this lens of 'Why did you treat me the way that you treated me?'" Mallory Yu, a radio producer in their mid-thirties, tells me. Yu is the eldest child of a Taiwanese father and Filipina mother who came to the United States prior to starting a family, and they grew up in a predominantly Asian-American "ethnoburb" in southern California. Yu has found therapy useful in processing their relationship with their family, even if their parents aren't exactly "comfortable" with the idea of talking about such personal matters with an outsider. "Instead of just accepting that this is the way that Chinese parents are, we're now wanting to untangle why they are the way they are, and in doing so untangle our relationship to them, hopefully giving ourselves, maybe, a better path forward."

I kind of love how Disney and Pixar movies have explored these complex dynamics—*Coco* and *Brave* could also fall within this category—because they're tapping into a very specific cultural moment that resonates loudly with my generation while simultaneously containing near-universal appeal. Mei and Mirabel's distress, as passed down by Ming and Abuela's own distressing pasts, is rendered viscerally and inventively, a refreshing departure from the many movies I grew up with that heavily emphasized romantic interests (Ariel and co. really did a number on young me's psyche, not gonna lie) alongside all those dead parents. If these movies are crafted with a young audience in mind first and foremost, they should probably more closely reflect what most young audiences might be experiencing at that time in their lives, no?

A Multiverse of Trauma

A daughter of Holocaust survivors recalls visiting family in a small German town as an adult in the sociologist Janet Jacobs's book *The Holocaust Across Generations*. "I apparently looked like Mother did when she lived there," the woman says. "I literally walked into town and people's heads turned and they called my mother's name, as if my mother had come back . . . It wasn't my favorite thing to go back as my mother. The scariest, creepiest thing was I knew who had done what, which neighbor had done what to whom."[10]

When she arrived at the house her mother and father had lived in before the war, she described meeting its current occupant, who attempted to greet her. "My hand developed atrophy at my side . . . I was having a hysterical reaction, I guess, my hand was not moving anymore."

Jacobs observes this account as a manifestation of traumatic memory, where "the child replaces the parent" and experiences the deep anxieties and fears of their antecedents. A return to a "site of terror" can connect generations in ways that oral histories passed down just quite can't, viscerally inflicting those who may not have experienced trauma firsthand but can feel it resonate nonetheless.

The series *Russian Doll* echoes this concept and imagines it within the sci-fi realm of time travel. In season one, Nadia (Natasha Lyonne) finds herself in an infinite loop of reincarnation on the night of her thirty-sixth birthday party, dying many times in many ways (getting hit by a car, a broken elevator, an air conditioner falling from a building, etc.) until she's able to figure out how to live a better, more fulfilling life. But season two is more focused on her complicated relationship with her late mother Nora (Chloë Sevigny) and the ripple effects of her family's history. Just a few days from her fortieth birthday, Nadia discovers a portal via the 6 train that takes her back in time to the early 1980s, where she inhabits her mother's body while her mother is pregnant with her.

Like that descendant of Holocaust survivors quoted in Jacobs's book, Nadia finds it understandably jarring to "become" her parent. "The universe finally found something worse than death—being my mother!" she kvetches. (She also travels even further back in time to inhabit her grandmother Vera, a Hungarian refugee during World War II.)

It's kind of like *Back to the Future* for a new generation, where instead of playfully exploring the social anxieties of WASP-y mid-century Americana, we're getting a dark exploration of mental illness and the aftershocks of the Holocaust via 1980s New York City. Intergenerational trauma is expressed in more academic terms than *Turning Red* and *Encanto*, with themes drawing explicitly from philosophical concepts and the heavily debated biological study of epigenetics, which is driven by the belief that trauma can be imprinted directly onto your genes and passed down through generations. Nadia lives out events she's only heard about via stories passed down from her relatives, and in doing so unravels a more complete picture of how things actually went down. A huge chunk of the plot hinges on an event that held significant consequences for Nora and, later, Nadia herself—Nora's unwitting assistance in stealing valuable gold coins from her mother, Vera, coins that were meant to go toward Nadia's college fund. Nadia becomes convinced that if she's able to track down those coins, she can change the trajectory of her life. But no matter what she does while being Nora or Vera, the coins wind up disappearing anyhow.

Living as her mother and grandmother serves two purposes for Nadia's personal growth: to generate empathy for their circumstances and life choices, and to come to terms with her own circumstances in life. In season one, there are glimpses of Nora's troubling behavior throughout Nadia's childhood, including a scene where she drags Nadia around the city as she manically buys watermelons from bodegas for unclear reasons. A key part of Nadia's path to self-discovery (and breaking her death loop) is admitting she's been living recklessly out of guilt; she feels she betrayed Nora, because as a kid, she wanted to live with Nora's stable and supportive friend Ruth. (Though she never admitted this to her mother.) Nora killed herself at the age of thirty-five, not long after losing custody of Nadia.

In season two, Nadia comes closer to understanding Nora, a schizophrenic, and letting go of all that guilt she's racked up, as she directly experiences one of Nora's psychotic episodes. As Nora/Nadia is evaluated by a doctor in a psych ward, Nora speaks to Nadia: "Nobody understood me until I had you." Nadia, overwhelmed by the disorienting state, becomes awash in sadness for her mother. "This is what it was like for you every day, huh Mom? I'm gonna finally find you and fix you."

Of course, Nadia cannot change the past and cannot "fix" her late mother, but that desire to do so echoes the burden and caretaker role so many kids from unstable upbringings can take on in relationships with their parents. And there's something about enduring the "site of terror"—her mother's illness or her grandmother's losses during and after WWII—that allows her to feel a stronger bond with her elders. As Jacobs notes in her studies of Holocaust survivors and their descendants, "Creating collective memories at sites of terror fostered the growth of intimacy between parent and child."[11]

When the universe throws cyclical death at Nadia, it forces her to process some of her own trauma; when it puts her literally in the shoes of her elders, she must learn how *their* trauma informed her own and grow out of that. In addition to portraying Nadia, Natasha Lyonne—born in 1979, just outside the arbitrary designation of the millennial generation—is a cocreator of *Russian Doll* and wrote and/or directed several episodes; she found inspiration in her own troubled relationship with her late parents and has connected their traumas to her struggles with substance abuse in her younger years. "Now that I'm an adult, I think so much of my being a wild thing was because I was trying to get in their shoes," she told the *New Yorker*. "I fully cleaned house on that type of behavior. I make sure that, at this point in my life, I just don't fuck with chaos."[12]

The movie *Everything Everywhere All at Once* is after a similar effect in eliciting empathy for its traumatized characters, though it stands out from other intergenerational trauma narratives by concentrating on the fractured parent-child dynamic mainly from the parent's perspective. At the beginning of the film, Evelyn (Michelle Yeoh) is dissatisfied with life. Her stale marriage to the meek but sweet Waymond (Ke Huy Quan) is on the brink of divorce, she disapproves of her daughter Joy's (Stephanie Hsu) queerness, and the family's laundromat business is being audited by the IRS. Here is where I'll pause to say two things:

1. This movie is way, *way* too complicated and twisty to sum up neatly and in less than a paragraph, or ten. The multiverses have multiverses! But I'm about to attempt to scratch the surface of it anyway. And,

2. If you somehow haven't seen this movie yet, stop what you're doing—which is reading this, duh—and go watch it, now. Because it's truly a fantastic, deeply rewarding journey, and the less you know going into it, the better it will be. I'll wait.

*

*

*

Okay. Lovely. You're back after having your mind exploded. Or you ignored my warning and don't care at all about spoilers.

Either way: In the middle of their disastrous meeting with IRS auditor Deirdre (Jamie Lee Curtis), an alternate expert fighter version of Waymond suddenly takes hold and pulls a baffled Evelyn into the janitor's closet to inform her that there's an infinite number of parallel universes out there, with a new one created every time a person makes a different life choice. (A different version of yourself makes the other choice in a different universe.) Their multiverse, the "Alphaverse," is under attack by the nihilistic Jobu Tupaki, an alternate evil version of Alpha Joy, who was born out of Alpha Evelyn's hostility toward her.

Evelyn learns to "verse-jump" by accessing different parts of herself as they exist in the other realms (i.e., life choices she didn't make in the Alphaverse)—a glamorous movie star, a kung fu master, and a chef, for instance. Because these parallel Evelyns represent the paths in life she might have taken but didn't, they also encompass Alpha Evelyn's regrets. They are what could have been had she not chosen to marry Waymond against her parents' wishes all those years ago, lives that may have been more fulfilling and exciting than toiling away in a laundromat with a "bland" husband and "disappointing" daughter, at least on the surface. The powerful Jobu Tupaki is the poisoned fruit of Evelyn's resentment, deeply enraged and unabashedly violent.

Everything Everywhere really understands that common disconnect between mother and daughter, first gen and second gen immigrants, straight parents and queer kids, and how these dynamics overwhelm and have the potential to destroy relationships and one's sense of self. It invokes the many examples of mothers who would not have become mothers if they'd had and/or made different choices in their past and the children who can sense this from time to time even with the most loving and supportive of mothers.

It's eventually revealed that Jobu isn't seeking destruction so much as the compassion and understanding she feels Evelyn hasn't given her; in one of many spectacularly chaotic sequences, Evelyn has to fend off Jobu's warriors (as well as those of her own crotchety father Gong Gong, who wants Evelyn to kill Joy—pun unintended but fitting) in order to get to Jobu and inspire hope in her daughter again.

The millennial filmmaking duo of Daniel Kwan and Daniel Scheinert, known collectively as Daniels, have described *Everything Everywhere* as "a dream about reconciling all of the contradictions, making sense of the largest questions, and imbuing meaning onto the dumbest, most profane parts of humanity." (Indeed, this movie contains butt jokes and fingers as hot dogs.) It's their attempt to "bridge the generational gap that often crumbles into generational trauma."[13] This seems like an apt way of looking at this batch of millennial-created fodder and how so much of it is driven by a need to stop the bleeding that emerges from the trauma. In previous generations, parents bought into the idea that the pursuit of the idyllic "American Dream" would mean their children and children's children ended up better off than they are, financially speaking (steady pay/career, homeownership, generational wealth). But how much emphasis was put on ensuring their children and children's children were better off emotionally speaking?

Trauma → Grace

A common thread among these movies and shows is reconciliation. Like many of the Disney-Pixar movies of the last fifteen years or so, *Turning Red* and *Encanto* are largely devoid of the traditional clear-cut villain character—your Scars, Ursulas, Gastons—those flamboyant, comical, dastardly Big Bads who have a specific evil ambition driving their actions as expressed through an excellent villain song. The switch-up from the cliché is welcome, though in transferring the "villainy"—or, more accurately in these cases, the antagonism—onto the parents, the stories have leaned into an arc of redemption that may not always feel entirely earned.

The climaxes of *Turning Red* and *Encanto* involve emotional showdowns where anger and resentment that have been suppressed for far too long boil over into, finally, confrontation. There's a catharsis to watching Mei, in giant panda form, assert her independence from her mother at the boy band concert she sneaks away to ("I LIKE BOYS, I LIKE LOUD MUSIC, I LIKE GYRATING! I'M THIRTEEN— DEAL WITH IT!") and Mirabel hit Abuela with the harsh truth that Bruno left the family because "you only saw the worst in him."

But not long after a war of the words and direct heightened conflict— wherein the elder speaks aloud their traumas for what seems like the first time—there is redemption and reconciliation. Ming and Abuela apologize for the overwhelming burdens they've unloaded upon their child/grandchild, and a relieved Mei and Mirabel find forgiveness and understanding. The only "villain" in need of defeat is the unhealthy behavior stemming from the trauma. This, too, is true of Joy and Evelyn in *Everything Everywhere*, and, despite her mother being no longer physically present, Nadia and Nora in *Russian Doll*. "If you could choose your mother all over, would you choose me again?" the spirit of Nora asks Nadia in the season two finale. Nadia, cradling her infant self in her arms, takes a beat and looks around that time-hopping 6 train car to get a glimpse of the older and younger versions of her surrogate mother Ruth, older and younger versions of her grandmother Vera, and the tweenaged version of herself.

"Yeah, I didn't choose you the first time, but I guess that's just how the story goes, huh, Mom?" Nadia finally replies with a wan but understanding smile before handing over her infant self to Nora.

These deliberately empathetic outcomes are an outgrowth of pop culture's wave of better-people-in-training. After years of "difficult men" antiheroes in prestige TV (Walter White, Tony Soprano, Don Draper, etc.), a new kind of central character arose in the 2010s to counter them. These protagonists are still flawed (and many of them could be slotted easily into the category of antihero-doing-horrible-things), but baked into the DNA of each narrative is their desire and deliberate attempts to become a better person, whatever that might mean—think BoJack in *BoJack Horseman*, Barry in *Barry*, the main casts of *Schitt's Creek* and *The Good Place*. They may or may not actually succeed in atoning for their bad behavior, but the journey is about the effort. The audience roots for them (to a point) for even trying in the first place.

Empathy is a precious, grossly underutilized resource. Yet to me, a naturally inclined cynic, the formula in many of these intergenerational trauma narratives can begin to feel a bit predictable and maybe a little *too* pat. The elders are often absolved of their destructive behavior following a few minutes of heightened conflict: Just duke it out in a war of words (or giant dildos, in one scene from *Everything Everywhere All at Once*), name your traumas for the first time, and . . . that's it? Is it ever this simple in real life? I'm not saying the parents need to plunge spectacularly into a fiery pit—and frankly, I don't expect animated Disney movies to ever be *that* cynical, dead Mufasa notwithstanding.

But when forgiveness in the face of an apology—perhaps not coincidentally, a recurring theme in Judeo-Christian theology—is treated as a given, it can undermine the immeasurable amount of pain and anxiety that's already been passed down to the kids and is never so easily smoothed over.

Mariam Georgis, an Assyrian-Canadian political scientist whose work focuses on global Indigenous politics and Indigeneity in Middle East politics, offers a counterpoint to my knee-jerk cynicism. Her family history includes stories of displacement: after Sayfo, the Assyrian genocide that occurred during World War I, her maternal grandfather made his way to present-day Iraq, where he met her grandmother. Decades later, not long after the Gulf War, Georgis's own immediate family fled Iraq, became refugees in Turkey, and eventually gained acceptance into Canada when she was around nine years old. Her childhood in Canada resembled Mei's in *Turning Red*; she recalls her mother always seeming anxious and nervous, which trickled down into an overprotective parenting style. She describes herself as having been an "angry teenager," and for a long time she resented her parents for the things she wasn't permitted to do ("My mom . . . helped me survive a war zone. There was no way this woman was gonna let me die in some bullshit called [summer] camp") and the things she had to do because of circumstance (like working multiple jobs as a teen to help the family make rent). There was this unspoken pressure placed upon her by her parents. "Even if they don't say it, immigrant parents kind of instill this drive in you to actually be their dreams," she told me.

But *Encanto* hits especially close to home for Georgis because of its themes around survival mode, which she touched on in an article for *The Conversation*. Abuela's trauma of having witnessed the murder of her husband while attempting to flee their under-siege village with infant triplets echoes the kind of trauma Georgis's parents experienced and also didn't talk about. "That scene at the river, where she's saying goodbye to her husband, standing there with three babies . . . when I left Iraq I never saw my grandparents again," Georgis explained to me. She has compassion for Abuela's need to control everyone around her and her resistance to dealing with those horrific events of the past, because living in and ultimately escaping a war zone had profound effects on how her own parents treated her, too. "Yes, I thought [Abuela] was a bitch, for sure," she said. "But I couldn't just see her as that because I thought, she needs help. She hasn't stopped survival mode.

"My mom now still lives like she's surviving a war zone and it's sad. Because I want her to live life fully, right? And she doesn't. And neither did Abuela, and neither did Mei Mei's mom, and neither did a lot of our moms, I bet."

Georgis is herself a mother now of two young children, and that compassion for the Abuelas and Mings of the world is also partially driven by her own efforts in breaking the cycle of trauma for herself and them. Through therapy she's been able to look back on her relationships with her parents and recognize that their approaches to raising her and her three siblings had its roots in the persistent economic and housing instability they endured as a family when she was younger. "My parents didn't sit there talking to me about my feelings. They kept me safe, they kept me clothed, and they kept me fed. And to them, that was loving me."

She's working on shaking herself from the survival mode she's internalized after all these years, but it isn't so easy. She says she had a visceral reaction when watching the flashbacks of Abuela being ripped apart from her husband. "I hope one day my children watch this movie, and you know, I hope they feel empathy, I hope they cry, because it's okay to cry—but I hope they don't feel it *in their gut*. I don't want them to be shackled by this expectation of perfection to survive that I inherited."

This seems to be the dream these movies and shows are promoting—of achieving peaceful resolution with the generations that follow. In practice, of course, it can be a little more elusive. In *Everything Everywhere*, Evelyn has to learn to focus on the now and not let what could have been spoil her outlook on life; it's the only way to defeat Jobu and bring Joy back into the fold. She must see, in the most out-there and visceral ways possible, how "her intense, insane expectations . . . completely caused her daughter to crumble," Mallory Yu tells me. "And to see how she could've mitigated that pain.

"It was a journey that I think [many millennials] wish all our parents could go on," they add.

Yu sees a lot of Evelyn in their dad, an industrial designer. Right before they were born, he received job offers from Disney Imagineering and Lucas Arts at the same time, a seemingly win-win conundrum to have from an outsider's perspective. Ultimately, he chose the former, because it was a "safer" financial choice for the family at that time—their mom was pregnant with them, and their parents were trying to buy a house—though Yu has long sensed "a hint of regret" within their dad.

"I can see how that regret and that—almost guilt—for wanting that different life, affects the way he relates to me and my brother, for example, and how that has trickled into and colored our relationships. It's hard to tell your parent that without sounding accusatory, so it's fantasy wish fulfillment to watch a movie where someone who is the age of our parents is going on that journey without necessarily needing us to kickstart it."

That's precisely it: Things like *Encanto* and *Everything Everywhere* function as fantasies of wish fulfillment. And these stories have their value.

On the other hand, there's value in representing the limbo and uncertainty, too. Jerrod Carmichael's *Rothaniel* proves there's space to tell stories of intergenerational trauma where reconciliation isn't necessarily a given. The comedian and actor's 2022 HBO special dispenses with the usual stand-up approach and finds him seated on a chair for the full one-hour set, divulging the details of extremely personal family drama and coming out publicly as gay for the first time. For anyone who'd been following Carmichael up to that point, many of these reveals weren't too surprising; in his previous HBO documentary specials, *Home Videos* and *Sermon on the Mount*, he filmed unscripted conversations with multiple generations of his family talking about themselves and how they see the world. One topic that arises in these segments is the rampant cheating and deceit practiced by the men in his family, including his father and grandfathers. And in a conversation with his mother, he reveals he's hooked up with men, a statement that's passed over as quickly as it's uttered.

But *Rothaniel* goes deeper, as if Carmichael's performing a therapy session upon himself, on a stage with an audience. There are "jokes" here and there, but that's not really why he's here. He feels the need to come clean and be more honest about who he is, and that means connecting the dots to his family's complicated, supremely messy history. Perhaps the most devastating segment of the special comes toward the end, when he describes his devoutly Christian mom's reaction to him coming out.

He wishes she would give him something, anything—even yelling—because that would at least be "acknowledgment" of his queerness. Instead, she's given him "nothing." After a long pause of shifting in his seat, while rubbing at his shoulder as if he were getting out a nasty knot, he morosely says, "She's nice. She's sweet. She ignores it. The worst of her is cold, like really, really cold." He admits that he can be this way, too: "I'm like my mom: fuck everybody."

A random audience member, whom we don't see, asks him to give her time. "I don't know how much time we have left," he says. "Just in general, one of my biggest fears is my parents' funeral, just the thought of one of them dying without saying everything, without contending, without expressing it all."

It's clear that at this very moment, when Carmichael is performing *Rothaniel*, his relationship with his mom remains uncertain, unsettled, and perhaps, untenable. He openly contemplates a future where he might have to cut ties with her, and the pain at this thought exudes throughout his body language and choice of words. This isn't Mei and Ming; emotional walls weren't torn down between Carmichael and his mother after a heart-to-heart. It's a little bit like Evelyn and Joy in the Alphaverse, in the sense of the parent choosing to actively ignore and dismiss their child's queerness rather than outwardly condemn it, except at the time he's making *Rothaniel*, Carmichael is still very clearly in the thick of processing it. He's well aware that talking about these things so candidly to the public could slow or completely derail a reconciliation with his mom and the other members of his family. But like many millennials have realized, there comes a point where you have to stand on your own apart from your parents and your family's lineage. You have to find happiness and peace, even if that means distancing yourself from where you came from.

To be fair, *Rothaniel* is the most directly autobiographical of any of the other examples I've mentioned thus far, so of course it's going to ring a little more realistic in its open-endedness. But Michael R. Jackson's more whimsical Broadway musical *A Strange Loop* rests easily alongside Carmichael's special in terms of how the parent-child relationship is rendered. Loosely based on Jackson's own life, it's a very meta meditation on what it can mean to be "fat, Black, and queer," about a young man named Usher, who's a Broadway usher with the dream of finishing his own musical theater play, *A Strange Loop*.

Like *Everything Everywhere All at Once*, there is *a lot* happening in this show: At times, the six supporting performers each represent one of his innermost thoughts (like "self-loathing" and "sexual ambivalence"), and at other times, they swoop in to play any number of other various characters, like one of Usher's hookups, or Whitney Houston, or members of his family (who are all named after characters from *The Lion King*). His father is disdainful of his queerness and wonders if his son is attracted to him; his devoutly Christian mother wants him to write gospel plays like Tyler Perry and believes she can pray away the gay. Both parents are convinced AIDS is quite literally God's punishment for homosexuality.

The climax of the show unpacks the guilt, anxiety, and self-hatred his family has passed on to him through a lengthy church sermon and scathing gospel tune. In this scene, the stage is designed to resemble his family's home on the bottom half of scaffolding, and on the top half, a church, with some of the cast dressed in choir robes and a casket carrying the body of Darnell, Usher's gay cousin who died of AIDS. Usher takes on the persona of a preacher, confronting his mother for how she's treated him after all these years.

"I can't help but reflect on the ways that I have lived a life without passion in fear of you and your husband's words to me that if I ever acted on my lust for another man, that I would meet the same fate as Darnell lying in that there box,"[14] he confesses. After unleashing everything he's ever wanted to say to her, the song comes to a halt, and there's a beat of silence. "You wanted a gospel play, and this is the only way I knew how to do it," he tells her.

Usher's mother embraces him and gives a spiel about how she loves him and then promptly returns to Darnell—how sad it is that he's dead, but there's still hope for her own son: "As long as you is sincere in your desire *to change your life for the better*, we go'n' work this gay abomination thang out." It's as if she never heard a single confessional word of what Usher has just laid at her feet. Somehow, after all of that, she's still got those same denigrating ideas and beliefs. Somehow, she's unchanged.

Eventually, Usher's thoughts wonder if he really wants to end his show on this note, raging against his closed-minded parents to a gospel tune. "Is this *really* what real life is like?" asks Thought 4.

"Maybe not," says Usher, "but that's what it *feels* like. To me. Or what it felt like. Especially when I was seventeen and telling my family who I was for the first time."

True to the show's title—which is taken from the scholar Douglas Hofstadter's cognitive science term to describe the cyclical nature of the self as well as the Liz Phair song "Strange Loop" (Usher loves Liz Phair)—*A Strange Loop* doesn't come to a definitive conclusion as to the relationship between its protagonist and his family. Instead, it comes back to Usher himself, how he processes his past, and how he can move forward apart from his parents: "Maybe I should regroup / 'Cause change is just an illusion . . . a strange loop."

Even after they've both formally concluded as pieces of art with a beginning, middle, and end, *Rothaniel* and *A Strange Loop* nevertheless live on afterward in a state of perpetual motion. The rest of the story has yet to play out—not the (possible) healing, not the (possible) reconciliation, or the (possible) cutting of ties. It's uncomfortably open-ended, like so many aspects of life.

Trauma → Oppression

Much of the research on intergenerational trauma has been concentrated on Holocaust survivors and their descendants, like Janet Jacobs's *The Holocaust Across Generations*, though such studies have also examined it through the lens of, say, the effects of slavery and Jim Crow upon Black Americans and the impact of Indian residential schools in the US and Canada on indigenous people and their descendants.

It seems not so coincidental then that so many of these trauma narratives are from the perspectives of those from traditionally marginalized groups—a potent combination of timing (more women, people of color, and openly queer people have opportunities to helm their own projects) and mutual sources of anxieties. Naturally, paradoxes emerge out of this movement, because these groups have a fraught history of being overrepresented on-screen through trauma in haphazard or voyeuristic ways. (Ahem *Game of Thrones, Boys Don't Cry, 12 Years a Slave*.)

A less forgiving way to observe this wave of narratives is as merely a more palatable version of a troubling trope. Yet the creators seem to have a keen awareness of how much Hollywood fetishizes this sort of thing and are careful to sidestep those most surface-level interpretations by pointedly considering the protagonists' emotional journeys and ensuring that, ultimately, survival and perseverance prevail. The aim is not to elicit empathy through shock but through familiar parent-child dynamics. (It also makes a difference that the locus point of the trauma in each of these specific movies and shows is emotional rather than related to any kind of physical or sexual violence; visually speaking, the audience is spared gruesome body horror.)

Another source of friction: As more and more of these stories are told, they must also contend with dismissive reactions to the rise in traumatic storytelling via pop culture and social media, which is tied more broadly to a general disdain for anything millennials touch or make popular. There's some truth to the feeling that the t-word is thrown around willy-nilly these days; just like "woke" and "canceled," in many instances, "trauma" has lost meaning. Heavily cited, quite convincing long-form essays have been written in places like *The Atlantic* and Vox criticizing the culture's obsession with labeling anything and everything trauma. (Jor-El Caraballo, the licensed therapist I mentioned earlier, believes it's crucial to talk about these things accurately because that informs our response. "It's like overcorrecting 100 percent—never acknowledging trauma, never acknowledging the impact of things on our lives to, 'Oh, the person didn't hold the door open for me as we walked into the grocery store; that is a traumatic racial incident.' Like, no, no, no—that's not what that is. It could be hurtful, it could be racist, but that's not trauma.")

Yet the point of these stories is to exude and relish in resilience. Because within immigrant and minority communities, therapy and other mental health–related exercises can be considered inappropriate, an unaffordable luxury, or both. Cultural and/or economic conditions render mental self-health low priority. "Being a dark-skinned Black boy raised in the Bible Belt who was naturally very sensitive wasn't necessarily the easiest thing," Caraballo told me. Caraballo is in his late thirties and grew up in North Carolina. Though his family is supportive of his career, as a kid he didn't feel encouraged to talk deeply about feelings and processing emotions. He specializes in destigmatizing mental health within marginalized communities, and much of his work with clients involves deprogramming and allowing them to give themselves permission to feel sad and angry about what's happening in their lives.

Both Mallory Yu and Mariam Georgis told me their parents don't quite understand why they were in therapy. Georgis says her mom was worried that all she'd do was "complain about them." Yu describes the "idea of 'saving face' in Chinese culture. It's like the proper mask you wear in front of everyone else that hides all of your messy emotions and your imperfections.

"That is saved for within the family, behind closed doors. That's not something for anyone to see. So the idea of sharing that with 'a stranger' or speaking openly about that with other people, it's definitely not something that my parents are comfortable with."

In a 2019 article, trauma psychologist Dr. Elena Cherepanov explained to the American Psychological Association that parents who have lived under oppression often internalize "survival messages" about who to trust and how to move about the world, i.e., "Don't ask for help—it's dangerous."[15] They then pass them on to future generations, and the cycle continues.

Yet many millennials understand there's a difference between surviving and thriving. Ideas around happiness and quality of life are more openly discussed and challenged among younger people, who seem to want more for themselves than what their elders could have previously imagined. "Mei's mom, her grandma, and her family, they grew up in a different generation where they had to get rid of their pandas . . . in order to live and thrive in a harsher environment," *Turning Red*'s director Domee Shi has said. "But Mei has what they didn't have. She has this great support system of friends. She's living in a different generation, and she doesn't have to follow the same path that her mom and her family has gone down."[16]

Are We All Traumatized?

At the risk of feeding fuel to detractors who believe my generation is too obsessed with trauma, yes, I believe we're all traumatized. How can we not be? We're existing in a post-pandemic world that wasn't all that great for many reasons in pre-pandemic times.

There are degrees to trauma, of course. According to Caraballo, a helpful way to identify it is on a scale of "big T" (the result of a direct traumatic experience) to "little t" (events that "really shift you physiologically" and significantly alter your worldview). Little-t trauma, he says, can stem from something like the loss of a loved one or being a child of divorce.

Whatever the scale, it's a common experience, especially as it relates to family. No matter how great your parents are or how loving and safe your childhood might have been, it's impossible to exist in this world without having some negative experiences imprinted on you as a kid, which you then must learn to unpack and decide to hold on to or let go of as an adult. And it's almost certain that whatever that stuff might be, it will stem at least in some part from the people who raised you.

Your familial elders don't have to have been on the level of Jamie Spears or even Abuela or Jerrod Carmichael's mom for you to feel the consequences of whatever unprocessed issues or detrimental choices came before you. This may be one explanation as to why these stories of intergenerational trauma have such broad appeal beyond just millennials like myself. I see a bit of my familial history in some of these fictional characters, especially in how *Russian Doll*'s Nadia and Carmichael contend with the similarities they observe in themselves and their parents and the overprotective parenting of Mei. (Ming showing up at school and lurking behind a tree outside Mei's classroom to give her menstrual pads instantly transported me to my first few days of seventh grade when my mom insisted on following directly behind my bus because she wanted to make sure I got to my new school okay. Absolutely mortifying behavior when you're twelve and already unpopular.)

Expressing creativity through the pangs of family lineage might turn out to be a defining mode of millennial culture, right alongside satires about vapid narcissists like *Girls* and *Search Party*. If the stories continue to evolve—let's get some more dad-child representation going here and more parents who never say "I'm sorry" at the end—the genre can flourish as more than just a product of its time.

It's too early to tell what Gen-Z's dominant traumas might be and how they'll materialize within pop culture, though there's evidence to suggest they'll do so in ways that are just as unflinching, if not more so. In 2019—right before the pandemic dampened a slew of childhoods and young adulthoods—a study by the American Psychological Association concluded that Gen-Zers were the least likely to report "very good or excellent mental health" and were most likely of all current generations to report having seen a mental health professional (37 percent to millennials' 35 percent).[17] Among the most stressful concerns for Gen-Z? Mass shootings. Their cohort has no shortage of anxieties to contend with as the world spins madly and angrily forward.

9

SANTA CLAUS IS A
BLACK MAN

My first pop culture obsession was *The Little Mermaid*. I was just under two years old when it was initially released, so I don't remember seeing it in theaters. But it and pretty much all of the other "Disney animated classics" became staples in our household, as my mom would buy each new movie or rerelease from the "vault" on VHS throughout the 1990s. For whatever reason, *The Little Mermaid* was the one movie she didn't purchase; instead, we had a recording of it from a time it aired on The Disney Channel, back when they didn't show commercials in the middle of movies. But I wore that tape out probably more than any other Disney tape we had.

I was drawn to everything about it: Sebastian's literal and figurative crabbiness peppered with occasional bouts of joy and empathy,

Flounder's flightiness, Ursula's seduction. But more than anything, I wanted to be Ariel, with or without the fins (though without fins would've been preferred). The bright red hair, the clamshell bra, the handsome prince . . . yeah, by the time I was three or four, I was already fully locked in, longing to be a Disney princess. You know, a walking cliché and feminist/anti-capitalist's nightmare.

I desperately wanted an Ariel doll, because like most only children, which I was for the first 4.5 years of my life, I liked to pass the time by playing make-believe. And I wanted to play make-believe by reenacting my favorite movie of all time, *The Little Mermaid*.

Now I have no memory of receiving my first doll, but old photos of a baby me suggest that it was a Raggedy Ann that had black yarn for hair (instead of the traditional red) and deep brown cloth for skin. My Barbies were actually Christies, the Black friend of the blond icon. There were no white dolls in our house, and that was deliberate; my dad was very aware of the infamous doll tests that had been conducted by psychologists Mamie and Kenneth Clark in the 1940s, which found that in a study of more than two hundred Black kids between the ages of three and seven years old, the majority assigned positive traits to white dolls and negative traits to Black ones.[1] That study became a crucial component in the *Brown v. Board of Education* case on school desegregation.

Okay yeah, but I was a kid, so I did not know or care about all of that. I just wanted that Ariel doll so I could sing "Part of Your World" to myself all day, every day. Yet no matter how many times I begged, I was never going to own an Ariel doll.

That wasn't going to stop me from reenacting my favorite movie of all time to my little heart's content, though. Oh no. And so I went with what was, to my wildly active kid imagination, the next best thing: the part of Ariel would be played by a tissue.

More specifically, a facial tissue. A Kleenex, Scotties, Puffs, or whatever brand you use to blow your nose with when you're sick or having a good, big ol' cry. Somehow, at some point, a receptor in my brain sparked another receptor in my brain that led me to project onto that delicate inanimate object as a half-fish, half-human teenage girl who longed for legs and a fully human prince. Don't ask me to explain it. I was just a weird kid trying to make the best of a crappy situation.

All the other characters were invisible, but I had my version of Ariel, whom I scrunched up and held as if she were a doll—except she wasn't; she was a piece of tissue. My tiny fingers wrapped around her "waist" so that her top half poked out of one end of my grip and the bottom half through the other.

I'd wave her around in the air as she swam through the ocean, defying her mean, overprotective daddy, King Triton.

swish, swishhhhh, shhhhhwishhhhh (This was my sound effect for the water she was swimming in.)

"Ah-ah-ahhhhhhhhh, ah-AH-AHHHHHHHH! *KEEP SING-INNNNNGG!*" (This was the part where Ursula takes her voice.)

And then, as the sea witch snatched that voice and it came time for Ariel to lose her fins and make her way to shore, I'd take the bottom of the tissue and rip it in half. Voila. Ariel had legs!

I went through a lot of tissues for a stretch there.

Where the hell is she going with this story? you're probably wondering.

Well, I see that whole weird thing as a formative experience in the evolution of my worldview on race, gender, pop culture, and my own self-identity. And I think you can trace a direct line from my this-tissue-is-Ariel era to the moment two decades later when I decided to pitch an idea that dared to challenge the depiction of an even more emblematic fictional figure: Santa Claus.

So it's 2013: I'm twenty-five years old, and I've been at *Slate* for a little under two years. It's around the holidays, and I'd been thinking about how Santa Claus's race had been a sticking point for me as a kid, and that it seemed outdated for him to still be depicted in most places as a fat old white dude all these years later. I had memories of feeling as though the reasons my dad gave me as a child for why Santa was Black at home but white pretty much everywhere else I looked, were bunk. (He was a shape-shifter, so my dad said, who took on the race of whatever household he was visiting. Clever, but I wasn't buying it, even then.) Now I wondered, what if instead of representing him as a human, we just avoided all that race stuff and made him some other kind of creature? And what other creature would be more perfect, more beloved—the kind of creature everyone, everywhere could get behind, no problem—than a penguin?

The pitch was an instant hit in the room. I wrote the piece, making my case lightheartedly while noting the very real bias embedded in our culture's "white-as-default" approach to everything, but especially fictional characters. Someone on the art team created a fun cartoon image of a fat penguin dressed up in a Santa outfit bearing gifts.[2] The piece went out into the world in December, and while I expected some snarky pushback—because when you work at *Slate*, you're basically inviting snarky pushback anytime you publish anything—I thought it'd come and go after a day or two like most news stories do.

And then Megyn Kelly got involved.

"*. . . yet another person claiming it's racist to have a white Santa, and—by the way for all you kids watching at home: Santa just is white, but this person is just arguing that maybe we should also have a Black Santa. But you know, Santa is what he is, and just so you know, we're just debating this 'cause someone wrote about it, kids.*"[3]

On her Fox "News" show *The Kelly File*, Megyn Kelly's producers corralled a panel of Fox contributors and commentators to bring my piece "Santa Claus Should Not Be a White Man Anymore" to the attention of the entire world. To be fair to the spirit of the mostly ridiculous discussion that took place, two of the panelists, Jedediah Bila and Bernard Whitman, defended my perspective ("our social fabric can take the elasticity of Kris Kringle," the latter said) and seemed to take it all as lightheartedly as I had in my article.

But no one remembers that part, and for good reason. Kelly (and less famously, the other panelist among them, Monica Crowley) was palpably incensed by what I'd written, as if she were a small child who'd just been told that not only was Santa not real, but the Tooth Fairy and Easter Bunny were also fakes. She said I'd gone "off the rails" in suggesting Santa Penguin, and insisted, with not even a modicum of irony, that "Just because it makes you feel uncomfortable doesn't mean it has to change."

Oh yeah, and then she added: "Jesus was a white man, too."

I was not watching Fox "News" live when that three-minute segment aired, because I like myself too much and that's not something I do except for the rare occasion when my work requires me to do so. But it didn't take long to feel the debris falling my way as the thing detonated all over the internet that night. What follows next is my particular experience alone, but the gist of this sequence is probably fairly typical of what goes down for any journalist who suddenly goes viral.

1. First, the general public reacts. I was at a Brooklyn Nets game at the time, and suddenly I was getting messages from friends and colleagues excitedly sharing the news of what had transpired. I wasn't much of a Twitter person at that point yet (god, what a time), but when I went to check my page, I saw that the praise and, more acutely, the vitriol were gushing forth. Pretty standard stuff when you're a Black woman— name-calling, racist and misogynistic slurs ("n———," "bitch," and the twofer, "n———bitch"), lazy sarcasm ("Do you also think snow shouldn't be white anymore, *derp*"). DMs and emails from strangers poured in, seeking to offer me either praise or belittlement or to merely drop more of those hateful slurs into my inbox.

2. Almost simultaneously, the outlets and online commentators react. In my case, Kelly's rant was blogged about by seemingly every major news outlet and then some, the greatest hits from the segment being the factory-made quotes "Santa just *is* white" and "Jesus was a white man, too." *The Daily Show with Jon Stewart* and *The Colbert Report* each did a segment on it, as did *The Rachel Maddow Show.* Most of them pointed out the ridiculousness and racism of it all, though of course, the Fox "News"–adjacent places like *Mediaite* and *Breitbart* presented it as though Kelly was Norma Rae speaking truth to power.

3. At this point, the story has grown beyond your wildest dreams (nightmares?) and you feel as though you have to respond to the hubbub in some way formally, in a follow-up post. The day after *The Kelly File* segment aired, I wrote up another piece, this one headlined "What Fox News Doesn't Understand About Santa." My tone was barbed and annoyed, as I addressed each of Kelly's silly talking points and chided her for getting all worked up about a fictional character who'd already been completely divorced from its historical origins long ago.

4. While *that's* happening, you're probably fielding interview requests from some of those same outlets—radio shows, podcasts, TV programs. In just a matter of days, I did the biggest number of public appearances I've ever done for a single piece I've written, including *All In with Chris Hayes*, *The Today Show*, *Reliable Sources*, and NPR's *Tell Me More*.

5. Occasionally in these instances, the furor gets so heated (or the news cycle is so slow, as it usually is as Christmas approaches) that you transcend the industry news cycle and bleed into mainstream culture, too. In my case, Kelly's rant made it as far as *Saturday Night Live*'s "Weekend Update" segment, where Kenan Thompson, dressed as Santa, revealed: "You heard of Secret Santa? Well here's a secret for you: I'm Black as hell." (The segment isn't all that funny, but to have Thompson star in a skit that was inadvertently inspired by my work is a surreal and kind of cool thing to take in.)

What would normally be a one-, maybe two-day news story stretched out over the course of about a week—a week of nonstop interview requests and emails from people I hadn't spoken to in years reaching out to say they'd been following the controversy. My colleagues and bosses were thrilled; my family and friends were ecstatic and proud, marveling at my sudden brush with fame. And why wouldn't they be?

This moment gave me the kind of publicity many people dream of and spend an inordinate amount of time and effort attempting to manufacture; meanwhile, I just stumbled into this attention merely because I said I wanted Santa Claus to be a penguin. This was an unqualified win for my budding career. And I hated nearly every moment of it.

After I politely turned down a request from Don Lemon's show a few days into the cycle, the producer replied: "Thanks for reaching back, Aisha. Are you just a little 'over' the story?"

My canned response: "I'm genuinely surprised at how much attention this continues to get but definitely glad that it sparked a discussion about how our culture is represented."

• • •

A decade later, I'm more than exhausted by the ongoing discussion about cultural representation. Because frankly, it feels like déjà vu, as if little has changed. Just as there's a formula for going viral as a journalist, there's a beat-for-beat playbook for how people react to the news that a character or story they've loved (or are merely familiar with) has been reimagined as non-white, gender-flipped, or explicitly queer:

1. Group A cheers on, deeming it a "win" for representation. Group B decries it as "woke" posturing and hypocritical. *So you're saying Spider-Man can be Afro-Latino now, but if we were to make Black Panther a white dude, the libs would be up in arms? Wow, not fair!*

2. Members of Group A pen blog posts and extensive articles breaking down the latest casting controversy, highlighting some of the most garbage tweets and podcast rants from angry randos on the internet and right-wing commentators. Late-night TV talk show hosts do the same, roundly mocking Group B.

3. The performers and filmmakers on the receiving end of the vitriol must expend their energy responding to the harassment on social media while promoting their project. Their celebrity friends speak out and come to their defense. If the trolling they're experiencing is dreadful and persistent enough, perhaps they'll even write an op-ed about the whole thing in a prominent publication or quit social media altogether.

4. Eventually, the furor dies down, only to be replaced by another cycle of outrage over a different "woke" reimagining that the trolls have set their sights upon. Subsequent articles about the new outrage inevitably refer back to the previous outrage cycle, like a snake eating its own tail.

We've seen it again and again and again. The women-led reboot of *Ghostbusters*. The women-led *Ocean's 11* reboot, *Ocean's 8*. *Hamilton*.

The third *Star Wars* trilogy. *Bridgerton*. The miniseries *Anne Boleyn*, with Black performer Jodie Turner-Smith in the lead. When Hollywood plays with IP or period pieces where whiteness, maleness, and straightness have traditionally reigned supreme, certain people are gonna get angry.

The summer of 2022 saw no fewer than four examples of this play-by-play take place at the same time, as if it were a battle for which property could get racist/misogynist/homophobic people most riled up: the miniseries *A League of Their Own*, which did a complete 180 from the 1992 movie by wholeheartedly exploring queerness and Black experiences within and apart from the All-American Girls Professional Baseball League; the *Lord of the Rings* and *Game of Thrones* prequels *Rings of Power* and *House of the Dragon*, where people of color exist in relative abundance to the movies and show that preceded them; and Disney's remake of *The Little Mermaid*, which has the young Black singer Halle Bailey stepping into the fins of Ariel. (Way to go, Disney—though your newish interest in practicing inclusivity is about thirty years too late for this former tissue-flying gal!)

Every last one of these properties has fueled antagonistic reactions that hardly seem worth wasting breath upon, but *The Little Mermaid*'s detractors just might take the cake for having the most absurdist takes. "From a scientific perspective, it doesn't make a lot of sense to have someone with darker skin who lives deep in the ocean," political commentator Matt Walsh opined with regards to the "science" of the mythical mermaid creatures. "I mean, if anything, not only should the Little Mermaid be pale, she should actually be translucent. If you look at deep sea creatures, they're, like, translucent. They have no kind of pigmentation whatsoever . . . And that would actually be a version of *The Little Mermaid* that I would watch."[4]

Not as pithy as "Santa just *is* white"—workshop your catchphrases, Matt!—but you've got to hand it to him for that Olympian-grade execution of mental gymnastics. That man's mind is so twisted as to have him convinced he'd rather watch a jellyfish-colored half human than a Black half human fall in love with a prince for two hours. This is the kind of logic we're dealing with.

To be fair, when you're used to being catered to and top of mind in pretty much every sphere of life, any minor detour or change of focus is perceived as a slight. The many cultural and societal myths America has told itself over the past couple of centuries have centered whiteness at the exclusion of everyone else. Fictional characters are no different. "The readers of virtually all of American fiction have been positioned as white," wrote Toni Morrison.[5] This is how she describes "literary whiteness"—as an identity that's been taught to see itself as "universal," the default. And who would want to relinquish such a powerful status?

• • •

Trolls acting big mad about female baseball players being queer on a TV show or a half fish having melanin in a movie pales in comparison to, say, real-life laws being passed that criminalize existing while trans. But being attacked by bigots on an individual level still comes with harmful repercussions.

In 2016, there was the infamous campaign against the remake of *Ghostbusters*, which angered fanboys because it cast four women in the lead roles. Leslie Jones, the movie's sole Black lead, bore the brunt of the harassment, which included comparisons to primates and doctored sexually explicit photos. Much of the harassment was fostered and encouraged by the right-wing attention-seeker Milo Yiannopoulos (remember him?), who gleefully shared many of the disparaging tweets and even went back and forth with Jones, at one point calling her a "hammy 80s black caricature."

Jones processed all of this abuse publicly, tweeting about the toll it was taking on her mental health; eventually, she announced she was "leaving Twitter tonight with tears and a very sad heart. All this cause I did a movie."[6]

Kelly Marie Tran and John Boyega both spoke publicly about the heated, racist backlash they received after being cast in the most recent *Star Wars* trilogy, and to an extent, their narratives became consumed by that backlash. Following the uproar, both actors found their characters Rose Tico and Finn sidelined in the third movie, *The Rise of Skywalker*, ostensibly a capitulation to the loud fanboys who'd complained about their presence. As Boyega told *British GQ* in 2020: "What I would say to Disney is do not bring out a Black character, market them to be much more important in the franchise than they are, and then have them pushed to the side. It's not good. I'll say it straight up."[7]

It's all gotten so predictable some studios are now warning their minority stars to be prepared for the worst, as if any performer of color could be surprised to receive racial harassment. "It was something that Lucasfilm actually got in front of," said Moses Ingram, star of *Obi-Wan Kenobi*. "[They said to us], 'This is a thing that, unfortunately, likely will happen. But we are here to help you; you can let us know when it happens.'"[8]

I can empathize. Never in my life had I been called a n——— more times than in the aftermath of Santa Penguin. I stayed off Twitter for a while and vowed never to read the comments under my own articles ever again. (I've mostly kept that promise to myself, and my mind is the better for it.) But my inbox was harder to avoid. For every encouraging, friendly, and sweet email I received from people far and wide (Brazil, Nigeria, Belgium, etc.), there was a soul-sucking message from a willfully ignorant racist to counter it and try to knock me down a peg. I deleted most of them, including the handful of death threats, because I don't really need that kind of energy clogging up my inbox. But I preserved a few; I guess because I'm still a little masochistic.

> I think Obama should be our new Black Santa. Nobody's better than Barry at giving other people's stuff away.

Another:

> In your "blog" you said Santa, i.e. white people, were pale, melanin deficient, and pink? How about black people are the color of fecal matter and mud? He continued: Maybe you're just upset that shockingly, ¾ of negro women aren't married to their baby daddy, and 48% overall have a sexual disease. And I'll stand behind the CDC's follow-up report, not token websites like "The Root" that try to skew the truth because it's so embarrassing.

(He enclosed a link to a news report about the CDC declaring that 48 percent of all Black women have genital herpes . . . one of the most common STIs among all races and one that most people don't even realize they have. But whatever.)

DJ Khaled voice Another one:

Why are you wanting to destroy the USA? You forget that you blacks have it better in my USA than any other nation on this planet.

And another:

Your argument about Santa not being "white" and how "white" shouldn't be the default color would be easier to digest if people who share the same ideas as yourself wouldn't try to default the color to being black. How about you try to add more ethnicity to your pool, try making him Hispanic, Indian or Asian . . . You may have been part of the gifted and talent program Miss Harris but maybe missed the class on the many ethnic cultures in this country. It isn't a black or white world Miss Harris.

LOL. My dude, did you just forget that my main argument was to make Santa a penguin?! *A penguin!* So that race wouldn't be a factor at all!

Reading is fundamental.

Then there's the person who proceeded to send me multiple emails *every day* with links to articles about Black-on-Black crime and welfare queens and Obama being a monkey from conservative blogs like

Breitbart. I blocked them soon after, but to this day, whenever I go to check my spam folder for a missing email, I can see that this person is *still* sending me these links with no context, no other message, just obsessively creepy vibes.

But while I can brush these people off as miserable and pathetic, I can't help but be filled with dread and despair over the fact that such people aren't really outliers, or at the very least, they don't seem like outliers. They are loud and wrong and proud, and their collective voice can't just be tuned out easily.

It takes little to nothing to set off some people. Merely offering critique or just, you know, existing as a woman or person of color can make you a target of extreme, reactionary vitriol. It's maddening to observe and even more infuriating to be dismissed by people who have co-opted "woke" to be used disparagingly as a catchall for anyone who pushes back against conservatism and rigidity.

I blame white supremacy and conservative heteronormativity. Shocker, I know. But we wouldn't be in this mess if our culture didn't subscribe to "literary whiteness" or deeply ingrained homophobia. Had there been no precedent for exclusion, no one would feel left out for not being in the majority, and the majority wouldn't feel as though they were being "erased" just because the minority was acknowledged.

Instead, we cling to the purity of myths and legends, which are inherently meant to be fluid and malleable, revised, bent, and subverted through subsequent interpretations. Part of the issue stems from the fact that, no matter how many times or ways a piece of art is appropriated, there will always emerge a dominant version (or versions) of that art, which prevails. When it comes to narrative storytelling, the versions that tend to prevail are white. (Perhaps because Black people are widely considered to be "naturally" gifted at music, this tends to be less true when it comes to pop music—"I Will Always Love You" ceased being Dolly Parton's song as soon as Whitney Houston's heavenly pipes graced those notes, as even Dolly Parton will admit.)

This is especially true when it comes to anything Disney-related; by nature of its near-monopoly on children's entertainment—and now all-ages entertainment, thanks to owning Marvel, Fox, and everything in between—the images they've created loom large. "The Disney version becomes the definitive version," animator Glen Keane once said.[9] Which partially explains why Disney keeps creating "live-action"/CGI remakes of its previous animated successes—audiences like what is familiar, and that includes the physical appearances of their favorite heroes and villains. It also makes me wonder—Disney may have re-imagined Ariel as a Black girl with red locks for its blatant cash grab of a remake, but if a little kid visits one of the conglomerate's theme parks, will they greet an Ariel who looks like the blue-eyed 1989 version, or the 2023 version?

It's frustrating to deal with conservatives arguing nonsensically about wholly fictional pop culture, but it's downright ominous when this strident insistence counters actual historical fact. We know that Hollywood's depictions of historical events take creative liberties. Yet those narratives can become the definitive accounts, "history" lessons obscuring truths and coloring how viewers see the world. One of the more sinister examples of this is *Gone with the Wind*, a movie that's helped promote Lost Cause rhetoric to generations of viewers and valorizes slaveowners (while depicting the Black characters on the plantation as servants there of their own volition rather than en-slaved people). At a 1988 screening pegged to the movie's fiftieth anniversary, a teenager, having seen it for the first time, was quoted as saying, "I feel bad for the Southerners. Before, I just assumed that the Northerners were in there doing what was right, fighting for truth and justice. This shows that it was a matter of people's lives."[10]

More recently, Will Graham, cocreator alongside Abbi Jacobson of the new version of *A League of Their Own*, wrote a Twitter thread responding to negative reactions to the show's overtly queer and diverse characters. (Unlike the 1992 movie starring Geena Davis, this version includes teammates who hook up with each other and frequent a gay speakeasy. It also has two Latine characters on the Rockford Peaches and a Black character who's denied a spot on the team because of segregation but finds her own way to fulfill her dreams of playing ball. They really went all out with this.) Providing the receipts (links to articles, etc.), he wrote in part, "For those saying that there were not Latine players in the [All-American Girls Professional Baseball League], I'd like to introduce you to Marge Villa, an incredible utility player of Mexican descent."[11] He eventually concluded, "What we're showing here isn't a revision of the story, it's not woke, it's not adding anything for contemporary audiences. This is, simply, the real story." Decades' worth of ignoring these stories in pop culture have made it that much harder for audiences to accept their veracity when they are finally presented with it.

• • •

On October 26, 2018, while minding my own damn business, I received two texts from a number with a Cleveland area code. The only thing they said was "n———" and "white Santa." It was super random and jarring. Who the heck even found my number, and why, nearly five years later, was this what I was getting targeted for?

This was the same day it was announced Megyn Kelly's NBC talk show had been canceled following remarks she'd made on air a few days earlier in support of using blackface for Halloween costumes. (Also, apparently, "Her weak ratings lagged those of the *Today* hosts she replaced.")[12] Clearly, all this time later, Santa Penguin was still able to touch a nerve. The myth of his whiteness dies hard.

Though it *is* dying, even if it's a slow demise: In 2021, Disney's US theme parks cast Black performers as Santa Claus for the very first time.[13]

And I was out of college by the time Disney introduced its first Black animated princess in *The Princess and the Frog*. (It definitely was not lost on me that she spent much of that movie as a frog! But we took what we could get back then.)

Today, Black kids have more characters to choose from than ever before, so it's moving (and heartbreaking) to watch viral videos of parents recording their Black children as they laid eyes upon Halle Bailey as Ariel in the trailer for *The Little Mermaid*.

"She's Black?" says one girl. "Yay!"

"She's brown like me," exclaims another.[14]

The joy, the recognition, the kinship these kids are finding in this new version of the character makes me so happy for them but also a little bit sad for my younger self, who didn't get to have this experience.

While writing the Santa piece, I'd emailed my dad asking him to send me a column he'd written for our local paper *The New Haven Register*, when I was just shy of three years old, titled "Black Kids Need a

Black Santa." In some ways, my article echoed his own, though his was from the perspective of a father imagining a more inclusive world for his daughter. He wrote about wanting to make sure I grew up with a "healthy image" of myself: "I do not want her to become one of those statistics that show Black children preferring white dolls to the dolls that look like them."[15]

He and my mom tried their best from the very beginning, and yet I still wound up wishing I had Ariel's red hair and clamshell bra and longing for an Ariel doll I could call my own. I never got it, so I made her into an image I could call my own, one that looked neither like her, nor like me, nor, for that matter, anything remotely close to human— or fish. (One more time for the back: It was a piece of tissue! My god, I was a weird yet impressively resourceful kid.)

In hindsight, I'm grateful my dad stuck to his stance and never purchased a white doll for me. It didn't exactly quell the pangs of desire I'd feel over the years of being able to wear my hair or do my makeup the way my white friends did theirs. (My mom caved in to my sister once, when she pleaded for a Baby Spice doll, but that thing lasted all of two days in our house before my dad insisted we go back to the store and exchange it for a Scary Spice doll instead.) My parents' best intentions couldn't triumph over the impossible beauty standards and overwhelmingly white representation that I encountered throughout the 1990s and into the 2000s. That's the power of white supremacy.

But that doesn't mean we should just give up on trying to resist that power; eventually it will (hopefully) be drowned out. There's this book I had when I was a kid—*Amazing Grace*, about a young Black girl who "just loved stories," like Joan of Arc and Anansi the spider. One day in class, the teacher announces they're going to put on the play *Peter Pan*, and Grace is determined to play the lead. But two classmates tell her she can't be Peter because "that's a boy's name" and "he isn't Black."

She goes home defeated, but her Nana is unfazed. She takes Grace to the local production of the ballet *Romeo & Juliet*, which features a Trinidadian dancer as Juliet. "I can be anything I want," Grace says to herself afterward.[16]

The point is, Grace is ultimately inspired to ignore her classmates and wins the part of Peter, and everybody—even her original naysayers—ends up agreeing she was the perfect person for the role. Is this a rather simple depiction of how things actually go down in the real world? Absolutely. Does it depict the power of reflection and representation and how it can be wielded for good, especially if you have a strong support group in your corner? Absolutely.

Ultimately, the strong guiding voices in my life—my parents, mentors, professors, and the bright, fierce critical minds I've encountered in my studies and career—would come into focus, even if it took some time to push through all the other mess. And growing up, there were movies and shows like the Brandy-starring *Cinderella* and *Living Single* that helped tip the scales a bit toward my developing pride in who I was. It wasn't a lot, but it had to be enough. These things helped me question who our society tends to prioritize once I entered adulthood, to look beyond whiteness and find self-acceptance in all realms of my life. And they indirectly led me to write about Santa and default whiteness and dream up Santa Penguin.

In a *New York Times* op-ed addressing the vitriol she faced from the most insidious corner of the *Star Wars* fanbase, Kelly Marie Tran wrote, "The same society that taught some people they were heroes, saviors, inheritors of the Manifest Destiny ideal, taught me I existed only in the background of their stories, doing their nails, diagnosing their illnesses, supporting their love interests—and perhaps the most damaging—waiting for them to rescue me.

"And for a long time, I believed them."[17]

Believing the lie will crush your spirit. And for a while, I believed the lie, too—the lie that my name, Aisha, needed some sort of profound (to me) backstory in order to be acceptable. The lie that I had to play Hollywood's version of the Black Best Friend to get white people to like me. The lie that I had to "act" like a man to experience equality with men. (Steve Harvey is a relationship coach hack!) So many unacceptable fictions were served up to me on a platter throughout my impressionable youth that I now know to send them straight back to the kitchen in demand of a new plate.

My spirit's no longer crushed, and I no longer wish to be anything other than who I am. Okay, maybe that's not totally true—I remain an incurable ball of anxiety in this post-pandemic world, and I still wish I was a little bit taller. (Did I mention I once dreamed of becoming a Rockette? I'm five foot one and shrinking by the day.) But what I mean is, I feel mostly comfortable in my skin these days. There is no doubt that immersion in pop culture had a lot to do with all the pain and insecurity I experienced back then. Yet it's also helped me emerge as a stronger, clearer-eyed version of myself.

Isn't that lovely?

Acknowledgments

I am both a procrastinator and a workaholic—which probably explains why it took me so very long to write this book. So I'd first like to acknowledge (and apologize to) every friend or family member I've encountered in the last few years who's had to hear me complain about the grueling process of writing a book, or has had me cancel or skip an important event or casual hang because I was writing a book. Your patience with me is greatly appreciated. I'm back, baby—I'm no longer writing a book!

I'm likewise grateful to my very patient editor, Daniella Wexler, whose out-of-the-blue email just a few weeks prior to the start of the pandemic inspired me to finally sit down and seriously consider writing a book, and to my very reassuring agent, Alia Hanna Habib. You've both helped shape this project in invaluable ways and I couldn't be happier with this collaboration.

There are a lot of people who contributed to my writing, research, and reporting in significant ways, and I so appreciate the time they took out of their equally busy lives to assist me with this project, including Jennifer Parker, Jenée Desmond-Harris, Odie Henderson, Kwame Opam, Antonia Cereijido, Natalie Hopkinson, Mallory Yu, Mariam Georgis, Jor-El Caraballo, Linda Holmes, and Marcia Abramson.

Of course, I must express gratitude for both of my parents—even if you are not nearly as pop culture–obsessed as I am, you are a huge part of how I became this way. If it weren't for all that early exposure to Motown, Turner Classic Movies, and yes, Kenny G, I probably would've turned out a very different person. Also, you've both always encouraged me to pursue the things I've loved, even though the things I love do not easily translate into lucrative employment—so thank you for all the many hours you spent shuttling me to various dance lessons and competitions, soccer/baseball games, voice lessons, and theater rehearsals, and not scoffing when I decided to get degrees in theater and cinema studies.

A very special thanks to my pups, Lucy and (Liz) Lemon, who have spent countless hours by my side as I composed this book, awaiting treats and belly rubs.

And finally, a very special thanks to my partner, Ari, who now understands firsthand what it's like to be with an anxious-depressive writer who needs to be reminded of when to sleep, hydrate, and take a break in her darkest of creative modes. (And I only listen mayyyybe 40 percent of the time. Still working on it.) You've cooked an untold number of meals and talked me through writer's block and done your best to make this entire process easier for me (and you), and this has not gone unappreciated by me. I probably could've written this book without your love and support, but it would've been *rough*. And why would I want to do that anyway?

Notes

Introduction

1. Roger Ebert, *"La Dolce Vita,"* January 5, 1997, https://www.rogerebert.com/reviews/great-movie-la-dolce-vita-1960.

1: Isn't She Lovely

1. Justin Pope, "'Black' Names a Resume Burden?," *CBS News*, September 29, 2003, https://www.cbsnews.com/news/black-names-a-resume-burden.
2. Stanley Lieberson, Kelly S. Mikelson, "Distinctive African American Names: An Experimental, Historical, and Linguistic Analysis of Innovation," *American Sociological Review* 60, no. 6 (December 1995): 930.
3. Lieberson, Mikelson, "Distinctive African American Names," 940.
4. Roland G. Fryer, Steven D. Levitt, "The Causes and Consequences of Distinctively Black Names," *The Quarterly Journal of Economics* 119, no. 3 (August 2004): 770.
5. Alex Haley, *Roots: The Saga of an American Family* (Boston: Da Capo Press, 2014), 2.
6. Stephanie Merry, "The Story Behind Why Prince Changed His Name to a Symbol," *The Washington Post*, April 22, 2016, https://www.washingtonpost.com/news/arts-and-entertainment/wp/2016/04/22/the-story-behind-why-prince-changed-his-name-to-a-symbol.
7. Robert D. McFadden, "Some Points of *Roots* Questioned; Haley Stands By Book as a Symbol." *New York Times*, April 10, 1977.
8. Arnold H. Lubasch, *"Roots* Plagiarism Suit Is Settled," *New York Times*, December 15, 1978.
9. Jervis Anderson, "Alex Haley's *Roots," The New Yorker*, February 6, 1977, https://www.newyorker.com/magazine/1977/02/14/sources.
10. McFadde, "Some Points."
11. Daniel Hautzinger, "From the Archive: Alex Haley of *Roots," WTTW*, October 9, 2018, https://interactive.wttw.com/playlist/2018/10/08/archive-alex-haley-author-roots.

2: Blackety-Black

1. https://www.avclub.com/adam-mckay-responds-to-backlash-to-his-response-to-the-1848357754

2. André Wheeler, "'Make Films Where Black Characters Don't Die': *Queen & Slim* Sparks Debate Over 'Trauma Porn,'" *The Guardian*, December 4, 2019, https://www.theguarian .com/film/2019/dec/04/queen-slim-lena-waithe-controversy.

3. "Red Tails," Box Office Mojo, https://www.boxofficemojo.com/release/rl1265468929.

4. "George Lucas," *The Daily Show with Jon Stewart*, https://www.cc.com/video/j67j6n/the -daily-show-with-jon-stewart-george-lucas.

5. Stephen Holden, "Pilots Who Sought to Soar Above Racism," *New York Times*, January 19, 2012, https://www.nytimes.com/2012/01/20/movies/red-tails-george-lucass-tale-of-tuskegee -airmen-review.html.

6. Marisol Bello, "Film on Tuskegee Airmen Gets Boost from Activists," *USA Today*, February 7, 2012, https://www.pressreader.com/usa/usa-today-international-edition/20120207 /284812167935927.

7. Jeremy Fuster, "*Eternals*: Best and Worst Case Box Office Scenarios After $71 Million Launch," *The Wrap*, November 7, 2021, https://www.thewrap.com/eternals-box-office-second-weekend-2.

8. Gene Demby, "Remember When You Had to Flip to the Back Page of *Jet* to Find Black People on TV?" National Public Radio, September 23, 2015, https://www.npr.org/sections /codeswitch/2015/09/23/442191706/remember-when-you-had-to-flip-to-the-back-page-of -jet-to-find-black-people-on-tv.

9. David Denby, "He's Gotta Have It," *New York*, June 26, 1989.

10. Alessandra Stanley, "Wrought in Rhimes's Image," *New York Times*, September 18, 2014, https://www.nytimes.com/2014/09/21/arts/television/viola-davis-plays-shonda-rhimess -latest-tough-heroine.html.

11. Peter Debruge, "*Girls Trip*," *Variety*, July 12, 2017, https://variety.com/2017/film/reviews /girls-trip-review-queen-latifah-tiffany-haddish-1202493340.

12. bell hooks, "Artistic Integrity," in *Reel to Real* (New York: Routledge Classics, 2009), 88.

13. William B. Collins, "Black Film Puzzle: Is *Sounder* the Answer?," *Philadelphia Inquirer*, October 29, 1972.

14. Clifford Mason, "Why Does White America Love Sidney Poitier So?," *New York Times*, September 10, 1967, https://archive.nytimes.com/www.nytimes.com/packages/html/movies /bestpictures/heat-ar.html.

15. James Baldwin, "The Devil Finds Work," in *James Baldwin: Collected Essays*, edited by Toni Morrison (Library Classics of the United States, 1998), 492.

16. Baldwin, "Devil Finds Work," 525.

17. bell hooks, "Mock Feminism: *Waiting to Exhale*," in *Reel to Real*, 74.

3: I'm a Cool Girl

1. "MTV Explains Decision to Pull Prodigy," *MTV News*, December 22, 1997, https://www .mtv.com/news/xpjl88/mtv-explains-decision-to-pull-prodigy.

2. Richard Harrington, "Critics 'Smack' MTV's Prodigy Video," *The Washington Post*, December 10, 1997, https://www.washingtonpost.com/archive/lifestyle/1997/12/10/critics-smack -mtvs-prodigy-video/e3b8a291-9cb0-450f-9a89-09c693e6a59b.

3. Michael Goldberg, "Prodigy Defense of 'Smack My Bitch Up,'" *MTV News*, December 5, 1997, http://www.mtv.com/news/cxa1hz/prodigy-defense-of-smack-my-bitch-up

4. Danika Maia, "The 'Smack My Bitch Up' Video Was Inspired by a Crazy Night Out in Copenhagen," *Vice*, November 18, 2014, https://www.vice.com/en/article/bn5aa8/we-heard -the-music-video-for-smack-my-bitch-up-was-about-a-night.

Notes

5. Katha Pollitt, "Hers; The Smurfette Principle," *New York Times*, April 7, 1991, https://www
   .nytimes.com/1991/04/07/magazine/hers-the-smurfette-principle.html.
6. bell hooks, "Power to the Pussy: We Don't Wannabe Dicks in Drag," in *Outlaw Culture*
   (New York: Routledge Classics, 1994), 25.
7. hooks, "Power to the Pussy," 25.

4: Kenny G Gets It

1. Andrew Tudor, *Image and Influence: Studies in the Sociology of Film* (New York: Routledge
   Library Editions: Cinema, 2014).
2. Jaclyn Peiser, "Fans Told Lizzo a Word in Her Song Was Offensive. She Changed the Lyrics,"
   The Washington Post, June 14, 2022, https://www.washingtonpost.com/nation/2022/06/14
   /lizzo-ableist-slur-lyric-apology.
3. Emily Yahr, "Taylor Swift's Stunning Statement: Famously Apolitical Star Slams Tennessee Republican, Endorses Democrats," *The Washington Post*, October 7, 2018, https://www
   .washingtonpost.com/arts-entertainment/2018/10/08/taylor-swifts-stunning-statement
   -famously-apolitical-star-slams-tennessee-republican-endorses-democrats.
4. Edwin Ortiz, "Drake Donates $100,000 to National Bail Out Collective," *Complex*, June 1,
   2020, https://www.complex.com/music/2020/06/drake-donates-100000-national-bail-out.
5. Dan Evon, "Did Eminem Kneel in Defiance at the Super Bowl?," Snopes, February 14, 2022,
   https://www.snopes.com/fact-check/eminem-knee-super-bowl.
6. Ken Belson, "NFL Was 'Aware' Eminem Planned to Kneel During Halftime Performance,"
   New York Times, February 13, 2022, https://www.nytimes.com/2022/02/13/sports/football
   /nfl-eminem-kneel-super-bowl-halftime.html.
7. *The Recount* (@TheRecount), "Eminem taking a knee for Kaepernick?," Twitter, February 13,
   2022, https://twitter.com/therecount/status/1493034072318296072.
8. Christopher Brito, "Eminem Takes a Knee During Super Bowl Halftime Show," *CBS News*,
   February 14, 2022, https://www.cbsnews.com/news/super-bowl-halftime-eminem-kneeling.
9. https://twitter.com/OccupyDemocrats/status/1493041337100234752.
10. "Americans Going Online . . . Explosive Growth, Uncertain Destinations," Pew Research
    Center, October 16, 1995, https://www.pewresearch.org/politics/1995/10/16/americans
    -going-online-explosive-growth-uncertain-destinations.
11. Alex Kuczynski, "Hold Me! Squeeze Me! Buy a Six-Pack!," *New York Times*, November 16,
    1997, https://www.nytimes.com/1997/11/16/style/hold-me-squeeze-me-buy-a-6-pack.html.
12. Lev Grossman, "You—Yes, You—Are TIME's Person of the Year," *TIME*, December 25,
    2006, https://web.archive.org/web/20120305133252/http://www.time.com/time/magazine
    /article/0,9171,1570810,00.html.
13. Joe Coscarelli, "How Pop Music Fandom Became Sports, Politics, Religion, and All-Out
    War," *New York Times*, December 25, 2020, https://www.nytimes.com/2020/12/25/arts
    /music/pop-music-superfans-stans.html.
14. Kat Bouza, "Rolling Loud: Kid Cudi Walks Offstage as Kanye Appears with Lil Durk,"
    Rolling Stone, July 23, 2022, https://www.rollingstone.com/music/music-news/rolling-loud
    -kid-cudi-kanye-west-lil-durk-1387184.
15. El Jefe (@guapgetterjeff), "We wanted @kanyewest anyway . . . . @KiDCuDi you soft," Twitter, July 23, 2022, https://twitter.com/guapgetterjeff/status/1550692206989688883.
16. Kurrco (@Kurrco), "The crowd was chanting 'Kanye' as Cudi was leaving . . . cmon man," Twitter, July 22, 2022, https://twitter.com/Kurrco/status/1550687558186803201.

17. Chris Lee, "Beyond the Creepy Teeth: How *Sonic the Hedgehog* Saved Itself," *Vulture*, February 14, 2020, https://www.vulture.com/2020/02/the-sonic-the-hedgehog-controversy-and -redesign-explained.html.
18. Walt Hickey, "*Ghostbusters* Is a Perfect Example of How Internet Movie Ratings Are Broken," July 14, 2016, https://fivethirtyeight.com/features/ghostbusters-is-a-perfect-example -of-how-internet-ratings-are-broken.
19. Kyle Chayka, "Can Monoculture Survive the Algorithm?," Vox, December 17, 2019, https:// www.vox.com/the-goods/2019/12/17/21024439/monoculture-algorithm-netflix-spotify.
20. Sean O'Connell, "In Pixar's Latest Comedy, Girls Just Wanna Have Fur," *Cinema Blend*, March 8, 2022, http://web.archive.org/web/20220307192648/https://www.cinemablend .com/movies/disneys-turning-red-review-in-pixars-latest-comedy-girls-just-wanna-have-fur.
21. Anastasia Tsioulcas, "Warner Bros. Kills Off *Batgirl* Movie, $90 Million In," National Public Radio, August 3, 2022, https://www.npr.org/2022/08/03/1115380005/warner -bros-kills-off-batgirl-movie-90-million-in.
22. Emma Nolan, "All the Times Mel Gibson Has Been Accused of Anti-Semitism and Racism," *Newsweek*, June 23, 2020, https://www.newsweek.com/mel-gibson-anti-semitism-racism -accusations-1512808.
23. William Earl, "Winona Ryder Accuses Mel Gibson of Making Anti-Semitic and Homophobic Remarks," *Variety*, June 23, 2020, https://variety.com/2020/film/news/winona-ryder -mel-gibson-oven-dodger-1234646288.
24. Kat Tenbarge, "YouTube Creators Are Pivoting Their Videos to Depp v. Heard Content and Raking in Millions of Views," NBC News, May 13, 2022, https://www.nbcnews.com/tech /internet/amber-heard-trial-depp-youtube-content-platform-algorithm-tiktok-rcna28016.
25. House Judiciary GOP (@JudiciaryGOP), Twitter photo, June 1, 2022, https://twitter.com /JudiciaryGOP/status/1532081904601669632.
26. Benjamin VanHoose, "Amber Heard Returns to Stand, Expresses 'Torture' of Online Mockery, Threats: 'I'm a Human Being,'" *People*, May 26, 2022, https://people.com/movies /amber-heard-returns-to-stand-talks-pain-of-johnny-depp-trial.
27. Jessica Wang, "Johnny Depp's Texts About Amber Heard's 'Rotting Corpse' Revealed During Defamation Trial," *Entertainment Weekly*, April 13, 2022, https://ew.com/celebrity /johnny-depp-text-messages-amber-heard-rotting-corpse-defamation-trial.
28. Anya Zoledziowski, "'I Will Fuck Her Burnt Corpse,': Johnny Depp's Violent Texts Surface During Trial," *Vice*, April 21, 2022, https://www.vice.com/en/article/y3v7mw/johnny -depp-cross-examination-texts-trial.
29. Kelsey Weekman, "Here's a List of All the Celebs Who Liked Johnny Depp's Instagram Statement," BuzzFeed News, June 2, 2022, https://www.buzzfeednews.com/article/kelsey weekman/johnny-depps-instagram-statement-liked-by-celebrities.
30. Gene Maddaus, "Why Was Depp-Heard Trial Televised? Critics Call It 'Single Worst Decision' for Sexual Violence Victims," *Variety*, May 27, 2022, https://variety.com/2022/film /news/johnny-depp-amber-heard-cameras-courtroom-penney-azcarate-1235280060.

5: Ebony & Ivory

1. Jonathon Green, "all that," *Green's Dictionary of Slang*, https://greensdictofslang.com/entry /ktfqsua#yGAAVMB0QdcUYZRR2ckAARPiFh-Jldnl.
2. George Fitzhugh, "Negro Slavery," in *Sociology for the South, or the Failure of Free Society* (Richmond, VA: A Morris, 1854).
3. Mark Twain, *The Adventures of Huckleberry Finn* (New York: Random House: 2010).

4. Twain, *Huckleberry Finn.*
5. Toni Morrison, *Playing in the Dark: Whiteness and the Literary Imagination* (New York: Vintage Books, 1992), 56.
6. Marsha E. Williams, John C. Condry, "Living Color: Minority Portrayals and Cross-Racial Interactions on Television," April 1989, https://files.eric.ed.gov/fulltext/ED307025.pdf.
7. Katie Storey, "*New Girl*'s Lamorne Morris Praises Show Writers for Addressing Police Brutality After He Started to Feel 'Weird' About Winston Being a Cop," *Metro*, June 3, 2020, https://metro.co.uk/2020/06/03/new-girl-lamorne-morris-felt-weird-winston-cop-praises -writers-address-police-brutality-12799987.
8. Twain, *Huckleberry Finn.*
9. Jose A. Del Real, "Some White People Are Pouring Out Their Hearts and Sending Money to Their Black Acquaintances," *The Washington Post*, June 6, 2020, https://www.washingtonpost .com/national/well-meaning-white-people-are-pouring-out-their-hearts--and-sending-money --to-their-black-friends/2020/06/06/05abc402-a67d-11ea-bb20-ebf0921f3bbd_story.html.
10. Chad Sanders, "I Don't Need 'Love' Texts from My White Friends," *New York Times*, June 5, 2020, https://www.nytimes.com/2020/06/05/opinion/whites-anti-blackness-protests.html.
11. David Margolick, "Through a Lens, Darkly," *Vanity Fair*, September 24, 2007, https://www .vanityfair.com/news/2007/09/littlerock200709.
12. Christopher Ingraham, "Three Quarters of Whites Don't Have Any Non-White Friends," *The Washington Post*, August 25, 2014, https://www.washingtonpost.com/news/wonk/wp /2014/08/25/three-quarters-of-whites-dont-have-any-non-white-friends.

6: This Is IP That Never Ends

1. Will Thorne, "*Parasite* Limited Series from Bong Joon Ho, Adam McKay in the Works at HBO," *Variety*, January 9, 2020, https://variety.com/2020/tv/news/parasite-hbo-limited -series-bong-joon-ho-adam-mckay-1203462319.
2. Josef Adalian, "How HBO Got to Yes on *Big Little Lies* Season 2," *New York*, December 8, 2017, https://www.vulture.com/2017/12/big-little-lies-season-2-why-hbo-decided-to-renew -it.html.
3. Chris Evans (@ChrisEvans), "And just to be clear, this isn't Buzz Lightyear the toy. This is the origin story of the human Buzz Lightyear that the toy is based on," Twitter, December 10, 2020, https://twitter.com/chrisevans/status/1337204197641629696?lang=en.
4. Isis Briones, "This *Jane the Virgin* Star Would Definitely Do a Show Reunion," *Forbes*, December 20, 2019, https://www.forbes.com/sites/isisbriones/2019/12/20/justina-machado -jane-the-virgin-puerto-rico/?sh=3ac738504394.
5. Carolyn Jess-Cooke, *Film Sequels: Theory and Practice From Hollywood to Bollywood* (Edinburgh, Edinburgh University Press, 2009), 16.
6. Jess-Cooke, *Film Sequels*, 20.
7. Jess-Cooke, *Film Sequels*, 23.
8. Frank S. Nugent, "Consider the Sequel," *New York Times*, May 31, 1936.
9. Rund Abdelfatah, Ramtin Arablouei, Julie Caine, Laine Kaplan-Levenson, Lawrence Wu, Victor Yvellez, Adriana Tapia, Miranda Mazariegos, Anya Steinberg, "The Nostalgia Bone," Naitonal Public Radio, October 14, 2021, https://www.npr.org/2021/10/13/1045812865 /the-nostalgia-bone.
10. Victor Hugo, *The Hunchback of Notre Dame*, translated by Isabel F. Hapgood (Project Gutenberg, April 2001), https://www.gutenberg.org/files/2610/2610-h/2610-h.htm#link 2HCH0014.

11. Abdelfatah et al., "Nostalgia Bone."
12. HRTVFan2, "1992 McDonald's Commercial Happy Meal (Nostalgia)," YouTube video, March 5, 2019, https://www.youtube.com/watch?v=QSgrIUV7GzA.
13. IMDbPro, "2016 Worldwide Box Office," https://www.boxofficemojo.com/year/world/2016.
14. IMDbPro, "2017 Worldwide Box Office," https://www.boxofficemojo.com/year/world/2017.
15. IMDbPro, "2018 Worldwide Box Office," https://www.boxofficemojo.com/year/world/2018.
16. IMDbPro, "2019 Worldwide Box Office," https://www.boxofficemojo.com/year/world/2019.
17. "U.S. Dept. of Retro Warns: 'We May Be Running Out of Past,'" *The Onion*, November 4, 1997, https://www.theonion.com/u-s-dept-of-retro-warns-we-may-be-running-out-of-pas-1819 564513.
18. Alex Ritman, "James Dean Reborn in CGI for Vietnam War Action-Drama," November 6, 2019, https://www.hollywoodreporter.com/movies/movie-news/afm-james-dean-reborn -cgi-vietnam-war-action-drama-1252703.
19. Friedrich Nietzsche, *The Gay Science: With a Prelude in Rhymes and an Appendix of Songs*, translated by Walter Kaufmann (New York: Vintage Books, 1974).

7: On the Procreation Expectation

1. Randall Balmer, "The Religious Right and the Abortion Myth," *Politico*, May 10, 2022, https://www.politico.com/news/magazine/2022/05/10/abortion-history-right-white -evangelical-1970s-00031480.
2. "In U.S., Decline of Christianity Continues at Rapid Pace," Pew Research Center, October 17, 2019, https://www.pewresearch.org/religion/2019/10/17/in-u-s-decline-of-christianity -continues-at-rapid-pace.
3. Jennifer Senior, "All Joy and No Fun," *New York*, July 2, 2010, https://nymag.com/news /features/67024.
4. Amy Cheng, "Don't Choose Pets Over Children, Pope Francis Says as Birthrates Drop," January 6, 2022, https://www.washingtonpost.com/world/2022/01/06/pope-francis-pet -children-selfish.
5. Anna Brown, "Growing Share of Childless Adults in U.S. Don't Expect to Ever Have Children," Pew Research Center, November 19, 2021, https://www.pewresearch.org/fact -tank/2021/11/19/growing-share-of-childless-adults-in-u-s-dont-expect-to-ever-have -children.
6. I Regret Having Children, Facebook group, https://www.facebook.com/IRegretHaving Children.
7. Jill Filipovic, "The Things We Don't Discuss," Substack, May 11, 2021, https://jill.sustack .com/p/the-things-we-dont-discuss.
8. Ayelet Waldman, "Truly, Madly, Guiltily," *New York Times*, March 27, 2005, https://www .nytimes.com/2005/03/27/fashion/truly-madly-guiltily.html.
9. Penelope Green, "Looking for the 'Bad Mother'? She's Still Here," *New York Times*, November 7, 2017, https://www.nytimes.com/2017/11/07/style/modern-love-looking-for-the-bad -mother-shes-still-here.html.
10. Ariana Romero, "The *Catastrophe* Series Finale Was Supposed to Blindside You—Here's Why," *Refinery29*, March 15, 2019, https://www.refinery29.com/en-us/2019/03/227182/ catastrophe-amazon-season-4-episode-6-ending-recap.

8: Parents Just Don't Understand

1. "Britney Spears Leaves Fans in Fits Over Funny Story Time About Her Clumsy Dog: 'One of Those Moments,'" *The News*, April 8, 2022, https://www.thenews.com.pk/latest/948439 -britney-spears-leaves-fans-in-fits-over-funny-story-time-about-her-clumsy-dog-one-of -those-moments.

2. Julia Jacobs, "Britney Spears, Out of Conservatorship, Says 'I'm Having a Baby,'" *New York Times*, April 11, 2022, https://www.nytimes.com/2022/04/11/arts/music/britney-spears -pregnant.html.

3. Leyla Mohammed, "Britney Spears Slammed Her Family with a Brutal Post About Being 'Drugged,' 'Threatened,' and 'Seen Naked When Changing' Under the Conservatorship, and Said She 'Won't Stop' Until She Gets Justice," BuzzFeed News, March 7, 2022, https://www .buzzfeednews.com/article/leylamohammed/britney-spears-drugged-conservatorship.

4. Julia Jacobs, Sarah Bahr, "The Britney Spears Transcript, Annotated: 'Hear What I Have to Say," *New York Times*, June 24, 2021, https://www.nytimes.com/2021/06/24/arts/music /britney-spears-transcript.html.

5. Kaitlin Reilly, "Britney Spears Says her Father Jamie Made Her Feel 'Ugly': 'I Was Fat and Never Good Enough,'" *Yahoo!*, May 4, 2022, https://www.yahoo.com/lifestyle/britney -spears-jamie-spears-criticized-weight-confidence-beauty-163332785.html.

6. Bruce Haring, "Britney Spears Vents on Instagram While Celebrating an Early Christmas," *Deadline*, October 15, 2021, https://deadline.com/2021/10/britney-spears-vents-instagram -early-christmas-celebration-1234856867.

7. Mohammed, "Britney Spears."

8. Peggy Drexler, "Millennials Are the Therapy Generation," *Wall Street Journal*, March 1, 2019, https://www.wsj.com/articles/millennials-are-the-therapy-generation-11551452286.

9. Lexi Pandell, "How Trauma Became the Word of the Decade," Vox, January 25, 2022, https://www.vox.com/the-highlight/22876522/trauma-covid-word-origin-mental-health.

10. Janet Jacobs, *The Holocaust Across Generations: Trauma and Its Inheritance Among Descendants of Survivors* (New York: NYU Press, 2016), 115.

11. Jacobs, *Holocaust Across Generations*, 122.

12. Rachel Syme, "In *Russian Doll*, Natasha Lyonne Barrels Into the Past," *New Yorker*, April 4, 2022, https://www.newyorker.com/magazine/2022/04/11/in-russian-doll-natasha-lyonne -barrels-into-the-past.

13. Daniel Kwan (@dunkwun), "Movies can change lives." Twitter, April 8, 2022, https:// twitter.com/dunkwun/status/1512496779098423296?s=20&t=MZxFOWkYZf3HaoFP mpRDBg.

14. Michael R. Jackson, *A Strange Loop* (Theater Communications Group, 2020), 82.

15. Tori DeAngelis, "The Legacy of Trauma," American Psychological Association 50, no. 2 (February 2019), https://www.apa.org/monitor/2019/02/legacy-trauma.

16. Tyler Treese, "*Turning Red* Interview: Director Domee Shi Discusses Film's Depiction of Intergenerational Trauma," Coming Soon, April 21, 2022, https://www.comingsoon .net/movies/features/1218994-interview-turning-red-director-domee-shi-generational -trauma.

17. Sophie Bethune, "Gen-Z More Likely to Report Mental Health Concerns," American Psychological Association 50, no. 1 (January 2019), https://www.apa.org/monitor/2019/01 /gen-z.

9: Santa Claus Is a Black Man

1. Leila McNeill, "How a Psychologist's Work on Race Identity Helped Overturn School Segregation in 1950s America," *Smithsonian Magazine*, October 26, 2017, https://www.smithsonianmag.com/science-nature/psychologist-work-racial-identity-helped-overturn-school-segregation-180966934.

2. Aisha Harris, "Santa Claus Should Not Be a White Man Anymore," *Slate*, December 10, 2013, https://slate.com/human-interest/2013/12/santa-claus-an-old-white-man-not-anymore-meet-santa-the-penguin-a-new-christmas-symbol.html.

3. *Slate*, "Megyn Kelly: Jesus and Santa Were White!," YouTube video, June 18, 2018, https://www.youtube.com/watch?v=vQXaP6Fm3F0.

4. Jason Campbell (@JasonSCampbell), "Daily Wire host says it is unscientific to cast a Black person as a mermaid," Twitter, September 14, 2022, https://twitter.com/JasonSCampbell/status/1570156771016065025.

5. Morrison, *Playing in the Dark*, xii.

6. Mike Isaac, "Twitter Bars Milo Yiannopoulos in Wake of Leslie Jones's Reports of Abuse," *New York Times*, July 20, 2016, https://www.nytimes.com/2016/07/20/technology/twitter-bars-milo-yiannopoulos-in-crackdown-on-abusive-comments.html.

7. Jimi Famurewa, "John Boyega: 'I'm the Only Cast Member Whose Experience of *Star Wars* Was Based on Their Race,'" *GQ*, September 2, 2020, https://www.gq-magazine.co.uk/culture/article/john-boyega-interview-2020.

8. Louis Chilton, "Obi-Wan Kenobi's Moses Ingram: 'If You've Got Talking Droids and Aliens But No People of Colour, It Doesn't Make Sense,'" *Independent*, May 22, 2022, https://www.independent.co.uk/arts-entertainment/tv/features/obi-wan-kenobi-moses-ingram-interview-b2088811.html.

9. Jason Cochran, "Pocahontas Needed an Ethnic Look," *Entertainment Weekly*, June 16, 1995, https://ew.com/article/1995/06/16/pocahontas-needed-ethnic-look.

10. Mary T. Schmich, "At This Theater, You'd Better Give a Damn," *Chicago Tribune*, December 13, 1988.

11. Will Graham (@WillWGraham), "We've had such an amazing positive first 4 days for the show, but predictably there are some people who are trolling the show," Twitter, August 16, 2022, https://twitter.com/WillWGraham/status/1559749097862492160.

12. John Koblin, Michael M. Grynbaum, "Megyn Kelly's Crash at NBC in One Word (Hers): 'Wow,'" *New York Times*, October 26, 2018, https://www.nytimes.com/2018/10/26/business/media/megyn-kelly-today-canceled-nbc.html.

13. Natasha Chen, "Black Santas Are Appearing in U.S. Disney Parks This Season for the First Time," CNN Travel, November 19, 2021, https://www.cnn.com/travel/article/black-santa-disney-parks/index.html.

14. Remy Tumin, "A New Ariel Inspires Joy for Young Black Girls: 'She Looks Like Me,'" *New York Times*, September 14, 2022, https://www.nytimes.com/2022/09/14/arts/little-mermaid-trailer-halle-bailey.html.

15. Frank Harris, III, "Black Kids Need Black Santa," *New Haven Register*, December 13, 1990.

16. Mary Hoffman, *Amazing Grace* (New York: Dial Books for Young Readers, 1991).

17. Kelly Marie Tran, "I Won't Be Marginalized by Online Harassment," *New York Times*, August 21, 2018, https://www.nytimes.com/2018/08/21/movies/kelly-marie-tran.html.